A Brief History Of
Castration

Second Edition

by

Victor T. Cheney

authorHOUSE™

1663 LIBERTY DRIVE, SUITE 200
BLOOMINGTON, INDIANA 47403
(800) 839-8640
WWW.AUTHORHOUSE.COM

First published by AuthorHouse 2/21/2006

ISBN: 1-4208-9720-9 (sc)

Printed in the United States of America
Bloomington, Indiana

This book is printed on acid-free paper.

The cover image is a reproduction of an ancient wall carving of a eunuch servant which was found in the ruins of a palace in ancient Ur dating to about 2000 BC. I included this image because it shows some of the physical characteristics of eunuchs such as: no beard, soft musculature and full head of hair like a woman. These characteristics are also shown on many other ancient carvings and pictures and are often the only records of eunuchs in many ancient cultures since the written records of eunuchs have been deliberately destroyed ... in some cultures.

Table of Contents

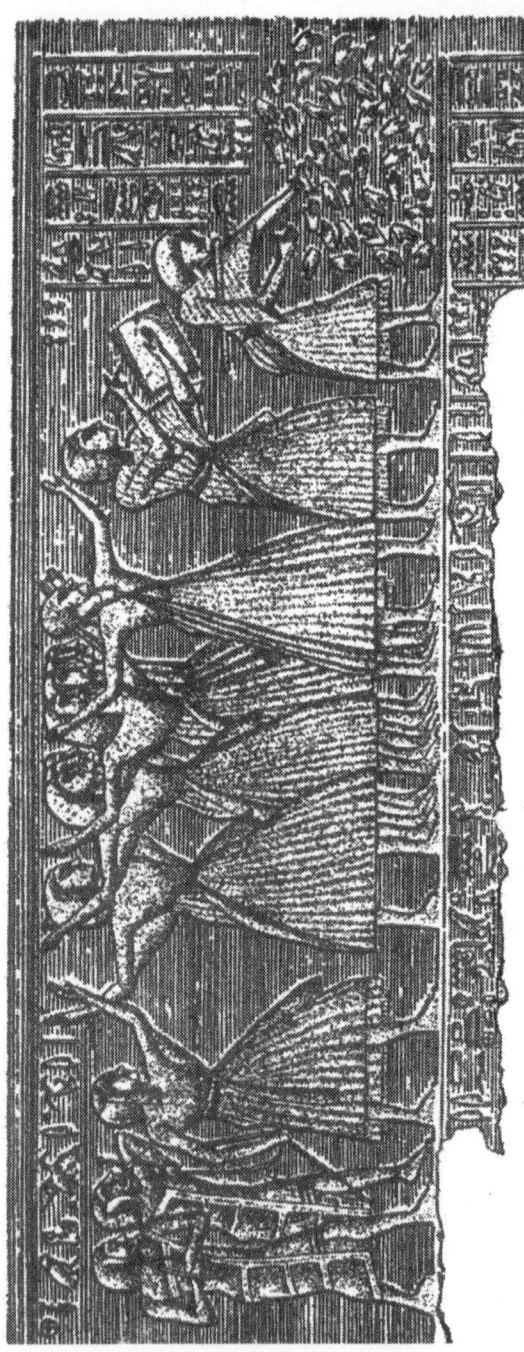

Illustrations from <u>Les eunuques a travers les ages</u>; Richard Millant; Paris: Vigot Frères Éditeurs, 1908.

The bas-reliefs and inscriptions at Thebes celebrated the victories of Ramases II (1304-1237 B.C.) in the same manner. One such sculpted mural shows prisoners of war tied with cords on the left side of the mural; in the center, Egyptians with their hands raised above their heads plead in supplication to their deity. They appear to be marching off before the officer in charge and the royal scribe, who are taking the inventory. In the right hand corner, the cut-off hands, penises and testicles are piled up in a jumble - a testimony of the corporal punishment inflicted on the vanquished. The inscription roughly indicates: 'Conducting some prisoners into the presence of his majesty; there are a thousand in number; phalluses, 3,000." Another sculpture gave the total number of 2,525 phalluses cut off.

Foreword

The subject of castration in contemporary discourse is almost always taboo, and its virtual absence in the social sciences as a research topic reflects both the neglect and shame that surround this practice. As Victor Cheney's book shows, this neglect is now being remedied, and the shame surrounding the issue is in the process of being dispelled.

From the perspectives of sociology, sexual deviance and criminology, orienting disciplines for analysis of castration, this practice has been widespread throughout history, re-emerging to perform different functions over different time periods. This book addresses the need to re-open the debate over its potential and current uses for our own time.

This study has five major themes. First, there is a copious historical record in both Western and non-Western literature that reveals its ordinariness in a variety of historical contexts; its positive acceptance and widespread usage by nobility, priesthood, and commoners alike. Second, whereas one function of castration is punishment, other equally commanding purposes involve social mobility, moral leadership, spiritual purity, disease prevention, crime reduction, pleasure enhancement, and profit.

Third, castration was often a survival technique in the ancient world and through the late Middle Ages in Western societies. For instance, rescuers of abandoned children may have preferred their charges to be castrated to avoid splitting their inheritance to non-family persons, or to avoid the possibility that the boy might be sold into slavery or prostitution if discovered to be expositio (exposed). Additionally, castrated slaves were viewed as more valuable, and treated accordingly.

A fourth point, the legal entanglements associated with regulation of the practice, helped clarify the role and status of persons, who might otherwise have been entirely marginal to the social order. In effect, boys who had no recognizable social status, and thus targets for death or slavery, received legal recognition, and occasionally protection.

A final theme, and in some instances, more controversial for contemporary lawmakers, is the use of castration as medical treatment. Apparently, when the matter entails a life-threatening disease, castration receives little or no attention. When it is proposed as a potential remedy for predatory adults who sexually offend children, it reenters the shadowland.

As a sociologist and educator, and recently involved with research on youth, both as victims and offenders, I can neither promote the cause of castration as a court-ordered intervention for the increasing number of young men who are sexually attacking children, nor do I turn my back on the possibility of such an intervention approach. I suspect my training has taught me to be more cautious; it demands that we wait until additional evidence becomes available.

This book, because it courageously presents a controversial topic, grounding it in rich detail in its social context, and does so in a careful, scholarly manner, is precisely the introduction that researchers and policymakers need to generate questions about the feasibility of such a procedure for repeat offenders.

Nanette J. Davis, Ph.D.

Portland State University

Preface

Castration is the oldest, most powerful, cheapest, quickest, most reliable treatment for preventing multitudes of crimes, diseases, violence and unwanted pregnancy. The procedure is also best for the overall health and longevity of the male. Unfortunately, very little has been published about it in the English-speaking world. This book—by reviewing the use of castration over the millennia in several different cultures—will serve to open the door, such that the public will be able to gain a better understanding of the effects of this simple surgery.

A defense of castration, or the state of being a eunuch, fails to resonate with most modern thinkers. For the most part, we identify the surgical removal of the testicles with serious, life-threatening disease. The idea of willful or voluntary excision of these organs may repulse or sicken people unaccustomed to this historical practice.

Yet the eunuch had an important spiritual role in many early religions, Christian and medieval periods, as well as being a firmly established political figure in Church and state affairs. Castrated men were the preferred harem attendants in Middle Eastern countries and were entrenched in public service as palace officials or state bureaucrats. Church choirs, largely devoid of women in the medieval epoch, depended on pre-adolescent males to provide the female voice. If castrated as a boy, this voice, forever rendered in feminine tones, was considered precious, a gift of the angels. Parents could unilaterally make a decision to have their son's testicles removed in the interests of purity or for facilitating a career. Sexual codes of many periods equated male and female virginity and male eunuchism as singular forms of moral purity, a bodily state of high merit.

However utilitarian their social involvement and highly regarded their spirituality throughout much of Christian history, eunuchs were distrusted. They were considered unnatural, overly sensuous, even promiscuous, and far too attached to women. Critics observed that *some* eunuchs took advantage of their condition to entice and corrupt women, inasmuch as pregnancy was no longer a threat. Their moral character, it was said, was far too defined by the absence of the male organ, a situation that lent itself to excesses, either ascetic or sexual. Additionally, many were heretics, either opposed to marriage and family life, or involved with deviant social circles. Because many eunuchs were slaves in the ancient world, their reputations may have been shaped by their lowly status.

The Church took a wholly contradictory position. On the one hand, early Christian canons and Church Fathers sharply rebuked eunuchs on biblical grounds, insisting that such voluntary action ran counter to God's laws. On the other hand, the Church had scores of men, castrated as children or adults, located across the spectrum of churchly activity. Entire monasteries were filled with eunuchs with impeccable moral credentials.

Because celibacy was held in such high regard in the medieval Church, it was bound to generate political and spiritual confusion. Thus, castration was perceived as both a higher and lower physical status. Even today, the Catholic Church faces major issues around sexual abuse of children by both gay and heterosexual priests. Invariably, celibacy as an externally imposed condition for purity, political career, or spiritual recognition, creates a major contradiction: an incessant struggle between sexual desire, which is natural, and denial of the sexual feelings, which is self-negating.

Exactly what relevance does the issue of castration have today? While some may view this procedure as archaic and barbarous, and certainly outmoded by contemporary standards, many do not realize that it continues to be practiced today for a variety of reasons, be they medical, sexual or spiritual. Most critics neglect to see its merits, particularly its primary application: as a viable treatment for sex offenders—at least in Western societies.

Castration for the sake of purity is an old idea. This book aims to reopen the debate today by presenting a brief history of castration as a normal procedure that has been widely used throughout history by Christians and non-Christians alike. This background enables us to perceive modern castration as a medical treatment that is especially effective as a remedy for serious sexual offenders. In this instance, we may wish to consider castration for public safety and protection of our children.

Chapter 1—An Overview of Castration

We need only look to the "cradle of civilization" for the beginnings of the phenomenon of castration. Research indicates that castration was initially used in the domestication of animals in the Eastern and Middle Eastern region during the Mesolithic period, about 8,000 or 9,000 years ago. Most animals tended to flock together and produce roughly the same number of male and female offspring. Since one male was all that was actually needed to service dozens of females for procreative purposes, castration served to be the ideal solution to the fighting and competition that resulted from males seeking to mate with as many females as possible.

The process of castration itself was relatively simple, and is still used in animal husbandry today. Shortly after the testicles descend in newborn males, a string or horse-hair is tied tightly around the scrotum, which causes the testicles to turn black and drop off in about three weeks time, apparently without discomfort to the animal. However, numerous other methods of castration have been employed throughout history, such as crushing the testicles by hand or between rocks, or by cutting them off with a knife. In the early Vedic records of India (c. 1500 B.C.), the term *vadhryasva* (he who castrated horses) was written. References are also found in ancient writings about the ox (a castrated bull), and its associations with words that signify the act of crushing, striking, shattering, and edging, as well as castrating.

The early herdsmen and farmers could easily observe the highly desirable effects of castration. The procedure not only eliminated the trouble of aggression in bulls, stallions, boars, rams and cocks (thus reducing the danger that came with handling the animals), but made the oxen, steers, geldings, hogs, barrows and wethers more tractable for pulling the plow, for riding and for other types of work. In addition, castration allowed the animals to fatten more easily, grow more quickly and taste better.

Human slavery originated in the same region not long after the domestication of animals. Some of the earliest records of the Old Kingdom of Egypt (c. 2600 B.C.) indicate that the sale of children or the selling of oneself to pay debts was widespread. Human slaves were regarded as merely a step or two removed from the status of domesticated animals, so it seemed only natural that consideration would be given to castrating them for similar purposes, thus making them more compliant and reliable servants, laborers or warriors. As slavery became more of an institution and the trade in slaves developed, it was found that those slaves who were castrated were more trustworthy and brought more money than those who were not. Although a high death rate was associated with the procedure, the added profit of the castrated slaves was sufficient to make the castration of slaves a regular feature of the slave trade until the final abolishment of slavery in the first decades of the twentieth century.

Herodotus (c. 484–425 B.C.) tells the story of Panionius, who castrated and traded slaves: "He sold the victims of his knife in Ephesis and Sardis, where they were much esteemed because of their honesty and fidelity in every way" (Book 8). One of Panionius' slaves, Hermotimus, became the chief eunuch of Xerxes (486–463 B.C.), and exacted his revenge on Panionius by instigating a family-wide castration in which he and his four sons castrated each other. Another account by Ammianus Marcellinus (c. 330-393 B.C.), says that Semiramis, the queen-mother of the Assyrian king of Mesopotamia (810-782 B.C.), was the originator of the practice of castrating slaves to make them more trustworthy (*Book XIV*, vi, 17).

The Greek historian, Xenophon (c. 430–355 B.C.) gave Cyrus, King of Persia—who captured Babylon circa 538 B.C.—major credit for proclaiming that eunuchs were the most loyal of servants. In his *Cyropaedia VII, he wrote:*

> He (Cyrus) drew his conclusion from the case of the animals: for instance, vicious horses when gelded, stop biting and prancing about, but are nonetheless fit for service in war; and bulls, when castrated, lose part of their high spirit and

unruliness but are not deprived of their strength, nor capacity for work. And in the same way dogs, when castrated, stop running from their masters, but are no less useful for hunting or watching. And men, too, in the same way become gentler when deprived of this desire, but no less careful of that which is entrusted to them.

The word "eunuch" itself is widely used to describe a castrated human male; several explanations of its derivation and significance are known to exist. One explanation is that it has evolved from the Greek words meaning "crush" and "cut." Another stipulates that the term is derived from the word *eunouchos*, meaning "chamberlain" or "guardian of the couch," whereas a different version states that the term originated from Semitic or Hebrew words referring to "trained," "tried" or "experienced"—literally "trustworthy," or "trusted."[1] Finally, the term eunuch is derived from the Assyrian expression, "he who is head or chief." The Septuagint version of the Bible translated the same Hebrew word 31 times as "eunuch," seven times as "official," and two times as a proper name depending on the context in which it was used.

The *Oxford Latin Dictionary* (1983) and *Harpers Latin Dictionary* (1907) both define the Latin word "eunuchus" as eunuch. Both *Britannica* and *Webster's* define eunuch as a castrated man: a man or boy whose testes or external genitals have been removed or who is deprived of testicular function because of physical problems (as in inflammation or injury). Hieronymus (c. 342–420 A.D.) was the first to translate the Bible into Latin from the original languages, and his version, known as the "Vulgate," used the word *eunuchus* in Genesis 37:36. In English this verse is rendered: "Meanwhile, the Midianites had sold Joseph in Egypt, to Potiphar, one of Pharoah's *courtiers*, and captain of his guard."[2] The *New Revised Standard Version* of The Bible renders the same verse: "Meanwhile the Midianites had sold him in Egypt to Potiphar, one of Pharoah's *officials*, the captain of the guard."[3]

Similarly, Genesis 37:36 and 39:1 (dating from c. 2,000–1778 B.C.) tells of the selling of Joseph to Potiphar, an "officer" of Pharaoh. Leviticus 21:20 and 22:24 (c. 1450 B.C.) speaks of excluding men and animals with crushed testicles from the religious ceremonies. Deuteronomy 23:1 (c. 1451 B.C.) states: "He whose testicles are crushed or whose male member is cut off shall not enter the assembly of the Lord." Yet, Isaiah 56:3–5 (c. 810–698 B.C.), a later book, includes eunuchs among those for whom religious practices elevate them in the eyes of God:

> ...let not the eunuch say, 'Behold, I am a dry tree.' For thus says the Lord: 'To the eunuchs who keep my Sabbaths, who choose the things that please me and hold fast to my covenant, I will give in my house and within my walls, a monument and a name better than sons and daughters; I will give them an everlasting name which shall not be cut off.'

Isaiah 39:7 foretells that King Hezekiah's sons are to become eunuchs in the palace of the king of Babylon. 2 Kings 20:18 (c. 600 B.C.) conveys the same prophecy. 2 Kings 9:32 tells that eunuchs throw Jezebel down to Jehu. Daniel 1:3 (c. 550 B.C.) recounts that Nebuchadnezzar's eunuch aids the captive Daniel. Browe[4] Esther 1:10, 12; 2:3, 14, 15, 21; 4:4–6; 6:2, 14; 7:9 describes the activities of King Ahasuerus' (the Persian King Xerxes I, 486–456 B.C.) many eunuchs. Jeremiah 29:2; 38:7–12; 39:15; 34:19 (626–585 B.C.) reveals the activities of the king's eunuchs. Matthew 19:12 (40 A.D.) details the words of Christ concerning eunuchs, words which were to become instrumental in inspiring hundreds of thousands to undergo castration for the sake of the kingdom of Heaven. St. Paul says in Acts 8:27–39 (63–64 A.D.) that Philip baptizes the Ethiopian eunuch who was in charge of the Queens treasure. In the Apocryphal book, *The Wisdom of Solomon* (3:14), Solomon (d. c. 943 B.C.) praises the eunuchs: "Blessed also is the eunuch whose hands have done no lawless deed, and who has not devised wicked things against the Lord; for special favor shall be shown him for his faithfulness, and a place of great delight in the temple of the Lord."

More specifically, the word "castration" seems to be derived directly from the Latin "castro." However, considerable speculation exists as to whether or not the term "castro" is connected with legends of the "castor, "which is Latin for "beaver." Even the great Juvenal (c. 60– 136 A.D.) seemed to accept this idea when he wrote, "He imitates the castor who makes a eunuch of himself—buying his life for the price of his organs." Legend had it that the beaver would castrate himself when he found himself in peril (the animal's scent gland are two pairs of membranous sacs between the anus and external genitalia).

Historically, most of the purposes of castration can be classified under six general headings: punishment, prevention of disease and crime, pleasure, profit, piety and purification (the latter will be discussed in greater depth in the Asceticism chapter).

King Merneptah established a monument at Karnak in Egypt circa 1225 B.C., which was inscribed with the lists of more than 13,000 phalli taken in battle with the Libyans and other Mediterranean peoples (see Chapter 3). The emasculation of a defeated enemy signified complete possession of the vanquished. A later offering of the severed parts to their god was a feature of the wars of several ancient civilizations.

Another example that may shed light on this notion of the emasculation of the conquered adversary comes in the form of a stone carving depicting Sennacherib after the siege of Lachish, Judea in 701 B.C. The cuneiform inscription reads: "Sennacherib, king of all, king of Assyria, sitting on his *Nimedu*-throne while the spoil from the city of Lachish passes before him." The king's face has been deliberately mutilated, presumably by his murderers. Two eunuchs, indentifiable as such by their sleek, beardless faces and soft, corpulent appearance, stand behind the king's throne fanning him. Sennacherib's (704–681 B.C.) inscriptions read:

> I cut off their precious lives as one cuts a string. Like the many waters of a storm, I made the contents of their gullets and entrails run down upon the wide earth. My prancing steeds harnessed for my riding, plunged into the streams of

their blood as into a river. The wheels of my war chariot, which brings low the wicked and the evil, were bespattered with blood and filth. With the bodies of their warriors I filled the plain, like grass. Their testicles I cut off, and tore out their privates like the seeds of cucumbers.[5]

Browe[6] a Jesuit priest, has studiously documented the history of castration in religion and law with copious references. His information is summarized here. The Babylonian king, Hammurabi (about 1955-1913 B.C.) Formalized the ancient law of retaliation "eye for an eye, tooth for tooth" known as *lex talionis* which called for castration for those who castrated someone else. Egyptian law called for the same punishment for anyone who had forced sex on a free woman. Late Roman law called for the same punishment for those who had sex with animals. The old pagan Frisian code of the Salic Franks, issued about 507 AD, used it for anyone who had stolen something dedicated to the gods. Self-castration was allowed in lieu of being buried alive or death by fire.

Browe wrote: "Most frequently castration was used to punish moral crimes to make a repeat crime impossible, primarily to punish the member that had sinned." Justinian (527-565) called for castration in his novellas for pederasts and for anyone who had castrated someone else. The Visigoth kings, Chindasvind (642-653) and Egica (687-702), also believed that pederasty should be punished like this. Norwegian law later prescribed castration for those who perpetrated bestiality. The Capitula Remedii, compiled around 843-850 in Chur-Raetia by secular and religious officials, prescribed castration for certain extramarital affairs. Some of the early Germanic people had the custom of allowing a husband to castrate the seducer of his wife. King Alfred (849-901) used this punishment for rape committed by peasants. The Breisgaugraf Duke Berthold II, in the battles of 1078, had some of the peasants castrated for adhering to his opponents. In one of the most famous cases. Peter Abelard was castrated about 1117 on the order of the Parisian Canon, Fulbert for seducing Heloise, his niece. The servants who castrated Abelard had the same mutilation done to them. Around 1010, the English King Henry I adopted castration as the punishment for counterfeiting, as well as moral crimes. Henry II renewed the law in 1180. William the Conqueror reduced several capital punishments to castration or plucking out of the eyes. Bishop Burchard of Worms (d. 1117) censured the crusader who had a priest castrated when he returned from the crusades. St. Aelred of Rievaulx (d. 1166) told a tale of the double monastery at Wattun where the nuns caught and castrated a monk who had seduced one of the sisters. The biography of St. Thomas a Becket (d. 1170) proves that such punishments actually occurred. The collection of laws put together by King Baldwin II of Jerusalem and the patriarch Warmund about 1120 prescribed castration for Christians who had intercourse with Saracens and Saracens who had sexual relations with Christians. Frederick II of Sicily (1272-1337) condemned to castration the servant who seduced the wife and maids of his master. The Tuscan codes of Chiaciano (1287) and Florence (1325) condemned pederasts to castration. In England and Western Europe, castration remained the punishment for rape until well into the Middle Ages. The 15th Century Waltpoden code in Mainz stated: When a bailiff finds a Jew trying to commit an indecency with a Christian wife or maid he can seize them both. Then he cuts off the Jew's tool and drives him out with sticks. Under Pope Alexander VI (1492-1503), Jews in Rome were castrated for the same crime. The laws of the middle Italian city of Macerate (1563) dealt such persons death after their genitals had been cut off. During the infamous Saint Bartholomew's Day Massacre of August 24, 1572, the victorious French Catholics cut the genitals from numerous wounded and dead Protestants.

After this time, no laws calling for castration for moral crimes could be found. Such mutilations became a sin for which absolution could be obtained from the bishop in certain cases under such laws as that which was passed in the Provinciate of Naples in 1576. After more than 3,000 years, laws calling for the castration of sex offenders faded from the records in Western countries. The practice probably continued in the unrecorded customs of primitive societies for which we have no record however. Only in modern times do we find records indicating that castration was employed in a punitive manner. Three states in the U.S., Washington in 1909, Nevada in 1911, and Indiana in 1917, introduced castration as an alternative or supplementary punishment. Denmark was the first to establish a comprehensive law on June 1, 1929, under Chapter XXIV of the Danish Criminal Code concerning punishments for rape, pederasty, and other sex crimes. This law was amended on May 11, 1935, with more details concerning permission to castrate offenders. Forced castration was never employed under Danish laws however.

Canon law abandoned castration as a punishment, but allowed it in the civil law as long as the enforcers of the law did not carry it to excess. Pius XI in his "Casti Connubii"" bull of 1930 did not speak against castration carried out by civil authority. The Nazi German "Law Against Dangerous Societal Criminals and Guidelines for Safety and Improvement of November 24, 1933" provided that a man who had reached his 21st birthday could be punished by castration if he was condemned to prison for at least six months for a crime of forced indecency, molestation of a child, or murder for the arousal or satisfaction of sexual desire. In Norway, the Act on Castration was passed June 1, 1934. In Finland, a castration act was passed June 13, 1935. In Iceland, the Act of June 13, 1938, laid down the rules for the use of castration operation. Sweden's Castration Act is dated March 24, 1944. The Danish, Finish, and Icelandic laws have specific provisions for compulsory castrations for certain categories of sex offenders. The Swedish and Norwegian acts have no formal connection with the penal code and are based purely on the medical-therapeutic considerations offering castration as a form of medical therapy for both sex offenders and others who may desire it.

Frenken[7] studied the patterns of sex offender treatments in Europe in the 1990s and found that the Northwestern European countries subscribed to a humanistic approach aimed at re-socialization of the offender, while in other European countries the more punitive approach still prevails. In North America, the court-ordered sentences for sex crimes are much higher than in Europe, but treatments are more readily available than in Europe. In the Eastern and Southern European countries, the old retribution and punishment viewpoint still prevails.

Plutarch (46–120 A.D.) recorded the narrative about a statue of Osiris' son at Coptos in Egypt that depicted him holding aloft the genitalia of Satekh, his uncle. Centuries later, in France, the victorious Catholics cut the genitals from numerous wounded and dead Protestants at the infamous Massacre of Saint Bartholomew August 24, 1572 A.D.

Castration for the prevention or avoidance of serious illness was advocated by Hippocrates in his work, *Book on Aphorisms*, and by Pliny, (*Book II*, chapter 37), for gout. Ancillon mentions in his *Treatise of the Eunuchs* that leprosy never attacks eunuchs and "…those whom leprosy threatens, on the advice of doctors, are permitted castration. This practice was sometimes authorized by those in charge of lepers and the experience has shown that the intervention had a happy effect on their life and health." Ancillon also reports that "…this antidote acts against the poison of elephantiasis."

Castration for pleasure has had many facets. The decadent aristocracy of ancient Rome initiated the use of eunuchs as objects of sexual pleasure. In addition to their historic duties of supervising their master's bedchamber activities, choosing his virgins, arranging orgies, and the like, the eunuchs became objects of desire in themselves (see chapter 5). As the eunuch's effusion in the Satyricon of Petronius (c. 66 A.D.) illustrates:

> O fairies, O buggers
> O eunuchs exotic!
> Come running, come running,
> ye anal erotic!
> With soft little hands,
> with flexible bums,
> Come O castrati,
> unnatural ones!

Juvenal mentions still another manner in which eunuchs were used for pleasure shortly after the advent of the *Pax Romana* in his celebrated

Sixth Satire. This verse, subtitled *The Anti-Sex*, was translated by John Dryden, 1631–1700):

> There are those who in soft eunuchs place their bliss;
> To shun the scrubbing of a bearded kiss;
> And scape abortion, but their solid joy
> Is when the Page, already past a boy,
> Is capon'd late; and to the gelder shown,
> With his two-pounders to perfection grown.
> When all the navel-string could give, appears;
> All but the beard; and that's the barber's loss, not theirs.
> Seen from afar, and famous for his ware,
> He struts into the bath among the fair:
> The admiring crew to their devotions fall:
> And kneeling, on the new Priapus call.
> Kerved for his lady's use, he with her lies;
> And let him drudge for her if thou art wise,
> Rather than trust him with thy favorite boy;
> He proffers death, in proffering to enjoy.

Castration was a fairly common procedure in the ancient world. First-millennium B.C. Assyrian officials installed eunuchs in positions of authority because they were thought to be less vulnerable than other men to sexual blackmail and corruption. Eunuchs also guarded harems and served as escorts for royal ladies. Cyrus the Great (559-529 B.C.) Selected eunuchs for every post of personal service to him, from the doorkeepers up.

Despite occasional bans on castration, youths were pressured by their families to undergo castration to enhance their career prospects. Most eunuchs, however, were castrated as punishment or to make them more tractable. Attractive slaves were sometimes gelded to serve as sexual toys for wealthy men and women. The emperor Nero (54-68 A.D.) Famously castrated a youth named Sporus and married him in a wedding ceremony in which the "bride" was garbed as an empress.

Apparently, in this famous satire against women, Juvenal was thinking of a young man castrated at a certain critical age after his two testicles had begun to grow large, but before maturation of the beard (probably between the age 14 and 16). Rome, at the time of Juvenal's *Sixth Satire*, was perhaps one of the most licentious places the world has ever seen. The poem clearly points out this degeneracy and women's contribution to the ribaldry. Juvenal was one of the early conservatives who found this kind of behavior particularly objectionable.

Edward Gibbon observed in his distinguished book, *History of the Decline and Fall of the Roman Empire*: "The use and value of the effeminate slaves gradually rose with the decline of the empire." The emperor, Septimus Severus (193–211 A.D.), had a hundred free Romans castrated so that his daughter might be attended by a train of eunuchs worthy of an Eastern queen. This use of eunuchs appears to be motivated more by a desire for prestige than for pleasure.

The historian, John Boswell, observing the link between child abandonment and castration, comments that abandonment practices have left an extensive historical record of brutality. Children may have been sacrificed to the gods, or simply exposed to die. Or they may have been sold as slaves, indentured servants, or child prostitutes. Some were even crippled or otherwise mutilated to become more effective beggars, because they could incite compassion in the hearts of almsgivers. Castration proved the lesser evil:

> Castrating boys to be eunuchs was a big business in the early [Roman] empire, although it, too, was limited by law, and eunuchs become steadily less common in the West throughout the Christian era, except from the end of the Middle Ages through the beginning of the nineteenth century, when they were again popular as singers.

The practice of removing the penis as well as the testicles of boys and young men to make them more pleasing to homosexuals, pedophiles and other sexual deviates has continued well into the present day.

Little is heard of the practice because of its shameful and illegal status, but those who have undergone radical castration often exist in the "red light" districts of some of the larger cities around the world. In 1961, the magazine *Eros* reported that the "eunuch colony" of the vice quarter of Bombay, India had more than 500 eunuchs dressed in women's clothing selling their services. The *Parade* magazine of March 14, 1982 reported that as many as 3,500 such eunuchs were working in Bombay as prostitutes and entertainers as recently as 1972.

In the chapters that follow, we explore the practice of castration in various countries and historical periods. Clearly, castration represents a contradictory practice—embracing both the highest virtues and lowest vices—but a practice that was deeply embedded in the religious and political life of early civilizations. What may shock readers is the realization that many great civilizations deteriorated when eunuchs were *removed* from the civil and military affairs of governments.

Endnotes—Chapter 1

[1.] James Hastings, *Encyclopedia of Religion and Ethics,* Volume 5. New York: Charles Scribner's Sons, 1912, p. 579.

[2.] *The Vulgate*, English Version by Msgr. Ronald Knox. New York: Sheed & Ward, 1948, p. 57.

[3.] *Holy Bible, The New Revised Standard Version.* Nashville, Tennessee: Thomas Nelson Publishers, 1990, p. 35.

[4] Browe, Peter. (1936). Zur Geschichte der Entmannung: Eine religions und rechtsgechichtliche studie, pages 19 and 20. Browe quotes the rabbinical records and early writers as his sources for this information

[5.] Charles Ancillon, *Traite des Eunuques.* Paris: Editions Ramsay, 1707, Reprinted in 1978.

[6.] Joseph Jacobs, *Eunuchs, the Keeper of the Bed.* London: Arlington Books, 1973.

[7] Freken, Jos. (1999). Sexual offender treatment in Europe: An Impression of cross-cultural differences. Sexual Abuse: A Journal of Research and Treatment, Vol. II, No. 1, pp. 87-93..

Chapter 2—The Eunuchs of China

The utilization of eunuchs was an important feature in Chinese culture. Indeed, the phenomenon became an institution, enduring for nearly 4,000 years. The use of eunuchs is thought to have begun as early as 2,000 B.C., and remained entrenched until 1924. Generally, the sources who have chronicled the history of castration and eunuchism in China were antagonistic toward the practice. The authors of several primary references even acknowledge their bias: Mitamura (1970) is scrupulously honest in revealing his own disgust with both his main sources of information and publisher.[1] Anderson (1990) points out that the Chinese mandarins who so despised the palace eunuchs wrote the histories that comprise the bulk of her sources.[2] Thus, allowance must be made for the prejudice and exaggeration that exist in the portrayal of these eunuchs.

It should be noted that castration was against the law on several occasions in Chinese history, namely during the reigns of Emperor Wen Ti (180–56 B.C.), Emperor Hsiau Wen Ti (472–499 A.D.), Emperor Yang Chien (589–604), Kublai Khan (1260–1294), Emperor Hung Wu (1368–1402) and Emperor Pu Yi in 1923.

The origins of the Chinese eunuchs can be traced to the Hsia dynasty (2205–1766 B.C.). Actual written records of the practice extend back to the pictographs of the Shang and Yin dynasties. The original eunuchs were not Chinese, but were Aborigines or other foreign prisoners. As the eunuchs achieved higher status in the imperial palace with the progression of time, great numbers of Chinese eagerly sought castration as a means of advancing themselves and their families.

Professor J. J. Matignon is another authority on Chinese eunuchs; he was attached to the French embassy in Peking for a number of years. He wrote: "The first mention of eunuchs in China was in 1,100 B.C. under the Chou dynasty. Emperor Chou-Koung confirmed that castration was one of the five punishments for serious crimes in his

Code of Edicts along with "branding of the forehead, execution and amputation of the hands or feet."[3] Matignon added in a later work: "Eunuchs castrated young have a round and plump figure, but the skin is flaccid, and he is apathetic. When they are old one could take them for old women…disguised in men's clothing. They are usually sweet, conciliatory, cheerful and of versatile character."[4]

Eunuchs were needed by the emperors as they were the only ones who could be trusted to serve and control their palace women properly. The ancient religious system and beliefs, as well as the strongly centralized form of government in China, required that the emperor have considerable numbers of women in his personal household. The emperor was considered to be a God-king, a son of Heaven, at the pinnacle of the religious, military and administrative hierarchies. His word was the absolute law of life or death over all his subjects. With such awesome power, he could have anything he wanted—especially the pleasures of the most beautiful and gifted women of the realm. Furthermore, it remained nothing less than essential that he have appropriate progeny in order to perpetuate his dynasty. These plentiful offspring were to come from the most select females so that the best could be chosen to govern succeeding generations of subjects. The prosperity and well-being of the entire nation depended on it. Much thought, inspiration and expense went into increasingly complicated systems of choosing wives and concubines for the emperor and his chieftains, as well as taking care of them in regal style.

The original "Yellow Emperor's" son (c. 2697 B.C.) was ordained to have four wives (the same number as in the Muslim system). Four was a sacred number symbolizing the four cardinal directions. In the Chou dynasty (1123–256 B.C.), the number of concubines in service to the throne was raised to 120; each had specific titles and ranks. In the Han dynasty (206 B.C.–220 A.D.), the custom of keeping concubines spread and emperors were known to have upwards of several thousand, feudal lords to have several thousand and wealthy officials to have a score or more. One source reported that an unprecedented 40,000 concubines were shared by the emperors Ch-ang An and Lo Yang. In an old Chinese saying, the matrimonial system was likened to a tea set: "Who in the world would think of having only one teacup for one teapot?"

The numbers of eunuchs required to serve these women in the imperial seraglio also increased. Their numbers are estimated to have varied from 3,000 to 13,000 in the earlier periods, and up to 20,000 in the T'ang dynasty. Documents indicate that more than 100,000 served in the late Ming dynasty from 1368 to 1644 A.D.[5] Such huge numbers of servants are incomprehensible to most until something is learned of the extravagant lifestyle of those who sat on the golden thrones in the "Forbidden City" and ruled over the world's greatest civilization of the time.

During the Ming dynasty, the palace's "Inner Precinct" occupied a walled area of about four square miles in Peking. The compound featured more than 360 brightly colored structures with tile roofs that housed the royal household as well as the staff of eunuchs, which were organized into four departments, eight sections and 12 bureaus. The Imperial Household Agency served the emperor's meals. The eunuchs in this agency were gourmets and culinary artists of the first order. The Nei Kuan Chien bureau was in charge of all construction, procured copper, tin, wood and iron utensils for use by the emperor and repaired mansions of local kings. The Yu Yung Chien bureau procured screens, chairs and other furniture. The Ssu She Chien bureau made the draperies, cushions, blinds, raincoats and umbrellas for the imperial cortege. Those in the Yu Man Chien looked after the emperor's horses, elephants and cows. The eunuchs in the Shen Kung Chien cleaned the Imperial Mausoleum, burned incense and lit the votary candles. The Shang Pao Chien were responsible for making the imperial seals with precious stones. Seals were symbolic of the emperor, and signified great power in the bureaucracy; well over 30,000 were used in a year. The Chih Tien Chien cleaned the outer court. The Shang I Chien fashioned the emperor's robes, headgear and footwear. The Tu Chih Chien swept the roads and acted as guards.

Next in order were the four *ssu*, or departments. The Hsi Hsin Ssu handled the firewood and charcoal for the palace and kept the fire-fighting tanks full of water. The eunuchs of the Chung Ku Ssu, clad in bright garments, played musical instruments, staged theatrics and performed puppet shows. The Pao Ch'ao Ssu merely produced toilet paper. The Hun T'ang Ssu operated the bathhouses.

The Chou, or sections, that were most worthy of note are as follows: The Ping Chang Chu manufactured the swords, lances, suits or armor, bows and arrows and firearms. Only eunuchs were allowed to handle the firearms, which were referred to as sacred weapons. The regular army did not have access to the firearms, and even during wartime, the eunuchs took charge of all gunpowder. The fact that eunuchs were the sole keepers of the firearms demonstrates how fully they were trusted by the Chinese rulers. The Wan I Chu was the only office located outside the Imperial Palace. Court ladies who had been expelled from the palace were kept in confinement here to prevent court secrets from leaking out to the public. The Yin Tsuo Chu produced the silver pieces that were to be given to especially meritorious subjects of the emperor. The Chin Mao Chu and the Chen Kung Chu constructed headgear and garments for the eunuchs. The Nei Chih Jan Chu made wine and flour and the Ssu Yuan Chu raised the vegetables. One chief eunuch supervised all of the departments and sections; his position was equivalent to the fourth official grade—immediately below the deputy minister of the external ministries.

Among the Chinese, the primary need for eunuchs involved the emperor's early upbringing and his later bedchamber activities. As soon as the imperial prince was old enough to leave his nurse's side, he would be instructed by eunuchs in speech, table manners, deportment and sex. During the Ming dynasty (1368–1644), the eunuchs used esoteric Buddhist statues of men and women in carnal embrace to teach the young men about sex. After the monarch's marriage, the eunuchs recorded each time the emperor had nocturnal relations with one of his consorts for later proof of conception.

The procedure for the concubines was different. Usually, after dinner the eunuch in charge of the imperial bedchamber would offer a silver tray of jade nameplates, which contained the names of some of the concubines, to the emperor. If the monarch was not in the mood, he would dismiss the eunuch. If he was interested he would turn one of the nameplates over, making his selection. Later, the eunuch would strip the concubine, wrap her in a feather garment and carry her to his majesty's bedchamber. After waiting a given time, the eunuch would call, "time is up." If the emperor did not reply after two such calls, the eunuch would enter the chamber. He would then ask the emperor if he wanted the concubine to bear his child. If the answer was negative, the eunuch would take proper contraceptive measures. If the answer was affirmative, he would record the date so that it could serve later as a confirmation of legitimacy.

"The familiarity that existed between the ruler and the eunuchs was of a special, intimate nature; nothing like it existed between the ruler and his other subjects."[6] They literally grew up together. Emperor Wu Tsung of the Ming dynasty called his chief of the imperial bedchamber "*pan, pan,*" meaning "friend." Hsuan Tsung, "the Brilliant Emperor" (712–750 A.D.), called his chief eunuch "our old servant." Emperor Ling of the later Han dynasty called his eunuch chamberlains "*chang jang—*my father" and "*chao chung—*my mother." These familiar terms show that a mutual feeling of respect existed between the emperor and his eunuchs. The eunuchs, who spent day and night at the emperor's side, often acquired considerable influence and wealth in their positions.

Historians maintain that several other reasons existed for the use of eunuchs in China: divine revelation, the jealous nature of Chinese men, revenge, and the use of castration as a punishment. Much of the Yin dynasty was a theocracy with the king acting as the divine agent, such that when he decreed ceremonial castration for prisoners of war, it was taken as divine revelation. The Confucian rules of decorum for women meant that the empress on the throne was not allowed to talk directly to her ministers. She had to use eunuchs as her sole medium of communication. The palace schools for women were staffed entirely by eunuchs. Only eunuchs were utilized in the women's quarters, "as a means of avoiding the suspicion of immorality and soothing jealous minds...."[7]

Emperor Wu of the second Han dynasty (25–200 A.D.) had many famous and capable men castrated as punishment so the quality of the eunuch corps increased more during his reign than at any other time in Chinese history. Some of these renowned men included: Ssu Ma Ch'ien, called the "father of Chinese history;" Tsai Lun, who invented the world's first usable writing paper in 105 A.D.—although paper was to remain unknown to Europeans until the twelfth century;[8] Li Yen Nien, a musical genius of the era; Chang Ho, son of a high official; and the prince of Lou Lan.

Many other instances throughout Chinese history indicate the special trust the rulers placed in the eunuchs. Eunuchs were regarded as the singular choice for serving as loyal confidants for the emperor's protection from consort families, domination by other nobility and moral supervision by Confucian religious leaders. In 717 A.D., Emperor Hsuan Tsung entrusted a eunuch with a precious manuscript library. During the Tang dynasty (757–902 A.D.), Emperor Tai Tsung gave eunuchs control over his personal treasury. Emperor Te Tsung put the palace guard under the supervision of eunuchs and had the eunuchs keep him apprised of distant military and provincial administrations.

In 1428, ruler Hsuan-te turned to his eunuchs as the only agents he could trust to thwart a princely rebellion. Emperor Ying Tsung (1438–1449) had only eunuchs for servants and intimate companions. Emperor Wan-Li (1573–1620) relied on eunuchs to perform essential business and to collect the taxes. An army comprised entirely of eunuchs was founded in 1622. Eunuch palace guards were employed as spies in 1635. About 1650, the throne had some 100,000 eunuchs in its employ nationwide. Emperor Kang Hsi (1661–1721) punished eunuchs more severely than other men so that they understood that their very lives depended on their trustworthiness. All eunuchs were thought of as "pure," but those under 10 years of age were termed "thoroughly pure," and prized by palace ladies, and allowed to perform the most intimate bedroom and bathroom duties.[9] Most monarchs trusted their eunuchs because they were "creatures docile and loyal as gelded animals."[10] A eunuch would always be childless, and thus would not covet political position in order to pass it on to sons.

Additional reasons for the use of eunuchs in Chinese culture can be found in the histories. In Tai Tsu's time (960–c. 975 A.D.), those who lacked the means for high levels of education necessary to pass difficult advancement tests could choose castration as a road to wealth. When these men were appointed to eunuch rank in the palace, the date of their emasculation was marked as their "birthday"—the beginning of their "second life."[11] In addition to harem and household duties, palace eunuchs, who had been castrated before the age of puberty and had high falsetto voices, were used widely as female impersonators in Chinese dramas. In the seventeenth century, descendants of banner chieftains were not only entitled to use eunuchs, but were compelled to do so to maintain the dignity of their stations.

Several specific methods of castration were used at different times in Chinese history. Originally, when applied as a punishment to prisoners or enemy soldiers, the procedure involved a simple slash of a dagger or sword. Due to the high mortality rate (60 percent mortality), this method was sometimes modified, such that only the penis or testicles were removed, rather than both at the same time. Indeed, total castration—being "swept clean"—was the favored approach. When a man had himself emasculated and paid for the operation, more care was generally given to him. In a more sophisticated technique, the subject was first given opium and then his penis and testicles were clamped between two pieces of bamboo as a ligature and severed by sliding a razor along the wood. The wound was washed in hot seed oil and covered with an oil-soaked cloth. The patient was left lying on his back and nourished with milk until he healed. Far fewer casualties resulted from this method.

Castrations in the later Ming and Ch'ing periods (1368–1911 A.D.) were usually performed by government-approved specialists, called *Tao Tzu Chiang*, who received the equivalent of about $84 per operation. They would prepare the patient by binding his abdomen and upper thighs with string or bandages and washing the parts three times in hot pepper-water. The specialist would then ask the client, "Will you regret it or not?" If the man showed the slightest uncertainty, the procedure would not be performed. If the man gave his full consent, both his penis and scrotum were quickly sliced off as close to the body as possible with a small curved blade. A plug was then inserted into the urethra and the wound covered with paper that had been soaked in cold water and bound up with bandages.

Afterwards, assistants would walk the new eunuch around the room for two or three hours before allowing him bed rest. No water could be drunk for three days after the operation. At the end of the waiting period, the plug would be removed and the patient allowed to urinate. Usually the wounds would be healed after 100 days and the new eunuch would go to the imperial household to learn his duties. At the end of the first year, the eunuch would be transferred to the Imperial Palace to begin his new vocation.[12]

Professor Mitamura draws on G. C. Stent's *Essay*[13] to provide an account of the preservation of the severed organs. Stent was an English scholar who had done extensive research on eunuchs in China during the 1870s and 1880s. The severed parts, known as *pao* ("precious" or "treasure"), were processed and sealed into a container of about three cups capacity that was stored away on a high shelf—symbolic of the original owner having attained a "high position." The pao would have to be examined by the head eunuch whenever an advancement was being considered. Another purpose in preserving the pao was so that it could be buried with the eunuch after his death. The eunuchs hoped to be restored to masculinity in the next world. The Chinese believed that Jun Wang, the king of the underworld, would turn those without their pao into female asses. According to Stent, 70 to 80 percent of eunuchs were castrated during childhood because of parental poverty. He noted that those who became eunuchs voluntarily after the age of 20 did so out of admiration for the wealth and position of high-ranking eunuchs.

Some of the Chinese terms used in referring to eunuchs were *haun kuan*, meaning either a castrated man or one who served in the Imperial Palace; *tzu Kung*, meaning one who is voluntarily castrated to show his devotion to God; and *ching shen*, defined as "purified body." A distinction existed between those castrated as children and those castrated later in life. The former were called *t'ung cheng*, or "pure from birth," and the latter were called *ching* or *cheng*, meaning "pure of body." The younger ones, regularly favored by the court ladies, had very little work assigned to them and often behaved and looked like young girls—soft, fat and beardless. *An gen* was the term for the eunuchs who were used to guard the Imperial Palace in the *Chou Li*, a book of law published in the Chou dynasty (1122–256 B.C.); *ssu jen was the term for the eunuchs who took care of the emperor's mistresses and handled the punishment of the court ladies.*

Eunuchs were frequently bed-wetters, had difficulties with urination and smelled bad as a result. The Chinese had a saying that a eunuch could be detected by his smell 300 meters downwind. "Stinky as a lao kung (eunuch)" was a common expression, as well. Eunuchs may have gained something of a bad reputation because of the practice removing both the penis and the testicles. The practice of cutting off the penis as close to the body as possible led to the difficulties in urination and to wetting the bed and clothing.

Historical literature reveals some of the more positive character traits among Chinese eunuchs.

- Exceptionally honest—not only were treasures kept in the palace, but the temptations presented by the numerous concubines also had to be resisted.

- Kind-hearted and benevolent to those in need.

- Seldom cruel, usually gentle and conciliatory.

- Warmhearted—many kept puppies as pets.

- Quick to shed tears, even over small matters.

- Easily irritated over minor things.

- Extremely sensitive about their condition. Any references to their "deficiency" insulted them. One did not speak directly of a "tail-less dog," but used a euphemism such as "the dog with the deer's tail." Broken objects like a teapot with a broken handle were not to be mentioned in the presence of a eunuch. The Chinese also avoided using the word for "cut" in a eunuch's presence because of its connection with castration.

- As a whole, eunuchs tended to be strongly united, helping each other and standing together against the rest of the world. During the reign of Emperor Yuan (48–33 B.C.), the eunuchs organized themselves so well that they succeeded in monopolizing state affairs, which caused great concern among the other officials. Li Shih, known as Ch'eng (33–7 B.C.), Yuan's successor, made changes and the eunuchs were once again relegated to the background.

The public's attitude toward eunuchs in China was generally one of disapproval. First, eunuchs were considered obscene by most morally conscious Chinese, who came to regard them with hatred. Second, since they were considered deficient by other Chinese, they were allowed greater freedom in their speech and manners. Remarks or actions that would normally bring stinging rebukes were overlooked because they were "just a eunuch." Third, eunuchs were often buried separate from their families, as they considered themselves akin to priests, even referring to castration as the act of entering the priesthood. The richer eunuchs formed fraternities so they could be sent off to the next world in style with a large chorus of chanting mourners.

Fourth, in the Ming dynasty (1368–1644 A.D.), filial piety and the continuation of the family line were fundamental Confucian principles. Since eunuchs automatically violated these tenets, voluntary castration was made a capital offense. In spite of these strong prohibitions, the old records show that eunuchs continued to be used by the emperors and their numbers actually increased. Another point is that most Chinese scholars shared the conclusion that eunuchs were a necessary evil, whose power had only to be controlled. Eunuchs were also accepted as a matter of divine destiny. Reference is invited to a new book by Shih Shan Tsm, The Eunuchs in the Mind.[13]

With so many people holding eunuchs in such low esteem, it remains almost surprising that any of their notable achievements were recorded in Chinese histories. Moreover, many of the eunuchs' accomplishments were undoubtedly expunged from the records— which is also the case in the Byzantine and Roman Catholic histories. Despite this fact, we have knowledge of some instances where eunuchs were given their due respect in the annals of history. Among these, we mention ambassador eunuch Cheng-ho, who led several expeditionary forces of up to 62 ships and 27,800 sailors into Africa, India, Ceylon and Arabia from 1405 to 1422 A.D. Ssu-ma Ch'ien (145-86 B.C.) is regarded as the grand historian of the Han court. Wang Chen became an army commander of distinction in 1449, while Wang Chih achieved greatness as a chief eunuch in the 1470s. Liu chin became a distinguished palace administrator in the early 1500s and Wei Chung-hsien was a trusted advisor in the 1620s. Eunuch Lao Ts'ai, a tax collector in the Fukien province, reportedly killed seven virgin boys on the advice of a necromancer and ate their brains in an effort to reproduce his own genitalia. Li Lien-Ying, the favorite of dowager Empress Tzu Hsi, wielded power for 40 years and is recognized as the last of the palace eunuchs who had historical significance. He died in 1912, the same year as the collapse of the Ching, the final imperial dynasty (1644–1912).

An exceptional record exists titled *Memorandum on Eunuchs* by Professor Tokio Hashikawa, which details the end of the practice of employing eunuchs in the palaces of China. Hashikawa tells of the exit of 470 eunuchs from the Tzu Chin palace on November 5, 1924—Emperor T'ung Ti of the Ch'ing dynasty, together with his retinue, were evicted by the Republican army general.

The practice of making and employing eunuchs waxed and waned with the fortunes of the various Chinese dynasties. In general, the periods of history when the barbarians from the north made their greatest inroads on the imperial Chinese culture were the times when the use of eunuchs would wane. Under the Mongols, Tartars, Khiton and Tangut conquests, the power of the eunuchs diminished. These nomadic, warring barbarians did not initially follow the Chinese custom. However, after having established themselves for a few years, they would gradually adopt the cultural convention of employing trusted eunuchs in the rulers' households.

Zheng He, the famed 15th-century Chinese explorer who made voyages from Asia to Africa. Zheng remains relatively uncelebrated, even in his home country. Zheng He was a skilled commander who stood nearly 7 feet tall. He was also a eunuch and a devout Muslim. He was the commander of the largest maritime expedition the world had ever seen: 28,000 people sailing 300 ships. In 1381, when Zheng was 10 years old, the imperial army attacked his province. The young male children of the enemy were castrated. The genitals were preserved in a jar, hopeful that after burial they would be made whole in the afterlife.

Eunuch Power. Though the custom of castration seems bizarre today eunuchs were actually a powerful force in the society of Imperial China. They had access to powerful women and their children. Child eunuchs often grew up with future princes and emperors. Indeed, eunuchs garnered so much wealth and political influence from close contact with royal families, that commoners sometimes had their sons castrated in hopes of improving the family lot. Ethnic Chinese will dominate the economies of many Southeast Asian countries.

In Indonesia, Zheng He is revered as a local god: thousands visit a temple dedicated to him every year.

Endnotes—Chapter 2

[1] Taisuke Mitamura, *Chinese Eunuchs: The Structure of Intimate Politics.* Translated by Charles A. Pomeroy, Rutland, Vermont: Charles E. Tuttle Co., 1970.

[2] Mary M. Anderson, *Hidden Power: The Palace Eunuchs of Imperial China.* Buffalo, New York: Prometheus Books, 1990, pp. 15 & 16.

[3] J. J. Matignon, *Les Eunuques du Palais Imperial de Pekin.* Clinical Archives of Bordeaux, No. 5, Fifth Year, May, 1896.

[4] J. J. Matignon, *Superstition, Crime and Misery in China.* Paris and Lyon, 1900.

[5] Jitsuzo Kuwabara, "Shina no Kangan (Chinese Eunuchs)." *Toyoshi Setsuen*, serialized in The*Mainichi* newspapers in 1923.

[6] Taisuke Mitamura, *Ibid.*

[7] *Ibid.*

[8] Anderson, *Ibid.*, p. 88.

[9] *Ibid.*, p. 308.

[10] *Ibid.*, p. 17.

[11] *Ibid.*, p. 184.

[12] *Ibid.*, p. 309.

[13] Shih-Shan Tsm (1996). The Eunuchs in the Mind. Dynasty. New York State University of New York Press..

Chapter 3—Eunuchs in Egypt

Egypt is comprised of the ancient lands along the fertile Nile River Valley. During most of its history, the country has been divided into two regions—Upper and Lower Egypt, with Caucasian peoples in Lower Egypt, and blacks in Upper Egypt. Those in Upper Egypt were frequently subjugated by those in Lower Egypt. The upper region was formerly called Nubia, and is now recognized as the Sudan. Much of the time, Egypt included the Sinai Peninsula. Presently, it is bordered by the Red Sea on the east, the Mediterranean Sea on the North and Libya on the west. The majority of the land is situated between 20 and 30 degrees north latitude (about the same as Jacksonville, Florida to Mexico City) and is subtropical.

The age of Egypt extends back to about 4,500 B.C. Some of this period of history has been traced by Egyptologists, beginning with Hecataeus of Miletus (late sixth century B.C.), who recorded some of this era in his *Periegesis*. However, this work is no longer available to contemporary scholars. The priest, Manetho, who wrote *Aegyptiaca* about 240 B.C., originally described Egypt's 30 dynasties dating from about 3,100 B.C. to 343 B.C. The Persians dominated Egypt from 525–332 B.C., the Macedonians and Greeks from 332–30 B.C., the Romans and Byzantines from 30 B.C. to 642 A.D., the Moslems through the middle ages, the French from 1798–1801 and the British from 1877–1936. Since a tendency exists for each succeeding administration to want to obliterate the records of the preceding rulers and replace them with their own, a tidy record of history is not available for Egypt.

The practice of castrating men and making them eunuchs was considered shameful and unlawful in Egypt. As such, chroniclers have largely avoided the subject. And though eunuchism has gone through various phases of acceptability, it has always been present to some degree in the history of Egypt.

Little material about the eunuchs of Egypt remains, mainly because of the willful destruction of the records of the practice of castration by Christian religious authorities. The Ptolomaic library at the temple of Serapis in Alexandria was probably the greatest such loss in 391 A.D., when hundreds of thousands of its rare old volumes were burned by the patriarch of Alexandria. However, some old wall paintings, carvings and statuary have withstood the ravages of time to give us some insight into the practice. Zambaco quotes Maspero as saying that the record is incomplete for the earliest Egyptian dynasties.[1]

Carvings on certain Egyptian tombs of the Third dynasty (2,686–2,494 B.C.) depict women dancing and being guarded by men who are clearly eunuchs. This is the earliest definitive record of the use of castration in ancient Egypt found by this author. The use of eunuchs, then, seems to have originated because of a need to have them serve the extensive harems of the aristocracy – similar to China.

The Ancient Egyptian Book of the Dead[2] contains a few cryptic references to castration. The funerary papyrus, known as the Book of the Dead of Ani, is one of the most famous of these dating to about 1250 B.C., which has been translated to read:

"What does it mean? It means the blood which fell from the phallus of Re when he took to cutting himself. Then there came into being the gods who are in the presence of Re, who are authority and Intelligence, while I followed after my father Atum daily.

I restored the Sacred Eye after it had been injured on that day when the Rivals fought.

It means the day when Horus fought with Seth when he inflicted injury on Horus' face and when Horus took away Seth's testicles. It was Thoth who did his with his fingers."

According to Millant, the pharaoh, Sesostris (c. 1970–1950 B.C.), was the originator of the custom of castrating vanquished enemies of war.[3] Sesostris was one of Egypt's greatest conquerors. He erected stelae or half-columns in the countries he conquered, with phalluses symbolizing courage and female genitals symbolizing weakness. Moreover, vanquished soldiers were castrated and made into subservient slaves. Sesostris himself was assassinated by one of the men whom he had castrated.

On the walls of the pharaoh Merneptah's (c. 1236–1223 B.C.) tombs at Karnak the numbers of genitalia cut off from invading Libyans and other Mediterranean peoples are listed:

"Courageous Libyans killed, phallus cut off and brought back....6

Libyans killed, phallus cut off……………….…...................…......……..6,359

Sicilians, phallus cut off…………………………………..…….........…...222

Etruscans, phallus cut off………………………………..…............542

Achaeians, phallus brought to the king………..…….................…......6,111."

The bas-reliefs and inscriptions at Thebes celebrated the victories of Ramases II (1304–1237 B.C.) in the same manner. One such sculpted mural shows prisoners of war tied with cords on the left side of the mural; in the center, Egyptians with their hands raised above their heads plead in supplication to their deity. They appear to be marching off before the officer in charge and the royal scribe, who are taking the inventory. In the right hand corner, the cut-off hands, penises and testicles are piled up in a jumble—a testimony of the corporal punishment inflicted on the vanquished. The inscription roughly indicates: "Conducting some prisoners into the presence of his majesty; there are a thousand in number; phalluses, 3,000." Another sculpture gave the total number of 2,525 phalluses cut off.

After a battle, the victorious Egyptians would fill their chariots with these phallic trophies. The foot soldiers would attach them to their spears and shields and the cavalrymen would attach them to their horse's heads. On returning to their own country, they decorated the doors of their homes with phalluses. A warrior who did not possess any of these hideous trophies was disdained and scorned, but those who could show numbers of the phalli cut off from their enemies became heroes and the women would sing their glory.[4] The custom continued down through history at least as far as the third century B.C., when records state that nearly 300 phalluses were taken from the battlefield.

Throughout Egyptian history, as in many other Middle Eastern countries, eunuchs were often found in high places. Although, some confusion has existed in interpreting the ancient Egyptian writing and statuary, fairly clear evidence exists that indicates eunuchs were widely used in the early days. For example, the statuary of pharaoh Ikhnaton (1379–1372 B.C.) shows many eunuchoid features: beardlessness, soft musculature, thin limbs, thick body, adipose thighs and general feminine shape. Yet, he is recorded as being a devoted husband of the beautiful Nefertiti, who gave birth to six sons. One bust in particular portrays him realistically with a melancholy expression, a refined head covered with a heavy *khoprash*, or war helmet, and beardless face, which could well be representative of the appearance of a born eunuch or a man castrated in early childhood. Photius, the teacher of Ptolemy XII Auletes (80–51 B.C.), was a eunuch who governed Egypt during years in which his pupil was underage, but later was condemned to death by Caesar in 47 B.C. Similarly, Kaufaur, the chief eunuch of King Abou-Kekr, succeeded the ruler and reigned for 20 years in the ninth century.[5]

> If any harm follows, then you shall give life for life, eye for eye, tooth for tooth, hand for hand, foot for foot, burn for burn, wound for wound, stripe for stripe (Exodus 21:23–25; Leviticus 24:19, 20).

What is recognized as the Mosaic law, or *Lex Talionis*, was codified sometime around 1512 B.C. Such is an expression of primitive, immediate vengeance, which imposes on the guilty punishment in exact measure to the suffering of the victim. This "eye for eye" retribution was extended in the ancient laws to punishment of the guilty part of the body that had assisted in the accomplishment of the crime. Specifically, the crimes of adultery and rape were punished by castration—cutting off the offending member. In ancient Egypt, rape was punished by the total excision of the penis and testicles of the guilty man. He was also beaten with a knotted, heavy stick called a *courbache* and, sometimes, the punishment would extend to cutting off his nose and ears. In some cases of adultery, the woman was whipped and sometimes disfigured by cutting off her nose.

Since 642 A.D., the principal faith of Egypt has been Islam, which allowed polygamy. As such, the need for harem eunuchs to guard the wives and concubines has continued in Egypt until very recent times. Millant states that the perpetuation of eunuchism in Egypt and other Moslem countries is due mainly to the Islamic faith. Islam, originated by the prophet Mohammad (c. 570–632), is a living faith and doctrine observed by nearly one-seventh of the world's population. More than merely a religion, Islam is a system for the organization of the entire community. While Mohammad himself had about 15 wives, it appears that he did not own any eunuchs, nor did he condemn the use of eunuchs. The *El Ktal*, book of Islamic laws, while recognizing that eunuchism is one of the indispensable cogs in the social organization of the area, still condemns the practice of castration.

Islam is not solely responsible for eunuchs in Egypt. Generally speaking, the country's climate is quite hot, and girls became fecund at an early age, as well as entered menopause at an early age. Thus, polygamy evolved with the laudable objective of safeguarding the continuation of the family and racial strain. Pregnancy, labor, birth and child-rearing often brought illness, debilitation and early death to the women, so substitutes and helper wives were almost a necessity. Observations of the animal kingdom, where one dominant male frequently has several females, also supported the idea of multiple wives. Polygamy has been defined by a number of societies as the natural order of things, and the number of polygamous peoples in the world was about four times that of monogamous people. Inasmuch as variety is arousing to men, the number of women in the harem was only limited by the wealth of the master. Wives had a status that was almost equal to the husband, but others in the harem did not have such high status—namely concubines and Ganymedes (young boys castrated and used as sex objects). These were usually slaves purchased on the open market. In addition, eunuchs more often were slaves.

Egypt's other major religion, the Christian Coptic Church, also contributed to the practice of castration in the region, mainly during the period from 300–1100 A.D. Some of the Coptic ascetic sects are believed to have practiced castration for the kingdom of heaven (per Matthew 5:27–30; 18: 8, 9; 19:12). Millant elaborates:

> For a long time the Coptic monks in the monasteries around Giza had a near monopoly on the manufacture of eunuchs and were the most renowned for this practice. The principal establishment of this group was on the left bank of the Nile, near Abou-Girgha, on the stone mountain called Djebel-Etter, thus named because of the ibis which lived there in great numbers. Several of the monasteries were built like forts on the sides of this mountain where the good monks established the central depot for mutilating the unhappy ones. The slave dealers stole the children or bought them for a low price in the Sudan. The head sacrificer was a Coptic bishop. The details of the enterprise were known to the government which let them be. Each year the viceroy bought at a specially low price 200 eunuchs for the Sultan's annual gift.[6]

Most of the black eunuchs came from Upper Egypt and surrounding countries, Abyssinia, the Sudan, Nubia, Carfour and Kordofan. Usually they were tall and thin, whereas the white eunuchs from the northern countries were normally hairless and fat. The price of the black eunuchs destined to be harem guards was in accordance with their ugliness and their degree of eviration. The most unattractive that were completely castrated would bring about the equivalent of 2400 francs and the partial ones with some remnants of a penis and no testicles would bring about 1800. Despite being castrated, some of the harem eunuchs were still capable of sexual function. A case in point: In 1877, a scandal was caused in the harem of the great sharif of Mecca when a black boy was born to one of the sharif's white concubines and presented as the sharif's own—although the sharif was also white. The white concubines of the harem would fetch 12,000 to 18,000 francs, depending on the beauty of their face and figure. The lowest price was for the black children, who might bring 300 to 500 francs.

The bronze and white eunuchs mostly came from the East. In 1659, about 22,000 were emasculated in the kingdom of Golconda, and the king of Butan sent more than 20,000 to the slave markets. Up to about the beginning of the 19th century, large tribes of Muslims occupied the provinces bordering Russia. Prisoners from their conquests would be included in these numbers and, sometimes, their raids on northern peoples would be motivated mainly for the purpose of gathering such slaves. The numbers of black eunuchs supplied by Egypt was estimated at 3,000 or 4,000 a year. The rate of survival for those who were castrated varied widely: only about 10 percent of the young boys survived back-woods butchery, whereas nearly 100 percent survived if they were operated on by the most clever physicians in Kartoum. Both Clot-Bey, physician-in-chief to the Pasha of Egypt, and the author, Paulitschke, have reported that at least a third survived the surgery on the average.[7]

In Egypt, where an omnipotent ruler could, over night, make his wine server into a minister of state, many poor parents saw castration as a means to a better life, a way of giving their sons or themselves an opportunity to gain wealth and power. Some eunuchs did, indeed, achieve status in society, but not without first having to overcome the various levels of the government hierarchy. Eunuchs were often appointed treasurers of the harem and of the whole realm; they were on the whole also well-respected. Frequently seen at the bazaar, the merchants were careful to treat the eunuchs with deference. Goddard cited the example of two eunuchs who became doctors and practiced successfully for several years.[8] The chief eunuch of the harem was even given the celebrated name of *dari seadet agasi*, which means "chief of the house of felicity."

On the first day of August in 1877, Egyptian and British officials signed the first convention to abolish slavery and eunuchism in Egypt. The document stated: "Every individual who is engaged in the commerce of slavery will be severely punished; and every mutilator of children will be prosecuted as a murderer by a court-martial." Another convention was signed in 1895 with even stronger wording. Despite the severity of the laws, Egyptians with money and influence continued to maintain harems, complete with eunuch guards and attendants. An article published in Cairo in the French newspaper, *The Egyptian Bourse,* dated June 29, 1909 emphasized this grim fact.

> In May, the government seized and liberated eight slaves which had been sold and kept in Cairo, and this is but a small representation of the reality that many are procured by high personalities. *Eunuchism and slavery continue to flourish in the houses of the pashas and beys.* A curious thing: these are called 'nationalists,' who claimed to give the slaves their freedom, who have given us this detestable example. In the time of the Muslim Khedive, the pashas were the greatest recruiters of slaves. This unclean work is still not effaced from contemporary history. Actually, it is by way of Tripolitania that is the main route from Turkey where they are then distributed throughout the country. In Egypt this leprosy continues to survive. The last two beys who have operated this breach of duty are Moustafa Rachid and Koutbe Baby Bey, two young, rich and well-educated men, so-called! We count on the government to inflict on them a punishment which will make them examples to the others. Today only the Muslims still persevere in this folly.[9]

The scholar Zambaco wrote about the winters he spent in Cairo for 12 years in the early part of the 20th century. He described the frequent captures by the fleets of the two governments that covered the Red Sea chasing black slave traders. Zambaco also remarked on the seizures of slaves and eunuchs, stories that would be discussed in the newspapers every month. Many of these slaves were bought in

Istanbul by the traders and transported to Alexandria and Cairo. The Philanthropic Commission would free them when found and place them in jobs with reliable households.

On September 16, 1909, the Cairo *Journal published the article, "The Traffic in Slaves."*

On the demand of the authorities of Mariout, a principal city of Egypt, the Minister of Justice issued an operational order for the arrest and provisional detention of a Bedouin named Chelatif, accusing him of making his living in the traffic in slaves between Tripolitania and Egypt. The Department for the Repression of the Traffic in Slaves had seized a dossier with a number of facts showing his culpability. A special tribunal will be formed to resolve his case.

Thus, in spite of the Egyptian government's concerted surveillance and the severity of the laws, the commerce in slaves and eunuchs continued in this period.

Endnotes—Chapter 3

[1] Maspero, *Histoire Ancienne des Peuples de l'Orient*. Quoted in Demetrius A. Zambaco, *Les Eunuques D'Aujourd 'hui et Ceux de Jadis*. Paris: Libraries de L'Academie de Medecine, 1911, p. 206.

[2] The Egyptian Book of the Dead. The book of going forth by day being the Papyrus of Ani (Royal Scribe of the divine offering. Translated by Dr. Raymond O. Faulkner. San Francisco: Chronicle Books, Plate 8 (Chapter 17).

[3] *Ibid.*, p. 94.

[4] Zambaco, *Ibid.*, p. 208.

[5] Millant, *Ibid.*, p. 227.

[6] *Ibid.*

[7] E. Goddard, *Egypt and Palestine*, 1867.

[8] Zambaco, *Ibid.*, pp. 69, 70. *Pasha* is an old Turkish title, derived from the Persian *padshah*. The title is always used with a proper name, and was given to high civil officials and was hereditary in 19th century Egypt. It also extends to the four highest military and civilian grades. *Bey* is another old Turkish title for gentleman or chief, and is a title of honor or courtesy in Egypt. In addition, the term can refer to a governor of a minor province.

[9] *Ibid.*, p. 74.

Chapter 4—Eunuchs in Persia & the Islamic World

The Persians are generally considered to be the people who intermittently occupied the Iranian plateau and much of the surrounding country at various times during their long and uneven history. Persian culture dates as far back as 4,000 B.C., which was the time of the ancient Akkadian and Ur dynasties, and continues today in the present state of Iran. The population is mainly Aryan, although the people are of mixed ancestry. Research indicates that castration was practiced in Persia, and that it may have had its origins in the region.

The custom of castration can be traced through the various periods of Persian history: from Babylonian and Sumerian times, about 3,000–600 B.C., the Achaemenid Empire, 559–330 B.C., the Macedonians, 330–276 B.C., the Parthian Empire, 250 B.C.–215 A.D., the Sassanian Empire, 224–651 A.D., the assorted Arab Caliphates, 651–1501, the Safavids, 1501–1736, the Zand Dynasty, 1757–1794, the Quajar Dynasty, 1794–1925, Reza Shah, 1926–1941, the Allied occupation, 1941–1945, to the reign of Mohammed Mossadegh, which ended in 1953. In fact, a eunuch, Agha Muhammed, was instrumental in overthrowing the Zend Dynasty and establishing—in violence—the Quajar house.[1]

In terms of religious faiths, Persians believed in the pantheons of Semitic gods from around 4,000 B.C. to the advent of Zoroaster (c. 618–541 B.C.). Zoroastrianism lasted in Persia until about 800 A.D., when it was gradually supplanted by Islam. (Remnants of the archaic religion still exist today around Bombay, India.)

Figurines of the "purified" eunuch priests from the temples to the goddess Inanna, dating back around 3,000 B.C., have been found in the Persian Gulf area. These statues and bas-relief carvings on the old palace walls from the Akkadian, Sumerian and Babylonian cultures clearly show the eunuchoid features that sharply differentiate them from the intact men of their era. The eunuchs' beardless face, corpulence, adipose hips, narrow shoulders and elongated arms contrasted with the heavy beards, angular figures and head adornments of most of the other men in the work. The eunuchs were not only shown as priests or worshippers, but also as musicians, singers, servers, cooks, military attendants, harem guards and other functionaries in the royal retinue.

Millant and Zambaco both discuss the use of eunuchs as sex objects for the pederasts. These authors refer to the Persian poets, Sadi, Rimi and Gulistand, and to the Indian writer, Vatsyayana, who mention this practice in their works.[2] However, the numbers who engaged in this practice must have been quite minor, because current studies show that across cultures pederasts and homosexuals account for a very small percentage of the population (one to five percent).

Eunuchs were demanded by Persian kings as part of the tribute from subjugated countries. Many were conquered, since Persians occupied most of the nations bordering it at various times in history. Assyria was obliged to send to King Darius I (522–486 B.C.) 1,000 silver talents, four months food for his army and 500 castrated boys every year, while Ethiopia was required to send 100 castrates yearly to Persia.[3] After each victorious campaign, the custom was to choose among the most intelligent and lively male children of the vanquished nation, castrate them and assign them to the seraglios, where they would be trained by adult eunuchs, learning the language and practices to carry out duties to their masters. This practice was still in use when Tavernier published a portrait of Persian life in 1675:

> Those who possessed positions in the Empire, came mostly from children captured in war, or sent as a present to the Shah, of about the age of nine or ten years. The Grand Leader had the choice of all of these young children, the best and most talented he kept, the others were distributed to the other princely seraglios. They would be instructed in religion, the law and all sorts of work. The healthiest and smartest were

given the best education so that they might serve their prince better. The others would be trained and employed in the offices where they were needed.[4]

When the young men reached manhood, they devoted their energy and loyalty to the country where they had been brought up and they were treated like adopted sons. Many were given important charges and delicate missions. They became the counselors of the princes— their "eyes and ears." They are found implicated in all the successions of the Persian aristocracy.

Herodotus, the "Father of History" (c. 484–425 B.C.), mentions the use of eunuchs several times in his histories. In *Book III* (2), he narrates the story of a particular eunuch, who was highly trusted by the Pharaoh Ahmose II of Egypt (also known as Amasis, who reigned from 569 to 526 B.C.), and sent as an envoy to the king of Persia. In *Book VI* (9), the author recounts how the Persians took the Ionian towns on the mainland and chose the most attractive boys to be castrated in order that they could become eunuch servants for the king. In *Book VIII* (103), Herodotus describes the chief eunuch named Hermotimus, who served King Xerxes (486–465 B.C.).

The Greek historian, Xenophon (c. 430–355 B.C.), favorably mentions the use of eunuchs by the Persian royalty in vital positions. Xenophon saw active military service with the Persians in 401 B.C., when he joined the campaign of the younger Cyrus against his brother Artaxerxes II. He later wrote a historical novel, the *Cyropaedia*, on the youth, training and career of Cyrus II (The Great, 559–530 B.C.). In this volume, he shows how true the eunuchs were to their masters, and how they deserved the crucial positions they occupied. This devotion to their master even included laying down their life, if the occasion demanded.

When Prince Abradate and his wife Panthea died, three of their eunuchs also died with them; and all were honored with a great funeral. Book VII of the *Cyropaedia* reads: "On a high column was inscribed the names of the husband and wife in Syrian characters, and on three smaller columns one could read 'here are the eunuchs.'"

Although the Persians and Assyrians had the highest regard for their eunuchs, most of the other writers throughout history have not been particularly kind to them. Both Plato and Polemon of Ilium (in the latter's *Portraits*) agreed that eunuchs were, for the most part, cruel, indiscreet and good for nothing—although they lived two centuries apart, one in the fourth century and another in the second century, B.C., respectively. Strato and Plutarch, who lived in the first century A.D., and the Roman satirists, who wrote in the second and third centuries, A.D., criticized eunuchs for their moral decadence and their role in contributing to the decline of Rome.

Claudian (Claudianus, Claudius, c. 370–c. 404) clearly had personal reasons for denouncing in scathing invective his rival at the Court of Arcadius, the Eastern Emperor, Eutropius, the eunuch. He secured a consulship by writing in praise of Stilicho, the Roman Western Emperor, and Honorius, chief minister.

Despite condemnations by the historians, eunuchs were produced and widely employed throughout the millennia of Persian history.

Bagoas (also *Bagol* and *Bagoses*) is the Greek form of an archaic Persian name often used for eunuchs. However, just as in disparate biblical writings, we find the word used as a proper name, which means "chamberlain," a job title that can mean a bedchamber attendant, a chief officer in the household of a king or one in charge of moneys, as well as simply a eunuch.

Chapters 12 through 14 of the Apocryphal book of the Bible, *Judith*, contain a discussion of how Judith was brought into the tent of Holfernes, the commanding general of Nebuchadnezzar (605–562 B.C.), about the year 587 B.C. by the eunuch, Bagoas, who was in charge of Holofernes' private affairs. Another Bagoas was a general in the army of one of the Ptolomies of Egypt. The best known of a long series of eunuchs named Bagoas was the confidential minister of Artaxerxes III. This particular Bagoas was commander in chief of the Persian forces in the conquest of Egypt (343 B.C.) and became wealthy by selling back to the priests the sacred writings looted from the Egyptian temples. He rose to such power that he became the real master of Persia. About 338 B.C., he murdered Artaxerxes and placed his son, Arses, on the throne. Two years later, he murdered Arses and made Darius III (336–330) king. When Darius asserted his independence, Bagoas attempted to poison him, but the king had been warned and made Bagoas drink the poisoned wine himself. Another eunuch with the moniker of Bagoas was the favorite of Alexander the Great (356–323 B.C.), as well as of Darius (according to the *Encyclopedia Britannica*).

Charles Ancillon quotes Vosius in his *Etymology of the Latin Language*, which stated that the Persians were the inventors of the custom of castrating men.[5] Vosius wrote that the Latin term *Spado*, a word that described eunuchs in their various forms, came from the Persian city of Spada, where the first castration was said to have been performed. The word *spado* and *spadone* are still used today to describe a castrated male—whether human or animal—or an impotent male. *Spay* means to remove the ovaries of a woman or female animal, and the word is sometimes used as a synonym for the word castrate.

Zambaco defines the *spadones* as eunuchs who had only the testicles removed; the penis (wholly or partially) was allowed to remain to facilitate urination.[6] This type of eunuch was deemed suitable for serving or defending his master, but not for guarding the members of the harem. Only the completely shorn eunuchs were assigned to the seraglio's inner precincts.

As in many other countries, eunuchism in Persia raised many poor men's names to immortality, which would have otherwise been long forgotten. In the biblical book of Esther, many of the eunuchs of the Persian king Ahasuerus (Xerxes I, 486–465 B.C.) were honored by having their names mentioned in the holy book. Hegia was the eunuch in charge of the king's women. Shaashgaz was the king's eunuch in charge of the second harem of concubines. Mehuman, Biztha, Harbona, Bigtha, Abagtha, Zethar and Carkas were the seven eunuchs who attended the king. Bigthan and Terish were two of the eunuchs who guarded the king's threshold. Hathach was the king's eunuch appointed to attend to Queen Esther. Harbona was one of the eunuchs who closely attended the king, himself. The names of these same eunuchs were also rendered in the Greek form in the version of the book of Esther that was presented to Ptolomy XIII and Cleopatra VII in 47 B.C. by Dositheus, messenger from Lysimachus, Ptolomy's son in Jerusalem.

Little information concerning castration was transmitted from the Macedonian (or Greek) dominated period of Persian history, which began with Alexander the Great's conquest in about 330 A.D., or from the Roman period, which is dated from about 2 B.C. to 330 A.D. However, references are made in later Byzantine history that indicate eunuchs were still in use in the harems and royal entourages during this era. Some authors have made it apparent that Byzantium borrowed the practice of castration from Persia. Menophanes, the general of King Mithradites the Great of Pontus (c. 121–63 B.C.), who sacked the island stronghold at Delos in 87 B.C., was one such eunuch official who was mentioned during this specific period of Persian history.

Persia has continued the custom of *Lex Talionis*—which is discussed in Leviticus 24:19, 20—throughout its history and even until the present day: the practice of cutting off the penis of the rapist and the hand of the thief. The soldiers of Persia also followed the ancient custom of cutting off the genitalia of both living and dead vanquished enemy troops until relatively recently (World War II).

The deplorable custom of destroying the previous regime's historical records, which occurred in Egypt and elsewhere, also occurred in Persia, and continues today. An article in the *Biblical Archaeology Review* discusses the subject: The story is told how the Waqf (Muslim religious trust) damaged and destroyed critical Christian and Hebrew archeological remains on the Temple Mount in Jerusalem. A lawsuit had been filed in 1986 to stop the destruction, but the decision was not handed down until November 1993, due to the political sensitivity surrounding the Temple Mount and the need to preserve public order. Structures that had been built by the Mamelukes, and the Crusaders, as well as the Second Jewish Temple, were irreparably damaged by the Waqf, who continued to inflict damage despite several earlier warnings by the government.[7]

In the case of Persia, the works of earlier Zorastrian, Christian, Buddhist, Hindi and other religious scholars were systematically destroyed by Moslem conquerors, as these writings were in conflict with the teachings of Islam. Most of the historical records pertaining to eunuchism in Persia and its possessions that are extant are from other Islamic nations. The vast majority of the surviving Arabic texts that contain references to Persian eunuchs have never been translated into English, and the ones that have are from the later periods of Persian history.

During this time, writers tended not to mention the physical condition of those men that filled the palaces of the Caliphs, Beys, Amirs and Nobles, a practice which tended to conceal the fact that many were eunuchs. Today we may find information about these castration practices available in English in the *Encyclopedia of Islam* (1979).

Scholz[8] reports that the reason castration is forbidden by Muslims is that the Koran (Sura 2:25) promises a heaven after death where they will be "Wedded to chaste virgins, they shall abide there forever." So the men must retain their virility in order to enjoy the company of these amorous huris. In spite of the prohibition of castration, there is still today a considerable use of castrated eunuchs as guards at Islamic holy places, as well as harems: The Ka 'bah in Mecca, the sacred shrine in Medina (the tomb of Muhammad in the Prophet's Mosque), and sometimes the Dome of the Rock in Jerusalem. As late as 1990 there wer 17 eunuchs in Medina and 14 in Mecca.

History According to the Encyclopedia of Islam

According to the text, the guardians of the harem were, at first, rarely referred to by their specific appellation of "castrate" (*khasi*) or "eunuch" (*tawashin*). Rather, they were usually designated by the more neutral term of "servant" (*khadim*), or referred to with the honorable title of "master" in the sense of "teacher" (*ustadh*), which gives some indication as to the function of some of the eunuchs.[9] Some eunuchs were called "master of audiences" or "master of ceremonies" (*amir majlis*) or "grand master of the armour" (*amir silah*). Other Arabic terms for eunuch include: *Abd* and *abid*, the usual word for "slave," and *ghulam* (plural *ghilman*), meaning "young man" or "boy," although this latter term was also used to describe young eunuch pages.

Khasi specifically designates the eunuch who has had only his testicles removed, "whereas the complete eunuch, deprived of all his sexual organs, is a *madjbub*," which means "'castrated by evulsion.'" The *Thousand and One Nights* contains descriptions of how men came to be eunuchs. Sometimes a man was mutilated "by a mistress (113th night), or a jealous husband (33rd night)," or because he seduced a young girl (39th night). In the folklore version, "a slave who refuses to be freed, is castrated and sold at a very high price (39th night)."[10]

While some males were even castrated on the orders of the king himself, many castrations occurred accidentally. "And it seems that some doctors practiced early on such an operation, when the state of illness made it necessary."[11]

The *Encyclopedia of Islam* reports that two methods were used for the emasculation of eunuchs that the author has been able to encounter: simultaneous ablation of the testicles (*mizwad*) and the penis or incision of the scrotal sheath (*safan*) *and evulsion of the testicles* first of all, then cutting of the male member; after this operation a rod of lead was placed in the urethra and replaced after each urination, until the healing was completed, in order to prevent tissues from joining.

However, the probability exists that the majority of eunuchs had only their testicles removed and their scrotum cauterized by "a red hot blade." Another form of castration, called *widja*, involved "binding the cord supporting the testicles and making them gush out," and subsequently crushed, after which they "atrophied naturally. Twisting the cord (*asb*) was also known."[12]

The same source states that some parents had their children castrated "in order to consecrate them to the service of the Church" and that "the religious origin of emasculation was not unknown," even though the "Council of Nicea (325 A.D.) had clearly prohibited eunuchs from the priesthood." Eunuchs were allowed to be "choristers and even priests in the Oriental Church."[13]

Scholars of Arab culture maintain that not only were large numbers of eunuchs castrated in Spain by Jewish peoples—as well as in locations including Abyssinia and Upper Egypt—then transported to the East, but that all eunuchs in Islamic lands were foreigners, not natives. "Until recent times, slavers from Muslim states situated further north raided Central Africa; women slaves and eunuchs passed clandestinely via Djibouti to people (in) the harems of the Hidjaz."[14]

A priori, these practices hardly appear legal. Before Islam, although some isolated cases of castration were reported and although the Arabs of the period without doubt possessed some eunuchs (it is sometimes thought that a reference to them appears in the Ku'ran, XXIV: 31, where it is said that women can show their finery to their male servants who have no carnal desire (*al-tabi'in ghayr uli l-irba*), [but] they cannot have had them produced regularly on their territory, so that the question of knowing whether emasculation of men was permitted was not put clearly to the first Muslims.

But, "prohibition of practicing emasculation appears to have proceeded by a sort of tacit consensus." That is, Muslims allowed Jews and Christians to produce eunuchs, "which the Muslims could then acquire without contravening their law."[15]

For the most part, Islamic law permitted the castration of animals. However, "some forbade the castration of horses only." Nonetheless, "gelded horses were always much appreciated, notably for war, for their endurance, their pace and silence." Similarly, calves were castrated, for when they reached maturity as bulls, it became rather difficult to make them work. In addition, the flesh of the castrated bulls (known as oxen) was considered to be more tender and flavorful. The same was also said of capons.[16]

Al-Djahiz is probably the first author to have recorded his observations on their characteristics and the transformations that they [castrates] undergo physically, morally and intellectually. He remarks rightly that if emasculation takes place before puberty—which is the most frequent case— the beard and body hair do not grow, but the hair of the head, eyebrows and lashes remain and never fall, exactly as with women, who do not experience baldness (I, 108, 114). Eunuchs have soft skin, florid complexion, but they become lined and thin very quickly with advancing age, which does not prevent them from enjoying a greater longevity, for they do not use their strength to copulate (I, 137). Their voice, having changed after the operation, is recognizable (I, 113) by everyone (which allows *hakiyas* to include them easily in their imitations (al-Masudi, Viii, pp. 162, 164). They have long feet...their musculature tonicity is weak and their flesh is flaccid; their walk is ungainly (*Hayawan*, I, 116) due to the weakness of their nerves. Because of the fetidness of their sweat, they give off a peculiar odor, contrasting on this point with the animals who, after castration, no longer smell bad (I, 106). Al-Masudi (VIII, 149) asserts, on the contrary, that the armpits of men who have been castrated do not give off a "fetid odor." Al-Djahiz adds that "urinary incontinence is their lot (I, p. 158). If the operation takes place in adulthood, the pilary system disappears, with the exception of the pubic hair (I, 113), and strength diminishes (I, 115)."[17]

Al-Djahiz goes on to discuss, at length, the nature of eunuchs' character, which he says iscomparable to children and women (I, 135–136); like them, they particularly like playing with birds. Finding in food and drink (they appreciate wine especially; I, 158) a kind of compensation for the deprivation of other pleasures, they have a tendency to eat and drink heavily, which, with their continence (VII, 223), explains their obesity (I, 111). They are avaricious, indiscreet, as quick to lose their temper as to show their joy or to weep (I, 135), inclined to gossip and slander. They despise the common people and accept only the powerful and the rich as masters (I, 136, 159). They like domestic work, but are ill-adapted to arduous trades (I, 117); on the other hand, they endure long horse rides better than the Turks and Kharidjis (I, 136) and are excellent at archery; especially devoted to that are white eunuchs, who deploy their warlike qualities against the Byzantines to avenge themselves for the mutilation that the latter have made them undergo; they dedicate themselves to harboring an implacable hatred (I, 125–125, 173–174). Appreciating the value of that which they have lost (I, 125), they are jealous of and hate the *fuhul* (I, 173), and do not lack cruelty; this trait of character shows itself in their taste for cockfights (I, 118).

Intellectually, they are superior to their normal brothers and are better at their trade, but one must not demand of them too much reflection (I, 117); those from Persia are highly appreciated (I, 118), but for the blacks of Abyssinia, Nubia and other parts, castration entails a complete physical, as well as moral decline (I, 119).[18]

The Encyclopedia discusses the eunuchs' "total loss of sexual faculties, and it is from this point of view that certain Muslims of early times had envisaged it; al-Mukaddasi thinks that emasculation, among the Rum [Europeans] consecrated to the Church, was intended to spare them the tortures of lust." But, according to al-Djahiz (I, 12), the mutilation was incomplete, reckoning "that it was intended simply to prevent the monks from impregnating the nuns." [19]

The Persian caliph, al-Amin (c. 780–813), is said to have bought many more eunuchs than his predecessors and with having had them constantly in attendance at his side, associating them in the affairs of state. His successors largely imitated his example, and the figures supplied, although to be treated with caution, remain very high; in the time of al-Muktaff (902–909), there were in the palace 10,000 *khadam*, blacks and whites (*Sakaliba*), and in the palace of al-Muktadir (908–932) 11,000 were sheltered, comprising 7,000 blacks and 4,000 whites. It is remarkable that al-Kalkashandi (V, 92) also mentions the figure of 10,000 for the court of Dihli (Delhi in India), but precise details of this kind are rare and are clearly exaggerated. However, the organization of the corps of eunuchs is well-known, particularly under the Fatimids.[20]

In terms of the black eunuchs, specifically,

their origin is sufficiently well-known, for it is evidently identical to that of the slaves, on which, moreover, there is some precise information. Al-Mukaddasi distinguishes three kinds: the first, which is, he says without any other specification, the best, was exported to Egypt; the second, that of the Berbers, was sent to Aden; the third 'resembles' the Abyssinians. Al-Istakhri, 40, remains equally vague in saying that the eunuchs sold in the Muslim lands are neither Nubians, nor Zandj, nor Ethiopians, nor Bedja, but belong to still blacker races. ...According to the *Hudud al-'adam*, p. 165, the Sudan is, without doubt, the land from which the majority of eunuchs came; in a lively passage, the author adds that the Egyptian merchants stole children there—or bought them from blacks that they had themselves stolen—took them, castrated them and imported them into Egypt where they sold them. A. Mez (chapter XX) mentions that in the 12th century, the town of Hadya, in Abyssinia, ranked as the only place where eunuchs were produced, but the region of Asyut, in Upper Egypt, is also cited.[21]

Al-Djahiz, in his work, *Hayawan* (Volume I, p. 125), is cited as reporting that, "as early as the 9th century," some eunuchs became so rich that they

bought estates in the border estates, recruited fighting men and made attacks on the Byzantines to revenge themselves for their very serious injuries. It may not be by chance that several governors of Tarsus (present Adana in Turkey), notably Bishr, *mawla* of Ibn Abi 'l-Sadj, were white eunuchs who launched expeditions against the Byzantines and that Thamal, commanding the naval forces in the Mediterranean, was also one. In the same way, in 919 the admirals commanding the Fatimid and Byzantine fleets respectively were both eunuchs (al-Kindi, *Judges*, 276). At this period, moreover, there were numerous generals who were *khisyan* (for example Mas'ud, Muflih al-Muktadiri, etc.); similarly some of them were leaders of the Hudjariyya.[22]

Kafur, a highly successful eunuch who attained the position of master of Egypt and Syria, died in 968. Historians have noted that he was black. [23]

Under the first Fatimids, Ustadh Djawhar, who was a Slav (c. 1169) eunuch, played a role so important that he merited a special biography. A little later, Bardjawan, who was also white, was the tutor of the caliph al-Hakim; having assumed the functions of the regent of the Fatimid Empire, he was killed by another eunuch, Raydan, on the orders of the caliph.[24]

According to al-Kalkashandi (*Subh*, III, 477) 1,000 eunuchs organized into a cohesive body during this era. "In the 12th century a number were to be found in charge of various forces, directing rival states and governing important towns."[25] B. Lewis writes that during Fatimid al-'Adid's reign, black eunuchs exerted considerable influence.[26]

> [I]t was his mu 'tamin al-khilafa, Djawhar, who, in 1169, hatched a plot against Saladin (Ibn al-Athir, vol. IX, 103). Eunuchs were still found among the troops of the latter (Imad al-Din, *al-Fath al-kussi*, 324; translated by H. Masse, 287), who took Karakush completely into his confidence (Baha' al-Din). It would be easy to multiply the examples.[27]

> In Persia, a notable case cited is that of Manucihr Kahn Mu'tamid al-Dawla, sometime governor of Isfahan during the reign of Nasir al-Din Shah (1848–1896); he had been taken prisoner in Fath 'Ali Shah's wars with Russia and castrated. On his death his property was claimed by the Persian crown on the grounds of his having been a slave, though this was disputed.[28]

"Aka Muhammad Khan, the founder of the Kajar dynasty, was a eunuch, having been castrated in childhood by Adil Shah, the nephew of Nadir Shah, into whose hands he had fallen."[29]

It should be noted that eunuchs occupying the throne is nothing less than "exceptional," and clearly in contradiction to Islamic law, "which demands the physical integrity of the ruler."

> A. Mez (chapter XX) mentions that a eunuch functioned as a *kadji* at Damietta, but it is certain that the *khisyan*, from the sole fact of their mutilation, were normally excluded from the magistrature. However, Nizam al'Mulk (*Siyasat-nama*, Schefer (ed.), Paris, 1891, 3, 41) considers that it is preferable to confer the functions of *muhtasib* on a eunuch and it will be noted that, under the Ottomans, the control of the *wakfs* of the Holy Cities and most of the mosques was assured up to the 16th century by the *kapi aghasi*, in the 17th century by the latter and the *kizlar aghasi*, respectively the Chief White

Eunuch and the Chief Black Eunuch, in the 18th century by the *kizlar aghasi* alone, after the weakening of the power of the whites (see below).[30]

Eunuchs continued to be used throughout Islamic lands from the end of the 10th century until the 19th century, although the "number had considerably diminished in Syria and also in Egypt, where there were no more than 300 belonging to the aristocracy who, alone, could afford such a luxury. Only very few castrated men were white. Similarly in the Persian Gulf, even the black eunuchs were very few in number."[31] The eunuchs, usually serving "as intermediaries between their master and his wives and concubines," had a great deal of freedom, such that they were able to become involved in political intrigue, sometimes conspiring with harem women.[32]

Eunuchs organized into a cohesive body as early as the ninth century. They were sometimes positioned between the soldiers and the Caliph, himself. On other occasions, they accompanied ambassadors during every visit.[33] Their positions were frequently lofty, and a clear hierarchy was established:

> At the court of the Fatimids, the eunuchs (*ustadh*) used to come immediately after the *amirs*. The officials in private service were eunuchs, of whom those of the greatest dignity wore a turban passing under the chin and were therefore called *muhannak*. 'The most exalted rank among the *muhannak* eunuchs was held by the one who had the charge of wrapping a special crown around the head of the Caliph for ceremonial purposes…Next came the *sahib al-madjlis* or master of the audience hall; the *sahib al-risala*, or master of correspondence; the *zimam al-kusur*, the intendant of the palaces; the *sahib bayt al-mal*, or director of the treasury; the master of the registry (*sahib al-daftar*) who directed the general offices (*diwan*); the bearer of the inkwell (*hamil al-darwat*); the superintendent of the Caliph's kinsmen (*zamm al-akarib*); the intendant of the table (*sahib al-ma'ida*)….'[34]

Under the Safavids, eunuchs (*Kh adjagan*, *Kh adja-sarayan*) played a particularly critical role in affairs of state. A. K. S. Lambton writes that, "in Persia, it was only under the Safavids" that eunuchs (*Kh adjagan*, *Kh adja-sarayan*) were in charge of the women's apartments in the royal palace, and began to play an critical role in political affairs.[35] Lambton quotes Chardin as stating that 3,000 eunuchs were in the court during this time, and that the majority were whites from the Malabar coast. However, during the reign of Shah 'Abbas (1587–1629), Georgian and other white prisoners of war were enslaved and castrated, usually serving in the royal harem. "According to the Tadhkirat al-Muluk, he was the first shah to introduce white eunuchs into the palace alongside the black eunuchs."

Eunuchs became especially powerful at this juncture, as the princes and heir apparents were secluded in the harems and the eunuchs were responsible for their education and training. One of the most famous of these eunuchs was Sarou-Taqi-Kahn Mirza, the first minister to Shah 'Abbas. Some historians have compared him to Richelieu, Emperor Louis XIII's minister. Like Richelieu, Sarou-Taqi (or Ali-Beck, as he was also known), made numerous enemies because of his zealous and vindictive way of breaking up intrigues among the aristocracy.

On the death of Shah 'Abbas II in 1667, the palace eunuchs contrived the succession of Shah Sulayman and seized control of the state. On the latter's death in 1694, with the connivance of Maryam Begum, Shah Sulayman's aunt, they placed Shah Sultan Husayn on the throne. He left the management of affairs of state entirely to them. They succeeded in extending their influence over military, as well as civil affairs, the only check on their power being the faction which prevailed in their own ranks and the rivalry of the religious party under Muhammad Bakir Madjlisi. The irresponsible character of their government and the faction to which it gave rise was one of the main causes of the decline of the Safavid dynasty. The *haram* of Shah Sultan Husayn, and with it the number of eunuchs, reached enormous proportions and swallowed up a large part of the revenue.

After the fall of the Safavids, the eunuchs never achieved any significant political power or prestige. By 1887, only 38 eunuchs in the royal harem were believed to exist.[36]

Orhonlu indicates that eunuchs—both black and white—first appeared in the Ottoman state "in the first half of the 15th century."[37]

> The use of negroes, that is black eunuchs, in the Ottoman Turk palace started during the reign of Mehemmed the Conqueror (1451–1481) and from the beginning of the 16th century we find black eunuchs employed alongside the white ones. In 1513 there were 10 white and black *khadims* (eunuchs) serving in the palace (Topkapi Sarayi Muzesi arsivi, N. D. 10052). The head of the eunuchs in charge of the Bab al-sa'ada of the palace was called the *kapi aghasi* or *bab al-sa 'ada aghasi*, which was the highest office in the harem. But in 1582 the superintendence of the harem and the office of *Dar al'Sa 'ada aghasi* passed into the hands of Habashi Mehmed Agha, and the black eunuchs and the white eunuchs were relegated to second place and had to be content with the office of *kapi aghasi*.

By the advent of the 16th century and into the 17th century, several white eunuchs ascended to the office of Grand Vizier, including: Khadim 'Ali Pasha, serving under Bayezid I from 1501–1503 for the first time, and from 1506–1511 for the second time; Khadim Sinan Pasha (1516–1517) during the reign of Selim I; Khadim Suleyman Pasha (1541–1544) during Suleyman the Magnificent's rule; Khadim Mesih Pasha (1585–1586) during Murad III's reign; Khadim Hasan Pasha (1597–1598) during Mehemmed III's reign; and Khadim Mehmed Pasha (1622–1623), under Mustafa I.[38]

As time progressed, black eunuchs became more dominate in the harems, and remained in the majority until the fall of the Ottoman

Empire. Eunuchs were employed not only in the palace, but in more common residences. In fact, they were found throughout Ottoman society.[39]

It has been noted that the Ottomans preferred black eunuchs who had been "castrated completely and who were physically ugly."[40] And black eunuchs generally remained in the majority. "By the force of circumstances, the white eunuchs were always less numerous than the blacks, and from the 16th century, they became more rare at the Ottoman court; the supply ceased completely with the annexation of the Caucasian regions by the Russians at the beginning of the 19th century."[41]

Black eunuchs were imported from Egypt, usually between the ages of eight and 11. The mortality rate was relatively low for young boys castrated before puberty, but rose to high levels for those castrated after maturity. As noted previously, most of the operations were done in Upper Egypt, although a group of professionals worked in Egypt during the 17th century called *djerrah-i djellabis*, because "a private person had no legal right in the empire to castrate his slave."[42]

Orhonlu states that "the process of abolishing slavery and the negro slave trade in the Ottoman Empire started during the reign of Mahmud II." Orhonlu quotes Dustur as writing that by February 1857, "a *firman* was issued prohibiting slavery and the slave trade in the Ottoman lands."[43] After the prohibition, the use of eunuchs—and of slavery, in general—waned, although they continued to be employed in the royal harems.

The Mamelukes of Persia

Beginning about 872 with the dissolution of the prosperous Tahirid caliphates and the coming of the Zanj rebellion in Iran (869–883), the former custom of taking slaves from the Russian and Eastern areas to the north, grew into the practice of forming them into regiments of guards. This was reminiscent of the old custom that dates back to at least the time of Cyrus the Great (c. 560 B.C.), who had wisely placed eunuchs in his personal guard. The ancient (c. 2500 B.C.) eunuchoid votive statues with fair skin and blue eyes are a testament to the Persian practice of castrating their white captives.

At this time, the Mamelukes (Mamluk and Mameluk, meaning "owned"), regiments of slave soldiers, were formed; they consisted of white slaves who had been converted to Islam. They were brought in by the Caliphs to compensate for the military inadequacies of the Arabs and Persians. These largely Ciracassian regiments were reliable soldiers who eventually formed their own caste. As each Persian dynasty weakened, the Mamelukes acquired a growing measure of control, occupying the chief political offices at the capital and in the provinces.

The method for castrating white slaves differed from that used for the blacks. Whereas the black slaves were forced to submit to a complete and barbarous amputation, referred to as "level with the abdomen," the white slaves were operated on with somewhat greater care, retaining the ability to perform coitus. (This distinction is also vouched for in modern times.) According to al-Djahiz, the operation encouraged all the *natural aptitudes* for the "Slavs," as opposed to the blacks. Parenthetically, the word "slave" came from "Slav," which originated in the early Middle Ages. White slaves were said to bring a higher price on the slave markets in the Islamic world than the black or mulatto slaves.

The main attributes of the Mameluke military society were apparent from the outset. They exhibited exceptional military ability and valor, as well as demonstrated a high level of unity against outsiders. However, internal dissension plagued their ranks. The Al-Bahriyya Mameluke regiment of 800 to 1000 horsemen, recruited by Sultan Al Salih-Nadim Al-Din Ayy ub (1240–1249) won battles at Al-Mansura in 1249 and Ayn Djalut in 1260, despite a split in their ranks in 1254, which seriously threatened their survival.

At this particular phase of Persian history, conditions were much like those in Europe. The power and authority of the central dynasty had been weakened by revolts and armed rivalries among the provinces. The Seljuks, warlike nomads, arrived from central Asia about 985 and defeated the Sultan Masud, with the support of the Persian nobles in 1040. The Seljuk, Togrul Bey, with a mixed army of Turkish and Mameluke troops unified the empire by 1063. His successor, Alp Arslan, completed the conquest across Egypt with his Mamelukes, defeating the Byzantines in 1071 and the Crusaders in 1096 and 1101. The Assassins (*Hashishin*, a taker of hashish) caused much destruction and internal strife beginning about 1094, and Genghis Khan sealed Persia's fate in 1220. His "Golden Horde" was stopped in one of history's most decisive battles on September 3, 1260 at Ayn Jalut in Palestine by the Mameluke commander named Baybars.

Baybars established himself as the Sultan of Egypt and began the world's most renowned slave dynasty, which ruled Egypt and several of the surrounding countries until 1517. During the Mameluke dynasty, one slave ruler would succeed another, much as a son follows his father. New slaves were regularly imported from Venetian trading posts in the Crimea (now Russia). Mameluke sultans ruled in Cyrenaica, Syria, the Hejaz, North Nubia and Egypt in this same fashion until Kansu Al-Ghuri (1501–1516), the last of the Mameluke sultans in Egypt, was overthrown by the Ottoman Turk Sultan, Selim I.

The Mameluke governors in the provinces intimidated the Ottoman governors, continuing to do so until about 1809, when the Ottoman sultan, Mohammed Ali Pasha (1769–1849), persuaded them to settle in the environs of Cairo. On March 1, 1811, Ali Pasha invited 300 of the Mameluke beys to the investiture ceremony for his son at the Citadel in Cairo. When they were all inside, he fastened the gates and they were killed in a hail of gunfire, thus putting a bloody end to Mameluke power in Egypt.

The Janissaries of the Ottoman Empire

The archaic custom of castrating prisoners of war and enslaving them produced not only the Mamelukes in Persia, but the Janissaries in the

Ottoman Empire, as well. The Janissaries (also Janizaries, *yeni ceri* or *yani ceri* in Turkish, which means "new force," "new troops" or "new army") were a disciplined and reliable military corps that were formed around 1340 under Sultan Orchan. The ranks were expanded and formalized during the reign of Murad I (1360–1385). Under the sultan's order in 1362, one in every five Christian boys captured was made available to the palace. Those not selected for service in the palace were destined for service in the Janissaries.

These *acemi aglans* (*adjami oglan* or *acemi oglan*, meaning "foreign boys") were later supplemented by another form of conscription under Sultan Murad II (1421–1451) to fill the ranks of the Janissaries when prisoners of war were no longer sufficient. This compulsory levy of Christian youths, 14 to 18 years old, was called the *devshirme* (meaning "conscription"), and lasted until April 1705, when the last *devshirme* was recorded in Greece. About this time, the ranks of the Janissaries became swollen with Muslim-born recruits, and conscription was no longer necessary.

As time progressed, the corps became increasingly unruly. They revolted and deposed their rulers on several occasions: Mustafa II in 1703, Ahmet III in 1730 and Selim III in 1807. When Mahmud II came to power in 1808, he secretly employed western artillery and troops. When the Janissaries revolted against these new troops, Mahmud destroyed them in their own barracks with cannon fire on June 15, 1826.

For more than 400 years, the Janissaries were the very core of the Ottoman standing army. Other units would be disbanded during peacetime, but their corps would remain strong, policing Istanbul and the frontier towns. They were rigidly disciplined during most of their history by strict rules of celibacy, religious service and confinement to barracks. Overall, the fact that some of them were eunuchs is believed to have played a part in their loyal and steadfast contribution to Ottoman rulers and employers.

Conclusion

In Persia and Moslem countries, castration has been utilized for nearly 5,000 years, and is still practiced in the harems of Morrocco and Arabia, although the harem became illegal in Arabia in 1962. Clearly, in this region of the world, eunuchs have proved to be a highly valued social group, such that the benefits of eviration are almost unquestionable.

Perhaps the reason why eunuchs have been portrayed as cruel, avaricious and haughty throughout Eastern history is now apparent. Considering that nearly all reported eunuchs in Persia and other Moslem countries were prisoners of war and captives who were forcibly castrated and enslaved, it would appear normal for the eunuchs to have had deep-seated resentment toward their captors, and thus exhibit reactive behavior.

Endnotes—Chapter 4

1. James Hasting, *Encyclopedia of Religious Ethics*, Volume 5. New York: Charles Scribner's Sons, 1912, p. 580.

2. Richard Millant, *Les Eunuques a Travers les Ages*. Paris: Place de LeEcole-de-Medicine, 1908, p. 113; Demetrius A. Zambaco, *Les Eunuques D'Aujourd'hui et Ceux de Jadis*. Paris: Libraries de L'Academie de Medicine, 1911, p. 211. Millant was a doctor, as was Zambaco, who was also a pasha. It should be noted that in the period from about 914–1150, the ethical climate of Persia condoned homosexual liaisons and sodomy was not punished. Masters of young slaves were free to indulge in unnatural and sadistic tastes. Resentments aroused by these practices were behind the murders of Zangi, born Ak Sonkur in 1146. Zangi castrated the sons of his Greek and Armenian prisoners to preserve their boyish and beardless appearance. The operation was usually done within their homelands, as well as within the borders of Islam, especially in the case of the Turks. (See H. A. R. Gibb, J. H. Kramers, J. Levi-Provincal and J. Schacht (eds.), *Encyclopedia of Islam*, Volume II. Leyden, The Netherlands: E. J. Brill. 1979, p. 1082.)

3. Millant, *Ibid.*, p. 93.

4. Tavernier, *Relations in the Interior of the Seraglio of the Grand Lord*. Paris, 1675.

5. Charles Ancillon, *Traite Des Eunuques*. Paris: Editions Ramsay, 1707, Reprinted in 1978, p. 54.

6. Zambaco, *Ibid.*, p. 77.

7. "Israeli Court Finds Muslim Council Destroyed Ancient Remains on Temple Mount." *Biblical Archaeology Review*, Volume 20, No. 4, 1994, p. 39.

8. Scholz, Piotr O. (2001). Eunuchs and Castrati a Cultural History. Princeton, NJ: Markus Weiner Publishers, Inc., pp. 20, 26.

9. *Ibid.*, Volume IV, p. 1087.

10. *Ibid.*, p. 1087. The authors refer to Al-Djahiz, *K. al-Hayawan (The Animal Kingdom)*, Volume I, pp. 121–123. Al-Djahiz (c. 776–869), a noted Arab writer of Basra and Baghdad, was the author of nearly 200 titles. Only about 30 have been preserved. His chief work was *The Animal Kingdom*. The seven-volume anthology includes trenchant observations of animals, including man, and is considered far ahead of its time in many concepts.

11. Gibb, *et al.*, *Ibid.*, pp. 1087–1088.

12. *Ibid.*, p. 1088.

13. *Ibid.*, p. 1089. The authors refer to L. Massignon, *Annuaire du Monde Musulman*, 1955, pp. 357, 385.
14. Gibb, *et al.*, *Ibid.*, Volume IV, p. 1089.

15. *Ibid.*, p. 1090. The authors refer to al-Kayrawani, *Risala*, translated by Bercher, 323. Oxen (castrated bulls) lived about three times longer than bulls.

16. *Ibid.*, p. 1090. *Hayawan* text appears in a more condensed form in *Mufakharat al-djawari wa'l-ghilman*, Pellat (ed.), Beirut, 1957, pp. 52–55, as well as in another edition by Hurun of Cairo, 1965, Volume II, pp. 123–125). Other sources note the smell of urine in eunuchs, due to their difficulty in urination and holding their water.

17. *Ibid.*, p. 1090. Kharidjis is a term for people from Eastern Iran.

18. *Ibid.*, p. 1090.

19. *Ibid.*, p. 1091. The authors refer to Hilal al-Sabi', *Rusum dar al-khilafa*, M. 'Awwad (ed.), 1964, p. 8.

20. *Ibid.*, pp. 1088–1089.

21. *Ibid.*, p. 1091. The authors refer to Vasiliev-Canard, *Byzance et les Arabes*, Volumes I and II, 1968, p. 130. The Hudjariyya was a tribe and administrative division of Arabia, found to the east of Mecca.

22. *Ibid.*, p. 1091. Kafur, who was originally from Lab in Nubia, was sold to the founder of the Ikhshidid Dynasty, Muhammad ibn Tughdj

al-Ikhshid. Al-Ikhshid recognized his great talents and raised him to command of the army, as well as entrusted his sons education to his instruction. Kafur enjoyed complete authority for 22 years and accomplished much for Egypt. Another famous eunuch also known as Kafur was Malik Kafur, who was the conqueror of the Deccan Plateau in India during the reign of Sultan 'Ala' al-DinKhaldji, from 1296 to 1316. This information originates from Gibb, *et al.*, *Ibid.*, Volume II, p. 1084, quoting for authority, Barant, *Ta'rikh-i Firus Shahi*, p. 376. From about 1206 to 1290, the Sultans of Dihli (Dehli) in India were all military slaves or their descendants.

[23.] *Ibid.*, p. 1091. Bardjawan's ancestry is uncertain, but he was probably a Slav. He rose to very high offices in Egypt and governed effectively, but made the mistake of calling al-Hakim his "little lizard." Hakim ordered his death and said, "the lizard is now a dragon." Bardjawan was stabbed to death on April 26, 1000.

[24.] *Ibid.*, 1091. See further, N. ElissŽeff, *Nur al-Din*, ii, 327, 340, 385, 484, 557, 657.

[25.] *Ibid.*, p. 1091. The authors refer to B. Lewis, *Race and Color*, p. 84 and bibliography.

[26.] *Ibid.*, p. 1091.

[27.] *Ibid.*, p. 1091. The authors refer to Great Britain, Public Record Office, F. O. 60/29. Murray to Clarendon, No. 60, Baghdad, 8 August 1856.

[28.] *Ibid.*, p. 1091. Agha Mohammed Shah (1794–1797), founder of the Qajar Dynasty (1794–1925) in Persia, is thought to have been only five years old at the time of his castration, since Adil Shah was killed about 1746. He attacked and defeated the remnants of the Zand Dynasty. he was succeeded by his nephew, Fath Ali Shah (1797–1834).

[29.] *Ibid.*, p. 1092.

[30.] *Ibid.*, p. 1091. The authors refer to B. Lewis, *Ibid.*, pp. 71–72.

[31.] *Ibid.*, p. 1091.

32. *Ibid.*, p. 1092. The authors refer to al-Kalkashandi, *Subh*, III, pp. 480–481.

33. *Ibid.*, p. 1092. The authors refer to M. Canard, *Ceremonial Fatimite...*, in *Byzantion*, XXI/2, 1951, p. 367. The authors also refer to B. Lewis, *Islam From the Prophet Muhammad to the Capture of Constantinople*, I, 1974, pp. 202, 204–205.

34. A. K. S. Lambton, "In Persia." In Gibb, *et al.*, *Ibid.*, p. 1092. Munis, a eunuch, was the commanding general of the Persian Armies during the caliphate of al-Muktadir (980–932). Little is known of his early life, but he appears to have been a castrated captive, who had come up through the palace hierarchy. He was named chief Emir, *Amir al-Umara*, being the first of several to bear this title. In 914 and 915, Munis was in command of the army that successfully defended Egypt from the Fatimid attacks. See Gibb, *et al.*, *Ibid.*, Volume I, pp. 11, 19, 446; Volume III, pp. 46, 120, 126, 619.

35. A. K. S. Lambton, "In Persia." In Gibb, *et al.*, *Ibid.*, p. 1092. Lambton refers to I'timad al-Saltana, *Ruznama-i khatirat-i I'timad al-Sultana*, Iraj Afshar (ed.), 1966, p. 644. Shah Abbas I (The Great) raised Persia from the depths of degradation to the status of a great power. His reign was remarkable, not only for his striking military victories (he took Baghdad back from the Turks in 1603), but also for the efficiency of his administrative system. He made Isfahan his capital in 1598 and it became a worthy city, rivaling even London in size.

36. *Ibid.*, p. 1092. The white eunuchs constituted the permanent staff of the palace these were slaves who had been castrated to make them eligible for service. Between 1451 and 1481, there were 20 in number, while under Selim I (1481–1520), there were 40. They were responsible for the protection of the sultan's person and personal attendance; they accompanied him wherever he went and guarded him as he slept.

37. Cengiz Orhonlu, "In Turkey." In Gibb, *et al.*, *Ibid.*, p. 1093. Ghadanfer Agha was another eunuch, who wielded enormous influence under Selim II and Murad II (1524–1595). See Gibb, *et al.*, *Ibid.*, Volume II, p. 1088.

[38.] Cengiz Orhonlu, "In Turkey." In Gibb, *et al.*, *Ibid.*, p. 1093. Orhonlu refers to E. W. Lane, *The Manners and Customs of the Modern Egyptians*, 1954, p. 137.

[39.] Gibb, *et al.*, *Ibid.*, p. 1090.

[40.] *Ibid.*, p. 1091. The authors refer to B. Lewis, *Ibid.*, p. 81.

[41.] Cengiz Orhonlu, "In Turkey." In Gibb, *et al.*, *Ibid.*, p. 1093. Orhonlu refers to M. Ertugrul Duzdag, *Seyhulislam Ebussuud Efendi Fetvalari Isiginda 16 Asir turk Hayati*, 1972, p. 120.

[42.] Cengiz Orhonlu, "In Turkey." In Gibb, *et al.*, *Ibid.*, p. 1093. Orhonlu refers to Dustur, *Istanbul*, First Series, Volume V, 1887, pp. 368, 396.

[43.] Gibb, *et al.*, *Ibid.*, p. 1093. According to Zambaco, *Ibid.*, p. 211, eunuchs could still attain very high positions in the Persian court—from antiquity to the 20th century. He cites a newspaper article from *The Times*, dated March 20, 1910, which told about a eunuch with the title of *kahn* named Garib, formerly with Zill-us-Sultan, who robbed a convoy of bank notes destined for the Shah and retired to a fortified position about 40 kilometers from Ispahan. On p. 77, he also notes that, "Down to the present time, the eunuchs attached to rich Turkish and Egyptian families, were playing roles, intimate with the chiefs of state, where they were able to acquire great fortunes, which, at their death, always reverted to their masters...."

Chapter 5—Eunuchs in Ancient Rome

The practice of rulers using eunuchs in a variety of capacities, extending even to marriage, in ancient Rome dates back to Tarquin, or Lucius Tarquinius Superbus, 534–510 B.C. Tarquin, the last king of Rome before the advent of the republic, had the young sons of exiled noblemen castrated for his sexual pleasure. In fact, Zambaco traces the origins of the *Scatinia* laws of present-day Italy—whereby both the active and passive partners in homosexual relations are punished—to Tarquin's widely reviled pedophilic practices.[1]

The emperor Claudius (41–54 A.D.) not only promulgated the laws that authorized Roman citizens to undergo castration as part of the Phrygian rites of worship of Attis and Cybele (see chapter 11), but also employed eunuchs extensively as court advisors. Another monarch, Vitellius (69 A.D.), sought the counsel of eunuchs, and employed them as his personal bodyguards. Claudius was later poisoned by the eunuch, Halotus, who had collaborated with Agrippina (the mother of Nero, 54–68 A.D.).

The now infamous Nero featured upwards of 60 eunuchs in his orgies, and eventually married one. The Roman historian, Tacitus, recorded the details of the marriage of the emperor Nero with the youth, Sporus, in 67 A.D. This young man had been totally castrated (penis as well as testicles removed), and renamed Sabina. "Sporus put on the bridal veil…the dowry, the marriage bed, the nuptial torch, everything was there…and during the consummation of the marriage, Sporus, who has been the love-boy of many others, imitated the cries and pleas of a maiden being deflowered." A saying that secretly made the rounds of the gossips of the day in Rome was: "The world would be a happier place had his (Nero's) own father had such a wife." Similarly, the emperor, Titus (79–81 A.D.) married one of his beloved eunuchs.

Hadrian (117–138 A.D.) was so enamored of Antinous, a eunuch of legendary beauty, that he raised a temple in the city of Antinopolis when the young man drowned in the Nile in 130 A.D. An official cult was established in his honor, and believers asserted that he became counted among the gods. Members of the Roman nobility participated in the rituals of the cult, including Heliogabalus (218–222 A.D.), also called Elagabalus, who had himself castrated for the priesthood of the Great Mother, and was known for participating in orgies with the eunuch Hierocles.

According to Saint Jerome (c. 347–c. 420), all of the Roman nobles engaged in sexual relations with their corps of eunuchs, or "stable litter." These eunuchs were referred to as *spadones,* having had only their testicles removed to retain sexual function, but not to inseminate.

Diocletian (284–305) is credited with introducing the Persian custom of confining women to their quarters under the vigilant guard of eunuchs. The eunuchs were admitted to the highest echelons of Roman society, including the imperial family itself, after taking on this role. They commanded respect, and were no longer abhorred, as was the case during the reign of Augustus (28 B.C.–14 A.D.). Constantine II (337–343 A.D.) later established what historians refer to as the "veritable reign" of the eunuchs, entrusting them with the secrets of state and the direction of government affairs.[2] Constantine's eunuch chamberlain, Eusabius, first governed the palace and, eventually the entire empire.

A considerable body of Roman literature exists, which details how eunuchs were both used and deeply integrated into society. Ovid (391–330 B.C.) Book X, lines 155–158, discusses Ganymede, while *Fasti,* Book IV, Pr. Non. 4th lines 179–389 depicts the worship of Attis and Cybele, as well as their eunuch priests.

Terence (Publius Terentius Afer, c. 195–159 B.C.) penned *The Eunuch,* a farcical play based on a Greek original by Menander (342–295 B.C.). In acts two and four, the author describes the derogation of old eunuchs, common at the time of his writing (161 B.C.). In the course of the work, a young man poses as an old eunuch to gain access to the women's quarters, in order to see the object of his desire.

Lucretius (Titus Lucretius Carus, c. 94–c. 50 B.C.), is the author of *The Way Things Are*. In Book II, lines 595–648, the Great Mother and her Phrygian retinue of eunuch priests are portrayed.

Valerius Maximus (flourished around 20 A.D.) notes the use of castration as a penalty for adultery, in *Factorum et Dictorum Memorabilium Libri IX* (*Nine Books of Memorable Deeds and Sayings*) (Book 6, chapter 1, article 13), which dates to c. 31 A.D.

Martial, or Marcus Valerius Martialis (c. 40–c. 104 A.D.) also elaborates on this punitive use of castration in *Epigrams*, Book II, Number 60. In Book III (Number 81, lines 3–6), he comments on the priests of Cybele, while in Book IV (Number 2), he writes, "The eunuch himself was an adulterer." Epigrams 7, 42 and 99 contain statements on marriage, as well.

Petronius Arbiter (Gaius Petronius, d. 66 A.D), who served as governor of Bithynia, and was an intimate acquaintance of Nero, cataloged the emperor's debaucheries in his effort, *Satyricon* (more properly *Satyrikon Liber* or *Book of Satyrlike Adventures*). While the work is primarily an amoral romance of debased hedonism, other chapters in the original book mention castration and the use of eunuchs (21, 23, 27, 108, 119 and 132). Petronius, often referred to as the *arbiter elegantiae* (arbiter of elegance) arranged festivals and parties for Nero. The ruler subsequently accused Petronius of conspiring against him, and ordered him to commit suicide, which was duly carried out.

Seneca (Lucius Annaeus Seneca, c. 4 B.C.–65 A.D.), in his *De Brevitate Vitae*, castigates Roman vice, namely the custom of members of the upper classes retaining castrated companions for sexual pleasure.

Lives of the Caesars, by Suetonius Tranquillus Gaius (c. 70–c. 122 A.D.), makes occasional mention of the eunuchs in the administrations of the Roman emperors. From Julius Caesar to Domitian (27–96 B.C.), including those in the households of contemporary wealthy Romans, eunuchs were key staff persons.

Justin Martyr, or Saint Justin, the first of the Christian apologists (c. 100–165 A.D.), charges the priests of Cybele with being sodomites in his *Apologia* (i, 27). St. Justin also speaks of a young man living in Alexandria who asked the governor to be castrated, so that he would no longer be suspected of impropriety (ii, 71). The governor refuses to honor his request because of the laws forbidding the procedure.

Juvenal (Decimus Junius Juvenalis, c. 60–c. 130 A.D.), examines the attitude attributed to the eunuchs who engaged in sexual relations with the Roman women of his day. *Sixteen Satires of the Ancient Harlot* (Satire VI, lines 365–380 and Satire X, lines 306–307) offer richly documented examples of this practice.

Lucian (c. 120–190 A.D.), author of *The Eunuch,* includes ample derogatory descriptions of eunuchs. In this maliciously satirical account of a competition for one of the chairs in philosophy established at Athens by emperor Marcus Aurelius, eunuchs are displayed in all their vanity and weakness.

History (Book XIV, chapter 6, section 17) by Ammianus (Marcellinus, c. 330–391 A.D.), contains a vivid portrait of the military forces during the years of 353–355 A.D., when a coterie of eunuchs were enlisted and actually participated in battle.

Macrobius (Ambrosius Theodosius Macrobius), who is believed to have completed most of his writing about the years 399 to 422 A.D., details the many reasons why eunuchs have lovely voices in his *Saturnalia.* Ancillon indicates that this is the primary reason Italians still had young men castrated as late as 1707.[3]

At the same time eunuchs flourished as tools and companions of those in the upper classes, Millant suggests that castration was held in very low esteem in ancient Rome. It was considered a misfortune, but nevertheless condemned under the penalty of death.[4] Edicts were so severe against castration that medical doctors who performed the illegal surgery were compelled to create a viable alternative. They found that the process of infibulation, which involved inserting a metallic ring through the end of the penis, would satisfy some of the purposes of castration, yet would not endanger the doctors in any way.

Infibulation was originally seen as a means to deter masturbation in young boys. In later years, it was used for comedians, singers and gladiators. Theatrical directors sought to prevent actors from being promiscuous, which would result in the spoiling of their voices. Gladiators were supposed to conserve their strength, which would otherwise be wasted in sexual excesses.

Celsus, the greatest of the Roman medical writers, composed a detailed set of instructions for surgeons on implanting the ring in the prepuce (foreskin) (Book VII, chapter XXV). However, Martial questioned the benefit of infibulation in his *Epigrams* (Number 25). It was later discovered that the implanted rings could cause ulcerations and accidents.

The use of eunuchs throughout ancient Rome has clearly had a detrimental impact on the modern perception of castration, particularly in the Roman Catholic world (i.e., Italy, Spain, France, etc.). Roman writers, whose teachings are still held in high esteem, condemned the practice, overlooking any advantages of the surgery to the castrated. As a result, many persons today regard castration much like Julius Caesar did: as a "sacrifice…worse than death."

Endnotes—Chapter 5

1. Demetrius A. Zambaco, L*es Eunuques D'Aujourd'hui et Ceux de Jadis*. Paris: Libraries de L'Academie de Medicine, 1911, p. 218

2. Edward Gibbon, *The Roman Empire*, Volume III, 1825, p. 380. (Translated into French by Jacob Artin, Pasha of Egypt, Ministry of Public Education.) Quoted in Zambaco, *Ibid.*, p. 218.

3. Charles Ancillon, *Traite Des Eunuques*. Paris: Editions Ramsay, 1707, Reprinted in 1978, p. 54.

4. Richard Millant, *Les Eunuques a Travers les Ages*. Paris: Place de LeEcole-de-Medicine, 1908, pp. 145–148.

Chapter 6—The Eunuchs of Byzantium

Byzantium, the name of the Christian Roman Empire of the East, was christened by Constantine the Great on Monday, May 11, 330 A.D. Its final conquest was by the Ottoman Turkish sultan, Mehmet II, on Tuesday, May 29, 1453. The empire, which lasted precisely 1,123 years and 18 days, took its name from the capital city of Byzantium located on the Bosphorus strait; the city was later called Constantinople, and is presently called Istanbul. Seldom has such a durable and significant empire received such an unfavorable reputation in the pages of our history books. Edward Gibbon persisted in inaccurately asserting that the enduring culture of Byzantium was one of constant decay in his celebrated work, *The Decline and Fall of the Roman Empire*, published in 1788. He saw the entirety of Byzantine culture as a betrayal of all that was best in ancient Greece and Rome.[1] W. E. H. Lecky was even more derogatory: Diner (1938) called Gibbon "hopelessly obsolete."

> Of that Byzantine Empire, the universal verdict of history is that it constitutes, without a single exception, the most thoroughly base and despicable form that civilization has yet assumed... There has been no other enduring civilization so absolutely destitute of all the forms and elements of greatness...The history of the Empire is a monotonous story of the intrigues of priests, eunuchs and women, of poisonings, of conspiracies, of uniform ingratitude, of perpetual fratricides.[2]

So poorly valued was the history of this era that its ancient coins would later be bought merely for the weight of gold they contained.

For all the criticism, Byzantium remained the primary power in the Christian world from the fall of Rome in the fifth century to the 15th century, flourishing while Europe wallowed through its "Dark Ages." Italy had become a comparative backwater since the time Constantine moved his capital and settled in Byzantium in 324 A.D. The period of actual decline of the Byzantine Empire occurred during the years of 1,025 and 1453, whereas the period between 843 to 1025 A.D. was, in reality, a golden age of prosperity, power and enlightenment.

Similar to the great expanse of time in the history of China, eunuchs were employed by the emperors of Byzantium in considerable numbers in the highest offices of the land. Tens of thousands of eunuchs of humble origins, who would have been doomed to short, hard lives of servitude, had they not been castrated, were raised to the heights of power, luxury and knowledge. Castration proved a survivor's tool for these men. The process made them trusted above other men by their rulers, made them relatively invulnerable to the temptations and diseases of other men. It also served as a means to achieving fame and fortune in the Byzantine empire. Throughout history, rulers found that only eunuchs could be relied upon for personal service and as a protective coterie. Over time, this custom expanded, such that eunuchs were instinctively relied on, although they were constantly reviled by others and historians continued to demean their admirable qualities with violent antipathy.

Ancillon quotes Lucian (c. 125–190 A.D.) in a description of the eunuchs of his day:

> He is neither male nor female. He is a wonder in Nature, but this is too general, we must have a more exact definition, one that tells more particularly and surely. A eunuch, then, is a person who can reproduce, by weakness, by frigidity or by removal of his reproductive parts. *Who cannot reproduce*, as the law expresses it (law 2, part 1 ff. concerning adaptations); one who has a thin and listless voice, complexion of a woman, and no facial hair; in whom courage and hardiness give way to fear and timidity; in a word, one whose customs and manners are completely effeminate. If a eunuch is so weak and contemptible with regard to his body, he must be still more so in his mind and heart.[3]

Ancillon also quotes Saint Basil in an even more vituperative excerpt:

>...[D]on't give me slaves and eunuchs, abominable men, without honor, who are neither men nor women, that love of sex drives them crazy; they are jealous, despicable, savage, effeminate, gluttons, greedy people, cruel, undependable, suspicious, furious, unsatisfied. They cry when deprived of a meal; to sum up, they are damned from their birth, people so crippled that can they have any right? Steel has made them chaste, but this chastity has no value, their depravity makes them furious, and they can bear no fruit.[4]

Research indicates that the words of the likes of Saint Basil contain many inconsistencies and accusations. Still, the damage has been done; generations of men and women seem to have accepted them at face value.

Ammianus Marcellinius was somewhat less derogatory in his portrayal of eunuchs:

>When Numa Pompilius and Socrates would say something good about a eunuch, they would not be believed, and would be accused of lying. In fact, even if Numa Pompilius said something good of a eunuch and supported his words with references to sacred sources, one would judge that he had withdrawn from the truth.[5]

Ancillon mentions that Marcellinius speaks well of the eunuch Menophilus, who was employed by Mithrades, King of Pont, and even praises Euthurius, one of the eunuchs of emperor Constantius (337–361 A.D.) as "Favotinus Mordonius" in the latter part of the same chapter, but does not give any detailed explanations, except the off-hand remark that "roses are born among thorns and some animals can be tamed among savage beasts."[6]

Indeed, writings favorable toward the eunuchs do exist. Theodore of Balsamone (c. 1105–c. 1200), who was the preceptor of Emperor Constantine VII Porphyrogenitus (905–959)—meaning "born in the purple"—wrote a tract titled "For Eunuchs and Eunuchism." Works such as this have been dismissed by Ancillon as undertaken merely "to praise what everyone despises and blames, imagining that this singularity would excite the curiosity and admiration of the readers. But all these books have not made the subjects whom they treated more praiseworthy, nor more legitimate. ...There is no one in Christianity who does not detest it...."[7]

This is the nature of the historical contradictions. The legal contradictions are even more curious. The making of eunuchs was against the law, but the practice continued nonetheless—apparently unhindered throughout the entire history of Byzantium. Domitian (81–96 A.D.) seems to have been the first Roman emperor to issue a decree against it, but some modern scholars attribute an increase in the use of castration during his reign.[8] Nerva (96–98 A.D.) renewed the prohibition, especially as it applied to citizens within the empire (Ammianus Marcellinius XVIII, 4). Hadrian went even further and applied the law to the physicians who performed the operation and those who tolerated its continuation. However, these deterrents did not cause the practice to disappear.[9]

Constantine (323–337) reviewed the laws concerning eunuchs and found them poorly observed. Leo I (457–474) forbade the sale of eunuchs of Roman nationality, but authorized the commerce of barbarian eunuchs. His edicts had the effect of flooding Byzantium with substantial numbers of eunuchs from foreign countries. Justinian (527–565) codified the laws into a more uniform system than formerly existed, but later issued supplementary enactments called "novels." In Novel 142, the emperor declared that the laws concerning eunuchs were not being observed, and that castration resulted in a frightful mortality rate (among 90 persons who received the operation, only three were said to have survived). Novel 142 punished the perpetrators and abettors of the operation with retaliation in kind under *Lex Talionis*—if the sentenced person survived, he was sent to the mines and his assets were confiscated. If women were found guilty of aiding or abetting castration, the state imposed deportation and confiscation penalties upon them. By contrast, those castrated as slaves fully recovered their legal rights. In effect, this statute resulted in restoring all the eunuchs in the empire to freedom.

Leo VI (886–912) observed that the laws of Justinian—despite the severe penalties they imposed—had not ceased the practice of making eunuchs. He subsequently reduced the punishment for this practice in his Novel 60 to a fine of 10 librae of gold and 10 years in exile. Under Leo VI's law, a free man could have the operation if it was done voluntarily, and according to a physician's decision. The law failed to mention the age at which voluntary consent could be given, and parents were empowered to authorize the operation for their children. Religious laws, dogma and canons as well as civil laws since the first council of the church at Nicea in 325 clearly prohibited the operation, but peculiar contradictions remained. The Church continued to utilize eunuch priests, while the emperor maintained his usage of eunuch administrators and officers in his army and navy. At the same time, the pope was enacting laws against the very procedure that made them eunuchs.

Tompkins quotes Runciman as saying that no evidence exists that the Byzantine eunuch's physical limitations had anything to do with warping his character. According to Runciman, throughout Byzantine history, eunuchs appeared "no more corrupt nor intriguing, no less vigorous or patriotic than their completer fellows...providing for the Emperor a governing class which he could trust. ...Even the noblest parents were not above mutilating their sons to help their advancement, nor was there any disgrace in it."[10] Guilland confirms this latter notion: "And, as a matter of fact, as soon as people realized that being a eunuch led to wealth, power and honors, parents, even those of the highest classes, consented to the mutilation of one of their children. The most renowned families in Byzantium, even the imperial family, had eunuchs."[11]

Guilland gives several reasons for the Byzantine's utilization of eunuchs:

- With the growing influence of the East over Byzantium, the gynaecea (women's quarters of the palace) required the services of many eunuchs.

- Once admitted to the imperial palace, the eunuchs rapidly gained the confidence of the emperor and empress in such a way that they had great influence over them.

- The elaborate ceremonials of the Byzantine court surrounded the basileus with eunuchs like seraphs.

- Eunuchs were barred from becoming the ruler by their condition, custom and the law, so they could not threaten to replace the empire's leaders, no matter how powerful or popular they might become. Eunuchs were unable to marry and have children as is incumbent on royalty, so they could not fulfill one of the first requirements. The emperors could appoint eunuchs to high positions, secure in the knowledge that these men would not threaten their own position—as members of the aristocracy were inclined to do.[12]

- Eunuchs were easily broken as soon as they stopped pleasing the emperor or empress.

- Eunuchs often made energetic and highly effective administrators(Evagrius IV, p. 2).

Ostrogorsky explains the role of eunuchs in court and state:

> The Byzantine state had at its disposal a unique civil service...Eight honorary titles, which begin with the *patricius* (Master of the Offices), were reserved for the eunuchs, and the patrician eunuchs in fact occupied a position superior to that of the other patricians and anthypati. The eunuchs played an important part at the Byzantine court. No office, however high, in Church and State (with the single exception of the imperial dignity itself) was withheld from the eunuchs on

principle, and many of the patriarchs, statesmen and generals who distinguished themselves in Byzantine history were eunuchs. There were, however, a number of court offices which were *normally* held by eunuchs. The most important of these were the office of the *paracoemomenus*, who slept near the imperial bed-chamber and who was usually one of the emperor's most trusted confidants, and the *protovestarius*, the head of the imperial wardrobe. Other officers with very important functions at court were the *rector*, one of the highest court officials..., the *protopraepositus*, or the Master of Ceremonies, the imperial *protostrator*, or the chief Master of the Horse....[13]

Other important positions usually reserved for the eunuchs were the titles of *sacellarius*, Chief financial officer, and *protoasecretis*, head of the imperial Chancery and bodyguard for the emperor and empress. By Novel 133 of Justinian, some functions had been reserved for eunuchs in monasteries. Even in the women's convents, the offices of treasurer and vice-treasurer were always held by eunuchs.

Eunuchs in the Byzantine Church

One of the most respected religious offices in the world is the Patriarch of Constantinople—equivalent to the Pope of Rome in the Roman Catholic hierarchy. The Patriarch is at the pinnacle of the Eastern Orthodox Catholic Church, which numbers some 250 million believers today. Orthodox and Roman Catholics hold many central affirmations in common, such as the Nicean Creed, but the Orthodox leaders trace their spiritual lineage to the Apostle Andrew, while the Roman Catholics consider themselves to descend directly from the Apostle Peter. Several of these Byzantine patriarchs were eunuchs (Makedonios II (496–511) per Nicephorus, *Historia Ecclesiasticus* XVI, c. 26, pp. 147, 168).

Germanus I, patriarch from August 715 A.D to January 730 A.D., was born into an important patrician family that had been implicated along with several other noble conspirators in the death of Constans II on September 15, 668. He was castrated on the order of Constantine IV (668–685)—although he was past the age when such acts were legal—and later raised to his high office in spite of edicts handed down by the Council of Nicea. Germanus I was the first figure of any real consequence in the iconoclast crisis and was later demoted for his attack against Iconoclasm on January 13, 730 by Leo III. Historians today are indebted to Germanus I for the most substantial writings on the question of icons in the first period of the Iconoclastic Controversy (Zonaras, III, 222).[14]

Nicetas I (November 766–February 780) was born of a humble Slavic family and was completely illiterate according to Zonaras (III, 277). A priest at the Saint Apostles Church, he was later raised to the patriarchal throne, against the ecclesiastical canons, by order of Constantine V (740–775). Nicetas was a notorious iconoclast who removed the last icons and mosaics from the monasteries and patriarchal palace (Theophanes, *Chronographia* 686).

Saint Methodius I (March 843–June 847) was castrated at an early age. He explained to a judge that he had miraculously acquired this condition from the princess of the apostles, Peter and Paul, that had done it to him to preserve him from sexual temptations. Methodius had been accused of seducing a woman, and in order to exculpate himself, took off his clothes and showed the judges his handicap (Cedrenus).[15] Methodius assisted the empress Theodora and Logothete of the Drome, Theoctistus, in settling the 132-year-old Iconoclastic Controversy by proclaiming the solemn rehabilitation of the veneration of the icons in March 843 and by excommunicating the most zealous of the iconoclast Stundite monks. He thus aided in ushering in the "Golden Age" of Byzantium. He died June 14, 847.

Ignatios, Patriarch of Constantinople from July 847 to October 858 and again from November 23, 867 to his death at an advanced age on October 23, 877, was the son of Emperor Michael I Rangabe (811–813), and castrated after his father was deposed in 813. He became a monk in the monastery at Satyros and rose to the rank of abbot. Appointed Patriarch by the regent empress Theodora, and after losing the position with a change in rulers, was re-appointed by Emperor Basil I (Cedrenus II, 172).

Stephanos II (June 925–July 928) had been the metropolitan of Amasya (a fertile region in present north-central Turkey) before being raised to the patriarchal throne (Theophanes, *Continuatus*, 410, 739, 902).[16]

Theophylaktos (February 933–July 928) was the youngest son of Emperor Roman I Lecapenus (919–944) and had been castrated at a very early age. He entered into the clergy, rose to an ecclesiastical secretary and advisor to the prelate, then ordained a deacon. Roman I had left the patriarchal throne vacant for two years, then raised Theophylaktos to this high office at age 16 (Theophanes, *Continuatus*, 409, 739). The youth was blindly obedient to his father's will until his own death in 956.

Polyeuktos (April 956–February 970) was also castrated at an early age by his parents and entered into holy orders before being elevated to the patriarchate. He was very firm in his resolve against the murderers of Emperor Nicephorus Phocas by making John Tzimisces do penance, expelling Tzimisces' mistress, Empress Theophano, from the palace and punishing his own coadjutors in the murder before he would permit himself to enter a church and be coronated.

Constantine III Leichudes (February 1059–August 1063) had been the protovestarius of Emperor Isaac I Comnenus before being raised to the position of Patriarch of Constantinople.

Eustratios Garidas (1081–August 1084) was also a eunuch patriarch, according to Anna Comnena (I, 149), who wrote a detailed history of her father, the Emperor Alexius I's life from 1069–1118. Research by Michael Glycas (p. 619), who was another contemporary chronicler of the period, confirms this point.

Bartholomew was a modern apostle of peace and love. He was the 270th successor to an actual apostle of Jesus Christ, St. Andrew, the first called apostle and brother of St. Peter.

Orthodox church leader. The head of the Orthodox church worldwide, the Ecumenical Patriarch's full title is Archbishop of Constantinople, new Rome and Ecumenical Patriarch's. When Constantinople became the seat of the Roman Empire, all the principle teachings of Christianity were put down in seven ecumenical councils held in or near the great imperial city.

The Orthodox church is the oldest Christian church in the world. The Great Church of Christ became a "church in captivity for more than 500 years (1453 A.D.). The Holy Orthodox church has millions of followers in North and South America, Central America, Caribbean, Asia, Australia, New Zealand, and Oceania. It is also growing in Western Europe. Orthodox faithful know they are part of a truly historic and global Christian community.

These patriarchs averaged about 10 years of service, which was slightly above the average for others in this position during the Byzantine era. Below the patriarchs in the Byzantine Christian Church hierarchy came the Metropolitans, then the bishops, priests, monks, deacons, and so on. Not surprisingly, many of these were also eunuchs. Stephanos II and Cedrenus (II, 705) tell us of John, the Metropolitan of Side who was chosen by Emperor Michael Ducas (1071–1078) to be the regent of the empire. Liutprand mentions in his *Legatio* (p. 371) that he had been received by a bishop in Latakia, who was a eunuch, and that other bishops who were eunuchs abounded, even though it was against ecclesiastical rules.[17] Cedrenus (II, 593) notes a eunuch priest, Nicephorus, who was raised by Emperor Constantine IX Monomachus (1042–1055) to command an army. Although Nicephorus had no military skills, Constantine knew he could depend on his fidelity.

Through the long history of Byzantium, the Christian church provided refuges, monasteries, hospices, asylums and religious foundations where deposed palace eunuchs were allowed—and sometimes forced—to go. Narses, Chamberlain of Justin II (565–578) had the monastery of Katharoi and several other shelters built that were reserved for eunuchs. Leo VI (886–912) had the convent of Saint Lazarus built in the Topoi quarter of Constantinople set aside for eunuchs. In most cases, they were tonsured in order to be clergymen or shaved in order to be monks. Such were the cases of the following notable monks.

- Antiochus, tutor and praepositus of Theodosius II (408–450). The basileus, in a towering rage, compelled him to take holy orders.

- Samonas, the favorite eunuch of Leo VI, was forcibly made a monk and confined in the convent of Martinakios (Theophanes, *Continuatus* 316).

- John was a eunuch clergyman whom Constantine VII (913–959) compelled to put on the monastic dress as a consequence of some misdeed. John abandoned the monk's dress and again put on clergyman's clothes when he entered the service of Romanus II (959–963), in spite of protests of the Patriarch Polyeuktos. After Romanus died, John quickly returned to monk's raiment (Cedrenus II, 339).

- The eunuch, Nicephorus, former protovestarius of Constantine VIII became a monk during the reign of Michael IV (1034–1041), and secluded himself in the famous monastery of Stoudios (Cedrenus II, 514, 480).

If we consider that the use of eunuchs was somehow improper or disgraceful in the Byzantine Church, the behavior of several of the Roman Catholic popes of Rome of the same period should be examined. Leigh Rutledge has documented that six of the popes were actively homosexual: John XII (955–964), Benedict IX (1032–1046), Paul II (1464–1471), Sixus IV (1471–1484) and Julius III (1550–1555).[18]

E. R. Chamberlain confirms the elicit behavior of three of the homosexuals and adds four more popes who acted immorally in other ways: Urban IV (1378–1389), Boniface VIII (1294–1303), Urban VI (1378–1389), Alexander VI (1492–1503), and Clement VIII (1523–1534).[19] Richard A. W. Sipe notes that Roman Catholicism's rule of priestly celibacy is not so much a doctrine as a clerical discipline, which was not required until the twelfth century. But even after this time, some priests, bishops, cardinals and even an occasional pope were married and "concubinage flourished for centuries among clergy vowed to celibacy."[20]

Eunuchs in the Byzantine Military

Given the unaggressive nature of most eunuchs, it may be surprising to find that they were frequently placed at the head of important military units, armies and navies. Eunuchs had the required qualities of trustworthiness and diligence, as well as administrative skills, and they were limited by their physical condition from ascending beyond a certain point in the government. The Augusti and Caesars who were the heads of the state could be secure in their dynastic power with the childless eunuchs placed at the head of the armed forces. On the other hand, the aristocracy, which surrounded the pinnacle of power, was full of individuals who thought themselves worthy of the throne and were quite capable of taking advantage of the opportunity if it presented itself. The basileis were acutely aware of the history of Rome and Persia, where victorious generals would return from the wars to the adulation of their troops and populace and depose the emperor.

Narses (c. 475–575 A.D.) was the most famous of all the Byzantine eunuchs, and has inspired much scholarly attention. He rose through the palace ranks to command the emperor's personal corps of eunuch guards, and on January 18, 532, this "deceptively frail" looking Armenian eunuch played a decisive role in quelling the "Nika" revolt at the Hippodrome in Constantinople.[21] By 538 he had been appointed Grand Chamberlain and was sent by Justinian to reinforce

General Belisarius in Italy. Norwich describes the eunuch Narses as not having the characteristics of a soldier; but more loyal and trustworthy than trained military leaders.

> His life had been spent in the Palace, and even his command of the bodyguard was more of a domestic appointment than a military one. The question therefore arises, why he was given the leadership of the new expeditionary force; and to it there can be but one answer. Justinian was beginning to have his doubts about Belisarius. The general was too brilliant, too successful—and, being still only in his early thirties, too young. He was the stuff of which Emperors were made; worse, he was the stuff of men who made themselves Emperors. In short, he needed watching; and who better to watch him than Justinian's most intelligent and trusted confidant, a man whose own age and condition alike debarred him from any imperial ambitions of his own? Even the eunuch's instructions from Justinian gave a hint as to the real reason for his presence in Italy: he was to obey Belisarius in all things, *so far as seemed consistent with the public weal*. In other words, he must accept the general's orders in military matters, but could overrule him in all major decisions of state policy.[22]

In 551, Justinian once again selected Narses, now well into his seventies, in his last attempt to bring all of Italy back into the imperial fold. According to Norwich:

> Narses was admittedly old, but he had lost none of his energy or his decisiveness. He was relatively inexperienced in the field; but there were several excellent tacticians—notably his old friend John—already in Italy. What was needed above all was a superb organizer, strong- willed and determined, able to dominate a team of ever-squabbling rivals and inspire them with new purpose and spirit. And for such a task Narses was ideally suited.[23]

Norwich concludes that the eunuch is actually a superior leader. "History offers few examples of a campaign as swift and decisive as that of Narses being successfully concluded by a general in his middle eighties; nor, surely, any more persuasive argument in favor of castration."[24]

Lawrence Herbert Fauber goes further than earlier historians in crediting Narses.

> ...[H]e was implicitly trusted. Furthermore he had conducted a successful military operation in 545, with the Heruls against the Sclaveni. His very fidelity assured him the great authority and powers of a general-in-chief whom all would obey, and who could secure united action in the war.
>
> In camp, he had proven his popularity with persons as different in temper and tradition as Persian deserters, erratic Heruls and intractable Thracians. In addition, the ascendance he had acquired over his fellow officers, and over the soldiers themselves, must have increased the good opinion that Justinian already had of him. It has been claimed that Narses handled men as though he had been born and bred in camp.
>
> Coupled with his financial resources as the Emperor's Treasurer, was the reputation Narses had as a man of 'princely generosity.' Furthermore, he was free from being reproached for avarice...; all during his tenure at Court he was well-known for his liberality, being more than eager to help those in actual want.
>
> Having proven himself to be one of the greatest generals of his era, if not of all time, Narses now entered upon a new career, that of the unrestricted ruler, or administrator, of the Italy he had reconquered for the Eastern Empire. Of the twelve years or so (554–567) that the Eunuch-Patrician held sway in the Peninsula, history has left scarcely any trustworthy details.[25]

Another tale of Narses' glory illuminates details about his subsequent activities. Some historians report that Narses, later in life, invited the hostile Lombards into Italy after Justinian's death and his demotion by Justinian II in 567,

...in revenge for an insult that he had received from Empress Sophia who, so the story goes, had sent Narses a distaff in pointed reference to his emasculation. 'I will weave her such a skein,' the old eunuch is said to have muttered, 'that she will not unravel it in her lifetime.'[26]

Fauber quotes William Plate (1849), whose writings appeared in *A Dictionary of Greek and Roman Biography and Mythology*, that Narses' disposition included an "irritable and resentful temper which is peculiar to women and eunuchs," in a theoretical explanation of Narses' seeming revenge in this legend.[27]

During the reign of Justinian, several other eunuchs occupied high positions in his government, among whom were Salomon and Kalopodius. Salomon, born near the town of Dars, Syria and neutered in a childhood accident, rose through the palace ranks, and was later placed at the head of an army that fought the Vandals in Africa. He was killed during the battle of Cillium in 544. Kalopodius was one of the ranking officers of the Nika revolt (Theophanes 279) and subsequently became *praepositus sacri cubiculi*—officer in charge of the imperial bodyguard (Theophanes 360).

The most notable and enduring achievement of the age of Justinian was the codification of the Roman law. The famous *Codex Justinianus*, which was first published on April 8, 529, recast some three million "verses" of the old law, reducing them to approximately 150,000. Justinian's code combined the old decrees, customs, laws and Christian commandments for the first time into a cohesive set of methods for administering a centralized state with clarity and forcefulness. In spite of the specific legal prohibitions against emasculation, Justinian's dependence upon eunuchs in affairs of state actually encouraged the practice, while his laws formally prohibited it. Indeed, eunuchs had been used in palace service long before the time of Justinian, but it appears that this emperor was the first of the

Byzantines to send them off at the heads of the armies to fight on the perimeter of the empire. This practice endured until late in the thirteenth century in the military, although eunuchs were far from being generally successful in their campaigns, and were often reviled by the soldiers under their command.

(The following biographical sketches of Byzantine eunuchs appointed to high ranking military positions are provided by Guilland; his ancient sources are also noted.[28])

The former chamberlain Novianos was commissioned a *strategi* (the third ranking military officer) during the reign of Heraclius (610–641) and charged with stopping the Arabs in Africa, but he was defeated and killed (Nicephorus of Constantinople, 28). Another chamberlain, Kakoritzos, was assigned to command a large army during the reign of Constans II, who ruled from 641 to 648 (Theophanes, *Chronographia*, 526). The former sacellarius (finance officer) John was appointed logothete of the army in 788 by Constantine VI (780–797); he led a military expedition to Calabria, but failed and was killed (Theophanes 718).

The eunuchs Stauracius and Aetius were the principle lieutenants of the Empress Irene (797–802). Stauracius had accompanied the Emperor Constantine VI on his military campaigns, and then led the army that successfully subdued the Slavs in Greece. Aetius led the army in vital campaigns in Asia Minor, but was killed along with the Emperor Nicephorus I (802–811) on July 26, 811, while fighting the Bulgar Khan near Pliska (Theophanes 730, 737, 764).

The former protovestarius Procopius was assigned command of an army by Emperor Basil I (867–886), but was killed as the army engaged in combat (Theophanes, *Continuatus*, 629, 805). The former headwaiter of Emperor Leo VI, Constantine, commanded an army that was sent to Italy around the year 888. The army was defeated and Constantine barely escaped with his life (Cedrenus II, 253). Damian, who had been chamberlain and master of the offices under

Michael III, was nominated drungarius of the city during the regency of Empress Zoe (913–919) (Theophanes, *Continuatus*, 386).

About 918 A.D., the eunuch Eustathius, military commander of Calabria, settled a treaty with the Arabs of Sicily (Cedrenus II, 355). Eustathius had assisted the Byzantine general, Nicephorus Phocas, in an action against the Bulgars in 896 by blockading the mouth of the Danube with his fleet.

Theophanes occupied several of the positions reserved for eunuchs during the reign of Roman I Lecapenus (920–944): protovestarius, paracoemomenus and paradynast. In 941, he led the Byzantine fleet against the Russian naval units that were raiding the Bosphorus area, and scored a decisive victory in a sea battle in which the Byzantines destroyed the Russian ships by "Greek Fire" (Cedrenus II, 52, 308, 310, 316). This event demonstrates that Byzantine rulers trusted eunuchs with gunpowder, just as the Chinese emperors did.

Constantine Gongylas had been a favorite of Empress Zoe and, under Constantine VII (913–958), was appointed to lead an offensive against the Corsairs off Crete in 949. The expedition was a disaster, due largely to the military incompetence of Gongylas (Cedrenus II, 336; Theophanes, *Continuatus*, 436, 753). Gongylas had originally come from the region of Paphlagonia on the south coast of the Black Sea.

Emperor Nicephorus II Phocas (963–969) sent the Byzantine fleet on an expedition to Sicily in 964 under the command of the patrician eunuch Nicetas. The navy was defeated and Nicetas was captured (Cedrenus II, 360). The emperor was so fond of Nicetas that he ransomed him for a higher price than he was ostensibly worth (Liutprand of Cremona, *Legatio*, 361).

In 968, Nicephorus II began the siege of Antioch, Syria, which had been under the control of the Arabs for centuries, but had to return to Constantinople before the attack was completed. He left his patrician eunuch Peter Phocas in command, and Phocas was able to finally conquer the city on October 28, 969. A few months later, Aleppo fell. Succeeding emperors John I Tzimisces (969–976) and Basil II (976–1025) were also served by Peter Phocas during several victorious engagements. Phocas was ultimately defeated and killed at the battle of Rhageas (Cedrenus II, 365, 417, 420, 422; Zonaras III, 508–510, 541–543). The former protovestarius Leo replaced Peter Phocas, but was defeated shortly afterward (Cedrenus II, 424, 427).

Antioch and Aleppo were again besieged by the Arabs in 970, but were driven off by a rescuing army under the command of Nicholas, one of the most faithful eunuch generals of John I (Cedrenus II, 383). Nicholas also briefly held other military titles under Constantine VIII (Cedrenus II, 480–481), Zoe in 1042, and Constantine IX. In addition, Nicholas commanded an expedition in Armenia—where he had a few victories, but was later discharged—due to the failure of one of his lieutenants (Cedrenus II, 552, 560). If Cedrenus is correct, Nicholas served in high military posts for more than 72 years.

Romanus, who was the son of the last Bulgarian Tsar, Peter (927–969), was castrated by the Byzantines to prevent his ascension to the Bulgar throne. Romanus surrendered the city of Skoplje in 1004 and was rewarded with the title of patrician and strategus of the Abydus theme (Cedrenus II, 435, 455). Nicephorus Uranus was a brilliant general under Basil II. He surprised and defeated the Macedonian Tsar, Samuel, on his way home from the Pelaponnese in 997.[29]

Around 1025, Orestes, former chamberlain of Basil II, was assigned to lead an expedition against Sicily. Since he was incompetent as a military chief, he was defeated near Reggio and discharged from his post (Cedrenus II, 503). Simeon, a third ranking eunuch, was appointed drungarius (second military rank) during the reign of Constantine VIII (1025–1028) (Cedrenus II, 495). Spondalus, Duke of Antioch, was replaced by the brother-in-law of the Emperor Romanus III (1028–1034) when he was defeated in battle (Cedrenus II, 490, 491). Romanus III also appointed the former chamberlain, John, to head the fleet that was sent to Italy in 1034 (Cedrenus II, 503; J. Gay, *The Meridional Italy*, 435).

Emperor Michael IV the Paphlagonian (1034–1041) was the son of a peasant father who had made Michael's three brothers eunuchs at an early age. All three were raised to high positions in the government. Constantine was one of these eunuchs; he was appointed Domesticus of the Scholae of the East (a first military rank) in 1037, and commanded the operations against the Abasgi. George Probatas commanded an expedition to Serbia in 1040; but all members of the military company were lost (Cedrenus II, 504, 515, 519, 527; Zonaras III, 590).

Emperor Constantine IX Monomachus (1042–1055) nearly lost his throne on two occasions to Byzantine generals whose troops proclaimed them emperor. This apparently made him more anxious to employ eunuchs than some of the other rulers of his epoch. In 1043, the emperor's former chamberlain, Stephen, was appointed to defend him against the pretender George Maniaces. The battle was as good as won by Maniaces when he was suddenly killed by a stray arrow. Thereafter, his troops lost their purpose. Another revolt by the "Macedonian party" under Leo Tornices besieged Constantinople before finally being put down by loyal troops under the eunuch, Constantine, in 1047. This Constantine was an Arab by birth and well known to the emperor before his ascension to the throne. Constantine was later defeated at Adrianople.

Nicephorus, formerly a clergyman, was placed at the head of the army fighting the Patzinaks with the highly regarded General Katakalon as his adjutant. Nicephorus and his troops were defeated at Diakene in 1049. Another patrician eunuch known as John the philosopher, who had been one of the chamberlains of the Empress Zoe, was designated to lead the makeshift army defending Constantinople against the incursion of the Patzinaks (Cedrenus II, 548, 560, 593, 597, 600, 603; Schlumberger, *The Byzantine Epoch* III, 578–585).

The Empress Theodora (1055–1056) tended to appoint eunuchs as her military commanders. Theodore was Domesticus of the Scholae (the most important military official of the empire), while Nicetas

Xylinite served as logothete of the drome and Manual Drungarius of the Night Watch (the second ranking military officer). Emperor Michael VI (1056–1057) kept these military commanders in their posts. Theodore was the supreme commander of the imperial army during the rebellion of Isaac I Comnenus (1057–1059), but was eventually defeated (Cedrenus II, 610, 619, 623, 627).

Emperor Nicephorus III Botaneiates (1078–1081) entrusted the command of the imperial armies to the protovestarius John in 1080, when Nicephorus Melissenus revolted, in spite of the warnings of his experienced military chiefs. The generals protested having to serve under the command of a eunuch, and the soldiers openly mocked him. John would not follow the advice of the experienced commanders and led his army to defeat. He became surrounded by the enemy and escaped only with the assistance of George Paleologus. While he was in danger, John promised Paleologus that he would adopt him and make him his heir, but failed to keep his word (Nicephorus Bryennius,[30] 159–166).

During the reign of Alexius I Comnenus, which began on Easter, April 4, 1081 and ended, 37 years later, in 1118, the eunuch Eustathius Kyminianus (sometimes spelled "Eustachius Cymnineaus") served as the drungarius of the imperial fleet. He played an active role in the warfare waged by the Byzantines, and was left in command of the capital while Alexius I was absent. Leo Nikezitus was another eunuch who was given various military assignments by Alexius I (Anna Comnenus[31], *Alexiad* I, 309, 339, 422; II, 21, 120, 177, 199, 316). When Andronicus II Comnenus (1183–1185) was in power, the imperial armies were under the command of four great chiefs, one of which was the former paracoemomenus, Nicephorus, a eunuch (Nicetas Choniates, 412).

Emperor Alexius III Angelus (1195–1203) is said to have taken the unwise advice of the eunuchs and their chief, George Oinaiotes—against the warnings of his generals—during the expeditions against Dobromir Chrysus (1096–1097). The expedition was a failure. The troops were under the immediate command of the protovestarius,

John, who deserted his military company at the first alert. George Oinaiotes commanded the troops that recaptured the imperial palace when it was invaded by the usurper John Comnenus (Nicetas Choniates, 608, 667, 670, 672; Nicholas Mesarites, 43, 46).

The last historical record of eunuchs commanding major military units was during the reign of Michael VIII Palaeologus (1259–1282). One of the imperial palace officials, Andronicus Oenopolitor, commanded one of the four armies in the battle of Belgrade in 1281 (George Pachymeres I, 512). Andronicus transported the mortal remains of Michael VIII to their final resting place in the town of Selymbria on the Sea of Marmora (Pachymeres II, 107).

While some may consider the Byzantine emperors decision to assign eunuchs to high military positions misguided, the record of those who did not use eunuchs for military purposes may repudiate such conclusions. The Roman emperors of the West were inclined to disdain the use of eunuchs in the military, and they may have paid dearly for surrounding themselves with virile officers. At least 20 percent of the emperors were lynched by their own troops. Galba, Vitellus, Pertinax, Elagabalus and Alexander Severus met this fate. Another 20 percent were assassinated: Caligula, Domitian, Commodus, Didus Julianus and Caracalla. Still another 20 percent were murdered: Tiberius, Claudius, Titus, Trajan and Marcus Aurelius. By contrast, only nine percent or 10 percent of the Byzantine emperors died at the hands of their own troops. In Byzantium, emperors were more likely to die of disease or be killed in battle (about 60 percent of them did so). Despite the shortcomings of eunuchs as military men—which historians have so strongly emphasized—the rulers seemly had valid reasons for selecting them.

Eunuchs in the Byzantine Civil Service

Scholars have established that eunuchs were frequently assigned important positions in the religious and military hierarchies of Byzantium, where they were both honored and defiled, but the role of eunuchs was even more pronounced in the civil bureaucracy, in terms of both numbers and rank. Foucher of Chartres, who visited Constantinople at the time of the First Crusade (c. 1096–1107), estimated the total number of eunuchs at 20,000 (L.I.c.IX). Ancillon quotes a figure of 5,000 eunuchs created each year in the kingdom of Boulan.[32] Some 1,200 were said to be in the postal service alone, acting as couriers, informers and tax gatherers. These eunuchs lived longer, kept the administrative machinery operating, assisted in the carrying out of significant ceremonial duties and made themselves indispensable to their emperors. Just as eunuchs in the Persian and Chinese cultures attained prominence—for example, Bagoas in 343 B.C., Hermotimus, circa 460 B.C., Ssu Ch'ien in 100 B.C. and Wang Chen in 144 A.D.—several eunuchs in the Byzantine empire rose to the peak of executive power. Sometimes this would be due to the weakness, illness or incompetence of the designated emperor; although such was sometimes achieved by the intelligence and ambition of the eunuchs themselves, or by a combination of circumstances.

Eusebius of Emesa was praepositus under Emperor Constantius (337–361), directing many of the state affairs (Ammianus Marcellinus XVIII, 4).[33] As an earnest adherent of Aryanism, he exiled Pope Liberius (337–352) (Theophilus 53, 61). He was put to death by Julius I (361–363), who expelled all of the eunuchs from the palace (Theophilus 71; Socrates III, i, 171 sq.; Sozumenus V, 187). Probatus was the chief eunuch during the brief reign of Jovian (363–364). The palace eunuchs attempted to have Jovian appoint an Aryan bishop of Alexandria, but without success (Sozumenus VI, 15).

Eutropius was Superintendent of the Sacred Bedchamber (praepositus sacri cubiculi)[34] during the reign of Arcadius (395–408) and arranged the marriage of the emperor and his protŽgŽ Eudoxia. Arcadius was only 18 at the time—slow of intellect, speech and movement, as well as weak in character—so the intelligent, ambitious and unscrupulous Eutropius was able to manipulate his young master quite readily. The eunuch, who was rather elderly with an utterly bald head and a wrinkled yellow visage, was accused by historians of having been born a slave and performing as a catamite and procurer earlier in life.

After the murder of Eutropius' chief rival, Rufinus, who competed against him for influence over the emperor, by the soldiers of General Gainas on November 27, 396, he was able to control Arcadius at will. Moreover, Eutropius received credit for repelling an invasion of Asia Minor by the Huns in 398, and was nominated consul in 399, the first eunuch ever to hold this high honor. As the highest officer in the empire, he was able to sell other offices and government lands at his convenience. The poet Claudian derided him in two poems for his unethical practices: "In the public antechamber of Eutropius there hangs a tariff, showing the prices of the various provinces...The eunuch seeks to wipe out his personal ignominy in the general disgrace and, as he has sold himself, now desires to sell everything else."[35] Both the Gothic General Gainas and the Empress Eudoxia finally prevailed on Arcadius to give up his chamberlain. Eutropius was exiled to the island of Cyprus, and despite assurances of his safety, was tried at Chalcedon, where he was condemned and executed (Zosimus 256 sq., 268, 269; Socrates, church historian, VI, 2, 67, 674; Sozomenus VII, 1520; VIII, 7).

Antiochus was the praepositus of Arcadius (Patria II, 241). He had originally come from Persia (Theophilus, 125, 127). At the beginning of the reign of Theodosius II (408–450), he was elevated to the title of Patricius and directed much of the public affairs of the state. He became wealthy, living in an opulent palace in the Hippodrome quarter, but was thought to have abused his authority. The emperor accused him of high treason, confiscated his property and forced him into a monastic order (Cedrenus I, 586, 600; Zonaras III, 100–102, Priscus, 227).

Lausos was a magistrate during Arcadius' regime and succeeded Antiochus as Patricius during the reign of Theodosius II. His palace was on the Mese, not far from the pretorium (Patria II, 170; Cedrenus II, 587). Inasmuch as Theodosius II was a mere seven years old when his father died and he inherited the throne, Anthemias acted as regent during the first seven years of his rule, and eunuchs assisted in the operation of the government in the top functions. Pulcheria, Theodosius II's older sister, was then named Augusta and took a strong hand in administering the government until Theodosius married Eudocia on June 7, 421, who became the new Augusta. Theodosius II, a weak, vacillating and easily led emperor who cared more for hunting than for governing, submitted to the domination of the eunuchs and women of the palace all of his life.

Khrysaphios was the foremost eunuch to have significant influence on Theodosius II toward the end of his reign. According to the historian Malalas, Theodosius loved Khrysaphios because of his beauty and named him to be his paracoemomenus (Malalas 363, 368; Pascale Chronical, 390; Patria II, 182). Khrysaphios attempted to have Attila assassinated, but the plot was discovered and Attila called for his head. Theodosius eluded the demand and Khrysaphios appeased Attila's anger by sending him gifts (Priscus 147–150, 212 sq.). Khrysaphios was a supporter of Eutyches and an enemy of the patriarch Flavian. Theodosius finally cut him off and Pulcherie was able to deliver Khrysaphios to his enemy, Jordans, who put him to death (Theophanes 160; Pascale Chronical 390, Zonaras III, 107–109; Cedrenus 601–603). (Theodosius II was killed on July 28, 450, in a fall from his horse during a hunting party.)

Urbikios, the chamberlain of Emperor Zeno (474–491), had been given the order to assassinate the Isaurian general, Illus, by the Empress Ariadne. The assassin, a member of the imperial guard, made his move in 482 at the Hippodrome, but the blow was deflected by Illus' armor-bearer, so that only Illus' right ear was severed. Illus discretely left the capital and Urbikios was still on duty when Zeno died in a fit of epilepsy April 9, 491 (Theophanes 197; Cedrenus I, 92, 421).

The eunuch Kalopodios surreptitiously removed the records of the Council of Chalcedon from the church of Saint Sophia and delivered them to his master, the Emperor Anastasius (491–518) (Theophanes 239). During the dominion of Justinian I (527–565), Kalopodius later became praepositus (Theophanes 279, 360; Pascale Chronical 620).

Upon the death of Anastasius at the age of 87 on July 9, 518, the praepositus Amanios urged one of his cohorts to the throne. Amanios made the error of telling Justin, then an officer with one of the leading assemblages of palace troops. The following day, the troops declared Justin their choice, and the people supported his selection. The new emperor put Amantios and his accomplices, the chamberlain Andrew and the pretender Theocritus, to death (Theophanes 255; Pascale Chronical 610–612).

The eunuch Margarites was one of the most honored personages in the court of the Emperor Maurice (582–602). He served as paranymph at the wedding of Maurice and Tiberius II's daughter, Constantina, in 582. Stephen, another prominent eunuch in the court of Maurice, had charge over the young princes (Theophylact Simocattes 52, 329 sq.; Theophanes 388 sq., 445).

Stephen of Persia was the sacellarius of Justinian II (685–695), a large and ferocious eunuch, rarely seen without a whip in his hand. As chief tax gatherer, Stephen was particularly cruel, sometimes torturing the reluctant aristocracy to extract a few additional pieces of gold for his master. When the citizenry finally rebelled, they cut off Justinian II's nose and slit his throat, and dragged Stephen by the feet behind a heavy wagon down the Mese from the Augusteum to the Forum Bovis—the modern Aksaray—and there burnt him alive (Nicephorus 42; Theophanes 562, 566, 575).

The paracoemomenus was tortured and martyred for his iconophile religious beliefs during the tenure of Leo IV (775–780). Several other highly placed eunuchs were tortured and forced to enter monasteries for adhering to similar beliefs at the time. The protospatharius Jacob and the chamberlains Leo and Thomas were three of these eunuchs (Theophanes 701 sq.). These virtuous and faithful men were a sharp contrast to the brutal Stephen, rapacious Eutropius or scheming Amantios.

Among the important eunuchs in the government during the reign of Irene (797–802), besides Stauracius and Aetius, were the patricius and later governor of Italy, Theodore, the sacellarius Constantine, the primate Mamelos and Leo Klokas, who played a vital role in the palace revolution that brought Nicephorus I (802–811) to the throne (Cedrenus II, 29; Theophilus 703–705; Dolger, *Regesten der Kaiserurrunden des Ostromischen Reiches*, 339). Many of these eunuchs died in the disaster of 811, when Stauracius and Nicephorus were fatally wounded at the battle with Krum on July 26 and Michael I came to power (Theophilus 765).

Theoctistus, patricius and governor of Caniclea during the reign of Michael II (820–829), was a eunuch, according to Theophanes *Continuation* (657). Theoctistus became Logothete of the Drome and was designated by Emperor Theophilus (829–842) to be the tutor of his three-year-old son, Michael III (842–867). The Empress Theodora became regent and she and Theoctistus exercised supreme power of the land until Michael III was able to govern himself at roughly age 17. Theoctistus led a naval force against Crete, which was successful in re-establishing Byzantine rule in the area for a time. In 855, Bardas, Empress Theodora's brother, surprised Theoctistus in the imperial palace and murdered him in the presence of the young emperor (Genesios 23 sq., 83, 86, 90; Cedrenus II, 139, 157 sq.).

Damian, who was originally a slave, became the Master of the Offices and chamberlain in the later part of the reign of Michael III. He became particularly influential after the murder of Theoctistus. Several of the other influential eunuchs while Michael III was in power included: Rentakios, chief of the imperial wardrobe, Michael Angure, master of ceremonies, and the koitonite, Ignatius, who subsequently became patriarch of Constantinople (Constantine VII, *The Imperial Administration*, 231; Theophanes, *Continuation*, 234, 657, 675, 831, 832, 836; Cedrenus II, 197 sq.).

Baanes was master of the offices and master of ceremonies during the reign of Emperor Basil I (867–886). Baanes was given the rare honor of riding in the royal carriage with the emperor and empress at the baptism of the young prince, Stephen, in the cathedral of Saint Sophia. Basil I delegated most administrative duties of the empire to Baanes, whenever he had to depart Constantinople on one of his expeditions. Nicetas was another indispensable eunuch when Basil I was sovereign. The ruler entrusted him with the crown of Armenia, which Nicetas delivered to Ashot, the king of the region (Constantine VII, *Book of Ceremonies*, Appendix, 231, 503; Dolger, *Regesten der Kaiserurrunden des Ostromischen Reiches*, 506; Leo Grammaticus, 354). The eunuch Basil was sent by Leo VI (886–912) as ambassador to the caliph Muktafi in 903 and 906 (Dolger, *Regesten der Kaiserurrunden des Ostromischen Reiches*, 539, 547).

Samonas, an Arab, began his career as a simple chamber attendant.[36] He gained the favor of Leo VI when he revealed a plot against the emperor and was promoted to protospatharius. In 905, at the time of the birth of Constantine VII Porphyrogenitus, Leo VI named Samonas Master of the Offices, where he wielded considerable power. Samonas intervened in the disgrace of the Patriarch Nicholas, the mystic. Since the eunuch secretly favored his countrymen and longed to return to them, but was finally dishonored and confined to a monastery; the eunuch Constantine replaced him as master of the offices (Theophanes, *Continuation*, 362–364, 369–370, 371, 373, 708–711, 725, 863–865, 878; Leo Grammaticus, 280–282).

In addition to Theophanes' role as a military leader, he was the outstanding minister of Romanus I Lecapenus (920–944), was granted the title "Anthypathus-Patricius" in 925, succeeding the mystic, John, as paradynast. Theophanes resolved all the questions of the marriage of Maria Lecapena—granddaughter of Roman I—with Peter, king of the Bulgarians, in 927, acting as paranymph at the nuptial ceremony. He was entrusted with recovering the celebrated image of Christ of Edessa in 942. In 934, Theophanes was sent as ambassador to the Hungarians and charged with concluding a satisfactory peace treaty. The sons of Romanus I removed their father to the island of Prote on December 16, 944; Theophanes attempted to bring him back to the throne, but his plan was discovered and he was exiled (Cedrenus II, 226, 307–310, 316, 319; Theophanes, *Continuation*, 413 sq., 423, 442, 746, 748; Constantine VII, *Administration of the Emperor*, 323).

The eunuch Salomon Kitonite was sent as a special envoy to Spain and Germany during the reign of Constantine VII (913–959), according to Bishop Liutprand in his *Antapodosis* VI, 4, 375–376, 712–713, 869–870; and Leo Grammaticus 283–284.

Constantine, a eunuch born in Paphlagonia, which is in Asia Minor, not far from present-day Armenia, was castrated probably because of his father's high aspirations for him (Cedrenus II, 271–273, 283; Theophanes, *Continuation*, 713–715, 386–391). Constantine was appointed chamberlain and master of the offices—practically directing the operation of the government—while Constantine VII Porphyrogenitus (913–919) reigned with the regent Empress Zoe Carbonopsina.

The eunuch Basil was one of the greatest statesmen at the height of Byzantine power, which was between 920 and 985. He was the oldest son of Emperor Romanus I Lecapenus (920–944) and a Slavic slave. His father ordered him to be castrated at an early age, along with his younger brother, whom Romanus I wanted to make patriarch.[37] During the reign of his father, Basil played an insubstantial role, working his way into the good graces of the co-emperor, Constantine VII (913–959) as Master of the Wardrobe. When Constantine VII became sole emperor, he elevated Basil to the posts of Chamberlain and Master of the Offices (Theophanes *Continuation*, 442, 754, 461 sq.). Endowed with Byzantine cunning and other gifts of statesmanship, Basil was also venal and greedy. He directed a victorious incursion against the Arabs and received the honors of his triumph at the Hippodrome. He remained in the favor of the emperor and was present at his final moments on November 9, 959. When Romanus II (959–963) mounted the throne, Basil discharged all the faithful old servers of Constantine VII, compensating them with gifts and titles.

Basil remained in a state of semi-disgrace during the reign of Romanus II, but was once again re-integrated in the power of the government as chamberlain by Nicephorus II Phocas (963–969) and honored with the newly created, high-ranking title of *proedrus*. When Bishop Liutprand was sent by the king of Rome as special envoy to Constantinople in 949 and 968, it was Basil who met and negotiated with him. Liutprand tells us in his *Legatio* (349, 350) that the chamberlain Basil was discontent with his position and seemed to have a clandestine relationship with John Tzimisces. Indeed, when John became emperor John I Tzimisces (969–976), he elevated Basil to Prime Minister and Chamberlain. Upon assuming these functions, he exiled all Nicephorus' relatives, confined the Empress Theophano to a convent, discharged all of the old functionaries and appointed his own men in their place (Leo the Deacon 94, 169, 174, 175; Cedrenus II, 271–273, 283, 288, 327, 379, 381, 414 sq, 416–418, 429–433, 444 sq.). Basil was successful in quelling the usurpation of Bardas Phocas during the reign of John I and the long, bloody attempt of Bardas Sclerus, which ended on May 24, 979. John I died of typhoid at Constantinople on January 10, 976, and Basil II (976–1025) was promoted to the throne.

Basil II, the royal, was 18 at the time and still dependent on the eunuch Basil to maintain the affairs of the state. However, a few years after Basil II assumed the position of ruler, discord developed between the young emperor and his puissant great-uncle. Finally, in 985, Basil II exiled the eunuch Basil to the banks of the Stenon and confiscated his immense riches. Basil died shortly afterward. In 996, Basil II found it necessary to invalidate all of the edicts of his former paracoemomenus: "For at the beginning of our own reign, until the disposition of Basil the paracoemomenus,...many things happened which were not according to our wish, for he decided and appointed everything according to his own will" (Basil's Novel of 996).

The eunuch Joseph Bringas directed government matters while the handsome but weak-willed and frivolous Emperor Romanus II (959–963) reigned. Bringas occupied the office of paracoemomenus and acted as paradynast during this period. He had come from the same Byzantine family that later produced the Emperor Michael VI Stratioticus (1056–1057). When Romanus II was assassinated on March 15, 963, Bringas had to relinquish his duties to Basil and take refuge in the cathedral of Saint Sophia. He was later exiled to Paphlagonia, and eventually confined to the monastery of Asecritus at Pythia, where he died two years later (Cedrenus II, 34, 339, 342–351; Theophanes *Continuation*, 445, 469). Bringas administered the empire during the interregnum, March 15, 963 to August 15, 963, when Nicephorus Phocas was acclaimed by his troops, marched on Constantinople, and broke the resistance of Bringas in bloody street fighting. Nicephorus II Phocas was crowned August 16, 963 in Saint Sophia, and married Empress Theophano shortly afterward.

Romanus II also retained the services of other monks while he was emperor. John, a former clergyman and de-frocked monk, was his constant companion for pleasure (Cedrenus II, 339; Glykas 564 sq.). John Khaevina had a critical role in Romanus II's entourage, serving as protospatharicus and grand hetaeriarch (Theophanes, *Continuation*, 469, 470, 757). Khaevina was also master of ceremonies during the reign of Nicephorus II Phocas (Dolger, *Regesten der Kaiserurrunden des Ostromischen Reiches*, 696, De Cer. I, 96, 437).

The patrician eunuch Christopher was praepositus sacri cubiculi when Nicephorus II governed, taking over many of the emperor's functions while he was engaged in distant military campaigns (Liutprand, *Legatio*, 362, 364). The brothers Michael and Nicetas were patrician eunuchs in the service of Nicephorus II as vestrymen and keepers of the imperial wardrobe. Unable to prevent the murder of Nicephorus II in his bed on the night of December 10, 969, they became discredited (Cedrenus II, 348, 377).

The eunuch, Serge, was sent by Basil II in 1014 on a vital diplomatic mission (Cedrenus II, 460; Dolger, *Regesten der Kaiserurrunden des Ostromischen Reiches*, 800), while the eunuch Ergodotus was entrusted to carry out a highly confidential mission in 1028 for Emperor Constantine VIII (1025–1028) (Cedrenus II, 484; Dolger, *Regesten der Kaiserurrunden des Ostromischen Reiches*, 829). Symon, Drungarius of the Night Watch, was a highly placed eunuch who advised Constantine VIII to choose Romanus III Argyrus (1028–1034) as his successor.

Three of Emperor Michael IV's (1034–1041) brothers were eunuchs—Constantine, George and John. Constantine was named Duke of Antioch circa 1036 and raised to the rank of Domesticus of the Scholae in 1037. Michael V gave Constantine a title that was the equivalent to the "greatest nobleman," an honor that had never previously been bestowed on a eunuch (Cedrenus II, 510–512, 535, 540). When the populace rose up against Michael IV, he and Constantine fled to the convent of Stoudio, but they were caught, tortured and blinded. Michael IV's second brother, George, replaced Symon as Drungarius, and was appointed master of the wardrobe. Symon retired to a monastery.

Michael IV's third brother, John, was the most intelligent and ambitious of all the brothers. He had gained the title of Master of the Orient during the reign of Romanus III in approximately 1029 and retained this title while Michael IV ruled. He was also granted the position of Orphanotrophus, which was semi-ecclesiastical in nature, and in control of the imperial finances as well as a considerable portion of the civil administration. In addition, a recent biography of John the Orphanotrophus contends that he harbored aspirations of being named Patriarch of Constantinople.[38]

John the Orphanotrophus, a greatly influential eunuch in the imperial palace, briefly controlled the destiny of Byzantium by placing his relatives on the throne. John was a peasant's son from Paphlagonia (the region around Sinop on the south shore of the Black Sea in present-day Turkey), who had risen in the palace hierarchy to a position where he was able to bring his brother Michael into the palace service. Michael was a handsome young man who caught the eye of Empress Zoe; she was about 56 years old at the time of their meeting. She married John on the same day (April 11, 1034) that her husband, Romanus III (1028–1034) died in his bath of unknown causes.

Michael IV was an able emperor from 1034 to 1041, but he suffered from epileptic fits, which increased in severity as time went on. During this period, John effectively oversaw the administration of the empire. He was especially adept at collecting taxes from the aristocracy. Realizing that Michael IV would not live very long, John induced the Empress Zoe to adopt his nephew Michael Caliphates who, as the heir presumptive, who was given the title of Caesar. When Michael IV died on December 10, 1041, Caliphates became Emperor Michael V. Ungrateful for the favors granted him by his uncle, he sent John the Orphanotrophus into exile and Zoe to a nunnery. Neither the citizens of Contantinople, nor the Church would stand for the behavior of such an upstart, and he was deposed and blinded on April 20, 1042.[39] John was entombed at the convent of the Mother of God Decapolitissa. Paradoxically, many years later (about 1058), Isaac I Comnenus allocated a donation to the convent for the upkeep of the tomb of the omnipotent eunuch (Zonaras III, 607, 624, 625; Dolger, *Regesten der Kaiserurrunden des Ostromischen Reiches*, 940).

Nearly all of the relatives of Michael V (1041–1042) were made eunuchs, including those who were already fathers of families, as a condition for promotion to the highest offices. Moreover, the emperor always traveled with a corps of eunuchs for guards (Psellus 3, 95; Dolger, *Regesten der Kaiserurrunden des Ostromischen Reiches*, 940).

John the Logothete was an individual of very low birth, without education or eloquence, yet Constantine IX Monomachus (1042–1054) entrusted him with a major share of the governing of the Byzantine state, appointed him paradynast and placed him at the head of the senate. John the Logothete had replaced the prime minister Constantine Likhoudes, another eunuch, who had displeased Michael IX (Zonaras III, 649, 650; Cedrenus II, 610).

When Theodora (1055–1056) came to power, she appointed her faithful eunuchs to positions of authority. Theodorus was named Domesticus of the Scholae. Manuel was designated Drungarius of the Night Watch. Nicetas Xylinite, who had been logothete of the drome, retained this position with Empress Theodora and into the reign of the following monarch (Cedrenus III, 623). Theodorus also maintained his position, as did some of the lesser eunuchs, during the years of 1056 to 1057, when Michael VI Stratioticus ruled (Cedrenus II, 615, 619, 620).

The eunuch Nicephorus, nicknamed Nicephoritzes because of his short stature, was originally from the Bucellas theme (near present-day Lisbon, Portugal). He had been brought to the palace during the reign of Constantine IX Monomachus (1042–1055), and rose through the brief intervening reigns to become Duke of Antioch and secretary under Constantine X Ducas (1059–1067). Nicephoritzes was clever, ambitious and resourceful, becoming the judge in the Hellas and Hellespont during the reign of Romanus IV Diogenes (1068–1071). He succeeded the eunuch John of Side as the first minister under the government of Michael VII Ducas (1071–1078). The corps of immortals (the Athanatoi) was formed on the initiative of Nicephoritzes. Such serious civil strife plagued Byzantium that the emperor took flight and joined Roussel of Bailleul at Heraclius, but Roussel turned him over to the new emperor, Nicephorus III Botaneiates (1078–1081). Botaneiates' grand heteriarch, Straboramanus, tortured Nicephoritzes on the pretext of forcing him to reveal where his treasures were hidden and he died, most likely in the year 1079 (Zonaras III, 707, 713, 720, 725; Cedrenus II, 705, 706, 719; Michael Attaleiates,[40] 180–182, 199, 200, 208).

A eunuchoid monk was charged by the mother of the future Emperor Alexius I Comnenus (1081–1118) to look after her son. The monk did not leave the side of Alexius I while he was young (Bryennius 150). Among the doctors who cared for Alexius I was the eunuch Michael. Other highly placed eunuchs in the service of the emperor included Basil Psellus, who discovered a plot against the emperor's life, Eustathius Kyminianos, Leo Kikezites and Constantine, who was headwaiter (Anna Comnenus, *Alexiad*, 180, 375, 420; Dolger, *Regesten der Kaiserurrunden des Ostromischen Reiches*, 1089, 1090).

John the Mystic served under Emperor John II Comnenus (1118–1143). His name was inscribed in the convent of Pantokrator at the instigation of the ruler (Chalandon, *Jean II Comnenus*, 30). The eunuch Thomas was sent as ambassador to the Sultan of Iconium (currently Konya, Turkey) by Emperor Manuel I Comnenus (1143–1180). Thomas was originally of low birth, but made his way up the Byzantine hierarchy and acquired a vast fortune, yet finished his days in prison (Kinnamons 269, 296, 297; Dolger, *Regesten der Kaiserurrunden des Ostromischen Reiches*, 1519).

The eunuch Pterygionitus performed the execution of Mary of Antioch and the Caesarina Mary in accordance with the signed orders of Alexius II Comnenus (1180–1183) and Andronicus I Comenus (1183–1185) (Nicetas Choniates 337, 348).

Two eunuchs, Constantine, who was sacellarius, and the former barbarian, Aluattus, were charged by Alexius III Angelus (1195–1203) with the onerous task of raising the huge sum of 16 hundredweight of gold demanded by the German emperor, Henry VI, as tribute in 1195. Alexius' position was so desperate that he ordered the eunuchs to plunder the tombs of his ancestors for their costly ornaments in the Church of the Holy Apostles (Nicetas Choniates 631, 632, 646, 703, 727). Alexius III also sent a eunuch on a diplomatic mission to Ibankos, which had rebelled (Nicetas 688 sq.; Dolger, *Regesten der Kaiserurrunden des Ostromischen Reiches*, 1655).

After the fall of Constantinople on April 12, 1204 to the diverted crusaders of the Fourth Crusade, the Byzantine line of emperors was resumed at Nicea from 1204 to 1261. No record exists of important eunuchs functioning in this period, although a new hierarchy of offices and titles had been established. The Protovestarii, cup bearers, and masters of the offices were not eunuchs during this period of Byzantine culture, as far as historians have been able to establish. With the restoration of the capital at Constantinople (1261–1453), the influence of the West was considerably stronger in Byzantium. The rulers adopted many of the usages and prejudices of Western culture. Henceforth, eunuchs were regarded as inferior, and their physical condition was considered more of a blemish than an advantage.

Guilland was able to find only a few references to eunuchs in the final centuries of the Byzantine empire. Emperor Andronicus II Paleologus (1282–1328) sent "one of his eunuchs" to confirm the status of the grand primicier, Cassianos, who was involved in high treason (George Pachymeres II, 107). Eunuchs also accompanied the Empress-regent, Ann of Savoy, and were present at the marriage of Theodora Cantacuzenus with the Sultan Orkhan, according to John V. Cantacuzenus (1347–1354) (I, 199, II, 588). While the Byzantine empire fell on May 29, 1453, the Turkish conquerors would continue to employ eunuchs in their harems in Constantinople for an additional 500 years.

Commentary

The zenith of the Byzantine empire was also the high point of the employment of eunuchs in high offices, despite the unfavorable commentaries of the ancient writers and the negative conclusions of modern writers. For example, Gibbon wrote in his *Decline and Fall of the Roman Empire*, that "...we shall find that the power of the eunuch has uniformly marked the decline and fall of every dynasty." Cedrenus passes on the old proverb: "If you have a eunuch, kill him; if you do not have any, buy one and kill him" (II, 29). Nicephorus Byrennius adds: "Until when the power will remain in the hands of the eunuchs, with effeminate spirit, perverse by natural inclination, clever enough to imagine all sorts of misfortunes and execute them, creatures with a cowardly soul, instruments of baseness, guides of the illicit acts and repositories of the vices" (*Alexiad*, Note 445).

In actuality, long after the heyday of the power of the eunuchs the administration of the Byzantine empire crumbled. Some historians have tried to convince us that eunuchs were not a beneficial element in society. However, for dozens of wise and powerful rulers in Byzantine culture, the advantages of eunuchs far outweighed their disadvantages.

The castration operation must have been a serious deterrent to recruitment, considering that the procedure was exceptionally hazardous to perform. Although no exact details exist on how the surgery was performed in Byzantium, we know that castration was a fearful, dangerous, painful, bloody and illegal affair. In Byzantium, septic conditions were poor, at best; instruments were crude, as were medications and techniques for controlling the excessive loss of blood. All of the technical problems must have been exacerbated by the illegal status of the surgery, which only served to make it a shameful and surreptitious procedure. Moreover, the general reputation of eunuchs must have been a deterrent to those who were considering the operation. Nicephorus Bryennius (*Hodoiporicon* 159) wrote in the 11th century that people would ridicule eunuchs when they passed by, crying out the equivalent of "carbuncle, carbuncle." Castration was also shunned because it was utilized for those vanquished in war and as a punishment for crimes. To illustrate: About 1,000 B.C., David had to take 100 foreskins from the Philistines to pay Saul for the hand of his daughter, Michal (I Samuel 18:25–27; II Samuel 3:14). Ultimately, the underlying reason for the extensive employment of eunuchs in a variety of state and social functions remains unclear.

Xenophon (c. 430–335 B.C.) sheds some light into at least one of the reasons why the imperial rulers used eunuchs in his historical story of Cyrus II the Great (559–530 B.C.) of Persia. When Cyrus became emperor, he gained an acute awareness that his security was in danger and that "men are nowhere easier prey to violence than when at meals or at wine, in the bath, or in bed and asleep." This insightful man also concluded that no man was likely to be absolutely faithful to his master as long as he was tied by love to some woman or child. Since eunuchs had none of these weaknesses, "he selected eunuchs for every post of personal service to him, from doorkeepers up" (*Cyropaedia*).[41]

Endnotes—Chapter 6

1. Edward Gibbon, *The Decline and Fall of the Roman Empire*, 1788. Quoted in John Julius Norwich, *Byzantium, The Early Centuries*. New York: Alfred Knopf, 1989, p. 25.

2. W. E. H. Lecky, "History of European Morals," 1896.

3. Lucian (c. 125 A.D.—c. 190 A.D.), *Dialogue on the Eunuch*. Quoted in Charles Ancillon, *Traite des Eunuques*, Paris: Editions Ramsay, 1707, Reprinted in 1978, p. 57.

4. Saint Basil (c. 330 A.D.–379 A.D.). Quoted in Charles Ancillon, *Ibid.*

5. Ammianus Marcellinius (c. 330—c. 391) wrote a famous series of books covering the period from 96 A.D. to about 390, but only books 14 through 31, covering the period 353–378 A.D. have survived. This excerpt is from book 16, chapter 7.

6. Charles Ancillon, *Ibid.*

7. *Ibid.*, p. 60.

8. M. K. Hopkins: "That with consistent use of the eunuchs as chamberlains and their exercise of power is likely to have begun with Diocletian and is to be connected with the elaboration of court ritual." *Eunuchs in Politics in the Later Roman Empire*, PcPhS, IX, 1963, p. 77.

9. Rodolphe Guilland, "Les Eunuques dans l'Empire Byzantin: Etude de Titulature et de Prosopographie" in *Etudes Byzantines*, Tome I. Bucharest: Institute Français D'Etudes Byzantines, Reprinted in St. Cloud, France by Europeriodiques, 1943, p 198.

10. Steven Runciman, *Byzantine Civilization*, 1943. Quoted in Peter Tompkins, *The Eunuch and the Virgin*. New York: Clarkson N. Potter, Inc., 1962, p. 28.

11. Guilland, *Ibid.*, p. 200.

[12.] *Ibid.*, pp. 205, 215.

[13.] George Ostrogorsky, *History of the Byzantine State.* New Brunswick, New Jersey: Rutgers Press, 1969, p. 249.

[14.] John Zonaras, a Byzantine historian who lived in the first half of the twelfth century, was an official under Alexius I. He retired to a remote island and wrote a history beginning at the empire's creation and ending in 1118, copying much of his material from Dio Cassius and other early writers. Guilland frequently makes references to his works.

[15.] George Cedrenus, who lived in the first half of the eleventh century, was a Byzantine chronicler. He wrote of the period from the empire's creation to 1057 in his *Synopsis Historiarum*, and is frequently quoted by Guilland. This quote is from book II, pp. 147–148.

[16.] Theophanes Confessor (752–817) was a monk who wrote several chronicles, mainly his *Chronographia*, which covered the period from 284 to 813 A.D. Several other authors contributed to the writing of *Theophanes Continuatus*, a history spanning the period from 886 to 963.

[17.] Liutprand of Cremona (mid-tenth century) was a bishop who had been appointed ambassador to the court of Nicephorus II Phocas. He wrote an account of his observations, which covered the years 949 to 969.

[18.] Leigh W. Rutlege, *The Gay Book of Lists.* Boston, Massachusetts: Alyson Publications, 1987, pp. 166, 167.

[19.] E. R. Chamberlin, *The Bad Popes.* New York: Dorset Press, 1969.

[20.] Richard A. W. Sipe, *A Secret World: Sexuality and the Search for Celibacy.* New York: Brunner-Mazel, 1990.

[21.] Corippus (c. 527–c. 580) was an African poet who wrote *De Laudibus Justini Augusti Minoris*, in which he describes Narses, "of a remarkable figure and face" (IV, 363). Corippus also wrote that the emperor had so much affection for Narses that people used to gossip about it in the court (III, 221; also noted by Theophanes 376).

[22.] Norwich, *Ibid.*, pp. 220–221.

[23.] *Ibid.*, p. 251.

[24.] *Ibid.*, p. 253.

[25.] Lawrence Herbert Fauber, *Narses—Hammer of the Goths: The Life and Times of Narses the Eunuch*. New York: St. Martin's Press, 1990, pp. 69, 70, 135.

[26.] Norwich, *Ibid.*, p. 268.

[27.] William Smith, editor, *A Dictionary of Greek and Roman Biography and Mythology*, Volume III. Quoted in Fauber, *Ibid.*, p. 182.

[28.] Guilland, *Ibid.*, pp. 206–214.

[29.] Tompkins, *Ibid.*, p. 29; Ostrogorsky, *Ibid.*, p. 308

[30.] Caesar Nicephorus Bryennius was the husband of Anna Comnenus, daughter of Alexius I and had proclaimed himself rival of Emperor Michael Ducas and Nicephorus Botaneiates. He wrote a history of the period between 1057 and 1118. Thus, his "historical" accounts were likely to be biased against opponents.

[31.] Anna Comnenus was the most intelligent daughter of Alexius I. She is recognized as having written an excellent history of her father's life, titled *Alexiad*, which covers events from 1069 to 1118.

[32.] Ancillon, *Ibid.*, p. 74.

[33.] This prosopography is taken from Guilland, *Ibid.*, with his ancient sources quoted. Additional details are provided by Norwich, *Ibid.*, and Ostrogorsky, *Ibid.*

[34.] "The wardrobe of the sovereign, the gold plate, the arrangement of the Imperial meal, the spreading of the sacred couch, the government of the corps of brilliantly attired pages, the posting of the 30 *silentiarii*, who, in helmet and cuirass, standing before the second veil, guarded the slumbers of the sovereign, these were the momentous responsibilities which required the attention of this minister" (T. Hodgkin, *Italy and her Invaders*, Book 1, Chapter 3, Oxford University Press, 1880–1899).

35. Claudanus, *In Eutropium*, i, 199–207. "But," warns Professor Bury, "we must make great allowance for the general prejudice existing against a person with Eutropius' physical disabilities" (J. B. Bury, *A History of the Later Roman Empire (395-800 A.D.)*, London, 1889).

36. R. Janin, "Samonas an Arab Minister in Byzantium" in *Etudes Byzantines*, Bucharest: Institut Français D'Etudes Byzantines, 1935, pp. 308–318.

37. Tompkins, *Ibid.*, p. 30.

38. R. Janin, "Un Ministre Byzantin...Jean L'Orphanotrophe, XIe Siecle," in *Etudes Orientales #34*, 1931, pp. 431–443.

39. Ostrogorsky, *Ibid.*, pp. 324–326.

40. Michael Attaleiates was a high official under Romanus IV Diogenes (1068–1071) and Nicephorus III Botaneiates (1078–1081) who wrote a personal account of the period between 1034 and 1079.

41. Much of what ancient Byzantine authors wrote in favor of eunuchs has been lost, and none of what remains has been translated into English. Two references in the field of Byzantine studies have been preserved in French, to my knowledge. One of these, Theodore Decapolites, writer and high government official (Patricius and Quaestor of Constantine VII (913–959), Porphyrogenatus and Romanus II (959–963), is the author of *Pro Eunuchismo et Eunuchis* (For Eunuchism and Eunuchs), according to Ancillon, *Ibid.*, p. 59. I have not been able to find a copy of this work in the United States. The only other author who wrote favorably of the eunuchs was Theophylactus of Orchrida (see next chapter).

Chapter 7—A Justification of Eunuchism:
Through the Eyes of Theophylactus of Ochrida

Translator's Note

Theophylactus of Ochrida, the writer of this treatise, is a witness to a scholarly presentation of opposing arguments about the true nature of euchunism. The treatise is dedicated to his brother who, as a eunuch, experienced much hostility and negative reactions to his condition. Although, the writer purports to be a simple scribe, remembering only what he has heard, we, the readers, know that he clearly favors the eunuch's position. His protagonist brilliantly takes up each of his accuser's arguments, and dispels them by sheer force of logic. A careful reading clarifies the intense historical role eunuchs played in medieval life, not only in relation to their Christian spiritual practices, but also to their political and military achievements.

In the prologue of the Apocryphal biblical book, *The Wisdom of Sirach, written about 132 years before Christ, Sirach writes:*

> You were invited to read it with good will and attention, and to be indulgent in cases where, despite our diligent labor in translating, we may seem to have rendered some phrases imperfectly. For what was originally expressed in Hebrew does not have exactly the same sense when translated into another language. Not only this book, but even the Law itself, the Prophecies, and the rest of the books differ not a little when read in the original.

This quotation is particularly appropriate for this translation, since we are dealing with Greek, Latin, French and other languages. For this reason, I took some liberty to modernize the phraseology, and to update the expressions. In some instances, I let the medieval phrase, humor or stylistic expression stand as is, and hope the reader will appreciate this historical note. Mainly, I aim to bring to contemporary readers some of the intensity and turmoil, as well as moral clarity, associated with the eunuch as an historical figure.

Background for the Treatise

This is a translation made from a book that was printed in both the Greek and French languages, which was written by Paul Gautier, and published in 1980 by the Association de Recherches Byzantines (Association for Byzantine Research). Gautier, a member of the French Institute for Byzantine Studies, titled his book *Theophylacte D'Achrida Discours, Traites, Poesies: Introduction, Texte, Traduction et Notes*, (This is translated as Discourses, Treatises, Poems: Introduction, text, translation and notes by Paul Gautier.)

Gautier used approximately 66 manuscripts and references in Greek, Latin, French, Russian, German and Bulgarian languages to explain and assemble the 8 treatises and 15 poems written by Theophylactus. He explains that the treatise, *Justification for Eunuchism*, was written for Demetrius, one of Theophylactus' three brothers, who had been castrated by his father to make him more acceptable for service to the Emperor.

Theophylactus was archbishop of Ochrida and is believed to have written the treatise on eunuchism shortly after the visit of the Byzantine emperor, Alexius I Comnenus (1081–1118), to Thessalonica (also called Salonica), a large city about 120 miles southeast of Ochrida. Alexius I is known to have visited Thessalonica at least twice while provisioning for the invasion of Normandy. The first visit took place from September 1105 to February 1106, and the next occurred in the winter of 1106 to 1107. Theophylactus preached to the emperor, and shortly after was invited to listen to a discourse on eunuchism at the court between a monk—believed to be Simon the Sanctified, a eunuch and leader of the monastery at Athos (about 80 miles southeast of Thessalonica)—and Stephan, a leading military commander of the city. The treatise takes the form of a dialogue between these two adversaries. The author's poetic Preface to the Treatise clarifies the purpose and source of this work.

The Justification of Eunuchism

Theophylactus of Ochrida (c. 1050–c. 1109)

My brother is the source of this treatise.
> He is a eunuch, a model of the honest life.
But irritated by the attacks against the eunuchs,
> that people inconsiderably throw,
he asks for appropriate consolation.
> To give it to him, I have composed this treatise,
a work for a pure and very scholarly friend,
> who appreciates the facts with fairness,
does not confound their nature in confusion,
> and does not understand criticism of the excellent eunuchs,
when by chance one sees a bad one.
> Because one has not failed to allow oneself
to crush the virile men with a thousand reproaches.

The eunuch's virtue rests on a more solid foundation.
> How many villains are there among men?
As much as the sand of the sea, the dust of the earth.
> If one wants to compare them with eunuchs,
who until now seemed villains also,
> they will be considered as lions in front of weasels and flies.

Even if certain laws and canons
> forbid the removal of the testicles,
search minutely for the meaning of these texts,
> examine the epoch of these laws
and consider all the various circumstances,
> as if you thoroughly knew the laws of rhetoric.
Because, during this examination you will find only one practice,
> which was not adopted as a security measure.

It is not primarily for the public that I have composed this treatise,
> but for my brother, a remarkable eunuch, because of his wisdom.
Even though this is a special favor to my brother,
> I nevertheless disseminate this work to all.
In reality, I am little affected by the malicious gossip,
> for I wish everyone to receive some benefit from my work.
To those who are not pleased by my proposals,
> I say you cherish these words and I will cherish those of you
who hear the message.

Introduction to the Treatise

Theophylactus of Ochrida

As the poem describes, this treatise is addressed to my brother, who is a eunuch, but remains unhappy because of the simple-minded attacks against eunuchs. He would like to silence those persons who accuse eunuchism of perpetrating a vice. Instead, he proposes that vice or virtue be determined according to each individual's merit. Rather than eunuchism causing evil, the author states that free will determines good and evil, inasmuch as it creates the condition that leads both intact men as well as eunuchs to violate God's laws. But, in eunuchs, free will actually reduces evil and violence, compared with non-eunuch males. At one level, I, Theophylactus, may be accused of exaggeration, because of my deep interest in the merits of eunuchism. Yet, I am motivated to seek information about the laws of the epoch, in addition to other information available at the time. But I do not see how this treatise would not condemn the judgment of those who only consider the text superficially, and do not consider the reality of these things deeply. This treatise, made in defense of my brother—for whom it is a nice gift— follows the plan presented at the beginning of the statement. If someone else also wants to profit from the benefits of this treatise, nothing will prevent it. And nothing shall prevent other people from benefiting from this work as well.

[The first argument, a critique of the eunuch condition, represents the negative stereotypes of the time about eunuchism as a moral and spiritual vice. Translator]

Critique of Eunuchism

I have found an honorable lawyer from Thessalonica to defend eunuchism. He was a protagonist when the emperor was there listening to two people intelligently discussing eunuchism. I paid close attention to their conversation so that I could remember it for your purposes. One of the two people, a eunuch, was accused of having permitted a nephew to be castrated in opposition to the laws of the Creator, believing that it was better to not conceive this sort of man than to offend divine and human laws.

The accuser cited the law of Moses,[1] which is for the Church a strong barrier against eunuchs and other castrated ones.[2] In addition, the canons of the Apostles,[3] the church fathers,[4] and a civil law decreed by Justinian also forbid this voluntary condition. This still does not include the views of the most ancient emperors of the Roman Empire, who forbade the ablation (surgical removal) of the testicles. In the eyes of this individual, eunuchism had corrupted the child's nature by preparing him to succumb easily to many serious passions.

The Accuser's Critique

Because of the cupidity and greed that exist in such people, eunuchs are the stingiest and most selfish of mortals. These negative qualities are naturally the thorny suckers of liberty, ambition, jealousy, love of pettiness, pretense, meanness, and undue sensitivity, all of which reigns unfortunately in the heart of eunuchs, as in a fortress. If, additionally, they haunt the palace, their low passions are either illuminated or deeply disguised. As for those who are the principle ministers of the emperors, I add this: To those eunuchs assigned to the women's apartments, this allows all kinds of vices. It does not matter that the individual eunuch is separated from other men, he will be as much a prey of his passions, and unduly sensitive to the feminine wiles as any man, as long as he is in physical contact with the women. Because weakness of the mind leads to increased vigor of the passions, one must make a concerted effort not to succumb to them. Moreover, if some women seduce him with their languor and general softness, I wager that the result will be an ungodly situation, similar to the dominance of the goddess Astarte among the Sidonians.[5]

Another group of eunuchs exist that are put on display in a theatrical manner. I refer to these cooers and warblers who have introduced their abominable ways—licentious songs and sweaty lust—into the Church. Do you still want another of their characteristics—to know what their customs are like? They comport themselves like comedians. In fact, among other things, these individuals are champions of drinking and carousing. Their behavior is indecent and unbecoming, and their language is full of obscenities. It has also been said that most of them practice repugnant homosexual intercourse. The accuracy of this rumor is affirmed mainly by those who are in charge of the women's quarters. There may be some truth to this rumor, because they frequently keep company with stage people. This would be similar to the grape, which only matures by contact with another grape. As if that were not enough, they murmur lascivious songs with the libertines. Is not speech a reflection of action? As for eunuchs who always dwell in the company of women, they exude from them an ardor, which enflames all who approach them. For these reasons, eunuchs are taken as bad omens, and targets for numerous attacks.

Justification of Eunuchism: The Eunuch's Perspective

With these words, the accuser quiets down, his facial expression showing how concentrated he is, and how strong his intentions are on binding the eunuch in chains. Smiling discretely, the eunuch presented himself as a polite man, but one who was highly animated in his denial of the accusations.

The eunuch said:

It seems to me that you are looking for the castrated ones who live somewhere in Persia or in the Arab countries. While you are heaping offenses on us, you crush us under their evil weight. We cannot confront you, as you have thrust your head back arrogantly in your attack. You speak, but do not see before you the archbishop of Thessalonica, the bishop of Pydna,[6] bishops of Petra, Edesse, Bulgaria, and several others of different ranks. In my opinion, when you mention these august persons, you should put down your dagger.[7] You roam into strange places, and see only the worst of everyone. Oh, come now, you the best of all men, do not act like this. Do not deride your friends because of the general social evil, which is the enemy of God and the law, and be so hostile to those nearest and dearest to you. These good men (i.e. bishops) who took this measure were voluntarily castrated to counter their own passions.

The Eunuch Explains That Castration is not an Offense Against God

If I am, in fact, according to your judgment, inherently against my creator, why not judge yourself in the same way, since you decided to remain a virgin, and with God's help kept your chastity. Marriage is the source of procreation. Consequently, if you do not use your sexual organs in view of their natural purpose, you too are against God's will, since you cut yourself short of his wisdom. Obviously, you consider your genital organs as superfluous. It follows then that we should not blame a man who castrates himself (Matthew 18:8,9, 19:12; Mark 9:43– 47). It is the same for a landlord who has good reason to cut down a fig tree that fails to produce fruit (Matthew 21:19). Neither should you blame those who cut off a sixth finger, on the grounds that whoever does so does violence to nature.

On the contrary, you have modified the nature of your genital organs because sperm formation is the natural function of the testicles, which were created so that man could procreate (Hebrews 11:11)— an act which you deplore. As you say, the production of sperm is superfluous because of your passion for virginity. You, who are in perfect possession of your reason, have decided not to use your genital organs for their natural purpose. So, why not accept their removal? You can hardly be criticized for it. You will no longer have to exhaust your body by dieting, or by avoiding baths, and by all sorts of spiritual asceticism. You have forced your body to be thin rather than fat, pale rather than having high color, feeble rather than vigorous. Do you suppose we are going to say that this transformation of your person defies the Creator's laws (Proverbs 6:1–3), simply because you have been created to enjoy good health, yet have been transformed into the opposite: an unhealthy person? If you blame me for eliminating the testicles, then I, on my side, reproach you for destroying your body. So abstain from accusing me, or you will be castigated among my friends. Hasten to the divine body that revived so many people. Then your lips will become solid red and the eagle that you are no longer becomes a prisoner of his own wings (Matthew 24:28).

When a Greek makes these reproaches, bear in mind we prefer nothing greater than nature, for living according to nature and its laws is the pinnacle of our mortal life. But to you who chose a life that transcends nature, you must work at it, you must practice to achieve it. Yet, you lack a spirit of fairness, because you silence those who speak out against eunuchs.

The Meaning of the Mosaic Law

When you frighten me, you do so by mentioning the holy readings, especially the law of Moses. I admire you for your directness. You accuse me of breaking the Mosaic law only because I am a eunuch, but you fail to grasp the real meaning of the law. My dear fellow, first the words of the law pertain only to those who are under the Law. Knowing that it is primarily a spiritual code, and points to the shadow of things to come, it remains imperative that we address the content of what is written on the tablets. Not according to the mere letter of the word (Romans 3:19; 7:14)—this is ultimately spiritually destructive—but instead examine the meanings presented on the tablets and interpret them in the broadest sense on behalf of the lawmaker (Hebrews 10:1), the eunuch, and all the castrated ones. Otherwise, God would not bestow special honor, which you know was awarded to the eunuch in the parable of Isaiah.[8] What Moses said about God forbidding the eunuch a place in heaven has been an old law, but it was superseded.

The Bible equates eunuchism with holiness: a eunuch as a servant of God. For example, who was Daniel? Who were his companions?[9] Who was Nehemiah?[10] And before them, who was Ebedmelech?[11] Are you going to exclude them from the assembly of the Lord (2 Corinthians 3:6)? Far from being sterile and fruitless, they were highly religious, and attended to their prayers and God's works (John 6:63). Their descendants and ancestors are in the terrestrial Jerusalem, where they have engendered many children because of their love. Or are they in the celestial, resplendent Jerusalem, where their heavenly condition is superior to that of many sons and daughters?[12] No one enters heaven who is insensible to God's reason that is within us, the divine seed of spirituality. Therefore, you and I, as well as all of us who hope not to be banished from the assembly of the first born, respect eunuchism. Let the Hebrews condemn physical eunuchism, for they have a limited view that abundant offspring are the highest good.

The Canons of the Apostles & the Church Fathers
(The Eunuch Continues)

As for the canons of the Church Fathers (Hebrews 12:20–24), I honor and worship them as life-giving rules. But I do not consent to be their prisoner. In fact, among adult men there exist those who have mutilated themselves (Sirach 17:11), because they believe that their sexuality places them in mortal danger.[13] If you think that this is our situation, speak up and hurl the daggers attacking our mutilated condition. Once you understand that we are not this sort of degenerate person, diminish the aggressiveness of your attacks against us.

If you presume that mutilation means removal of the testicles, and insist that the canon uniformly punishes this practice, I must clarify our situation. Yes, those men who are castrated while still youths, with the intention of seducing women lost in iniquity, may assume that they can conquer them primarily because they have been castrated, and the dangers of pregnancy abated. These eunuchs are profligate in satisfying sexual desires. For in reversing Paul's law (1 Corinthians 7:27–31) of marital chastity, they aim to have women like they never had before they were castrated.

This is why ancient and Biblical teachings called such eunuchs enemies of God's creation. Not only do they not use their body parts according to the Creator's plan, but they also reject the idea of ejaculation as the proper goal of copulation. Why should they, seeing that they are familiar with the most agreeable gratifications other than intercourse and can satisfy even the most sensual women. To expose one to the evident dangers, they do not escape the grief of their own murderers.[14]

On the other hand, if someone were still a child or adolescent, and has their testicles amputated because it is their parents passion and zeal to preserve their chastity and purity, who would condemn him? If parents fully collaborate in their desire to have their son be a eunuch, it is to eliminate the danger of sinning. Do you really think the canon sees this act in a bad light, and sharply criticizes it?[15] We think not.

The Historical Justification of Castration

Ah, well, I rest my case. We (eunuchs) admit that eunuchism was prohibited because of the circumstances, which pushed the Apostles to proscribe it as a cause of Simon's downfall.[16] The Church Fathers, and those that followed took this line of reasoning because of the aftermath left by early heretics (who rejected the married state).[17] The entire heretical doctrine appeared to rest on the removal of the testicles. Now that set of erroneous ideas has vanished.

We do not sin. We practice the ablation for the love of purity and piety, just as you do your virginity, shunning marriage as a desecration. If you order me not to scrutinize the intention of the law, I reply that you offend the essential laws of rhetoric. This is analogous to striking the giver of your life. Do not forget that the letter and intention of the law deal with a number of serious problems. But I no longer pay attention to these matters: others can defend themselves.

Economy and Legislation

What amazes me is how you mistakenly perceive that I have departed from the early Hebrews. I seek the height of science and wisdom of Christ in which one finds the treasures and wisdom of knowledge (1 Corinthians 1:4–7; Colossians 2: 2, 3). I know that the Church has admitted many accommodations, which appear to run against the contention of the divine laws, but which learned ministers of Logic (the Holy Word) have established. I naturally do not rigidly adhere to the letter of the law, but rather leap over it in an act of faith. Thus, in reviewing the law, I penetrate the darkness and see its deepest intentions (Psalms 36:23, 24). You, who impose these laws as from the height of the Acropolis, imply that the Fathers of the Fourth Council agreed that the promise they made to the Egyptian bishops was negated.[18] To those who glorify our Gospel, this promise is not valid (Matthew 5:33, 34).

How did the Fathers of the Fourth Council determine that the women who fornicate will submit to a severe punishment, but not treat men in the same way? In effect, we annul their union. Why should God punish men any less for dissolving marriage (Matthew 5:32), notwithstanding the case of fornication, as the great Basil once wrote?[19] It seems obvious that only when we move into the spirit of the precepts, can we learn to understand and live by the Word. Accordingly, when I explore the *spirit* of the law, in view of the epoch in which these restrictive legislations were made, I am instructed by God to follow my own soul.

Tradition and the Eunuchs

What tradition holds, and what our interpretation of the laws shows is truthful and straightforward, I find repeated by the secular tradition. This reveals remarkably high status achieved by the eunuchs in the State as well as in the Church.[20] In effect, the doctors of the New Testament, the initiators and explorers of the mysteries of God, and true bishops of the soul, have seen that men of ancient times, had a great faith. In protecting their purity, they were able to carry out the ministry of God and the handling of saintly things. Also, far from reducing the multitude of eunuchs made expressly for church-related functions, another reason is the disappearance of perverse intentions—a point I made earlier.

There exist other doors that are open to the practice of eunuchism, inasmuch as it contributes to sanctification. In fact, I can verify that physicians today administer treatments to their patients, which are considerably different from earlier ones. If you ask them the reasons for this change, they will reply that treatment changes have to do with varying resistance to illness, and the changes in the lifestyles of contemporary people.

In the same manner, the doctors of the Church have similarly changed their conduct to adapt to contemporary life. Is this change toward accepting eunuchism a transgression? Is it negligence by all the bishops, and this, despite their openness regarding this issue in the Church? It is perhaps that the emperors have closed their eyes on this practice of eunuchism, because they were more interested in increasing the numbers of these young men than of holding onto an outmoded belief? Eunuchs are also well disposed toward their master, a practice clarified by etymological explanations.[21] Should we plant the belief that all the bishops have failed to awaken to this shift in Church practices? Their aim surely remains that of keeping the form and appearance of the Church pure and unstained.

The Legislation of Justinian

Emperor Justinian I (527–565), after earlier emperors had proscribed eunuchism as sinful and destructive, changed this practice by law. I wonder about the law of this brave emperor, inasmuch as he may not have known that his empress, Theodora, neither promoted the eunuchs nor honored their dignity, but instead treated these men like slaves. Nor did she praise General Narses, the greatest military leader.

The emperor's edict immediately changed the laws, stigmatizing those who castrated themselves. To my mind, this new law was one of the strategies of the crafty Tribonian.[22] Possibly, I may have heard a rumor that the law was issued under a peculiar circumstance—the high mortality rate among those castrated. But consider the excessiveness of this decision. If castration is clearly deadly, where do the many palace eunuchs come from, as well as those army leaders who have enlarged the frontiers of the Roman empire? If the operation is so deadly, why not outlaw the taking of drugs and all the other medical treatments, since they also put people in danger?

I say to Justinian: I will show you that the eunuchs are useful for your majesty who has created this legislation. If you are unable to see my position because you are not a clever enough magician for luring those many eunuchs all standing strong at your side, simply abolish these laws, which only you can eradicate. In effect, you must necessarily choose one of two things: Either abolish castration and never use eunuchs, or transfer them to the highest posts and favor castration because it is very advantageous to your regime.

Critique of Anti-Castration Legislation *(Simon the Sanctified Speaks Directly to the Emperor)*

We cannot accept the fact that you maintain castration as a sin for others, but employ eunuchs on the basis of their abilities. Although many men have been castrated, due to illness, this is evidently not condemned, because you lack the time to examine the causes of their castration. But we refuse to accept these arguments because the emperor must not neglect the bad conduct of his subjects. When you refuse to investigate the causes of castration, you become like Miltiades and Koroibos[23] of old, for then you mock your own legislation and strive to deceive us. If your decree genuinely proscribed castration, it would inspire great fear among the doctors who had been performing the operation, even in front of witnesses.

Otherwise, if you see eunuchs as strangers who exist merely to colonize the barbarian countries,[24] you will soon see that the people in your entourage, and those who direct the affairs of your country, are not the same. How can a sensible man with intelligence choose magistrates who would relinquish the most important posts at the first onset of the barbarians? This move provokes great and small individuals alike. To whom do you confide the treasures of the Romans? Certainly not to the estimable people, whom you have in your palace, and who are incapable of receiving any important instruction, because they are endowed neither with independence nor judgment, and who attack freedom. Your stupidity is great and very dense, if you do not believe the tragic poem that asserts: "The slave is nothing compared to the free man." Listen to the song of the lyrical muse: "Never does the fawn-colored fox and the roaring lion exchange between them their nature." Thus, the Nomisma (Byzantine gold coin) of your decision rings falsely with the sound of a copper coin when it strikes. This is certainly why one rejects it like a rotten shoe. As the judge recognized, "Nothing is absolutely unusable in the empire that is in the Church of God."

Older Legislation

If I examine the older laws, I discover a mundane and entirely vulgar motivation that does not reflect princely aspirations. The sentiments focus on how to populate the empire; to hold a military force together; to recruit a multitude of soldiers; and to attract wise men to join them by stepping aside from the laws of Christ (1 Corinthians 2:6, 7), and our own peace. These are at the heart of the lion (Psalms 25:9; Ephesians 2:14) and caused these emperors to forbid castration. This is not simply conjecture on my part; I can interpret the truth very well. It is guaranteed by another Roman law, which did not impact on older persons of privilege and advantage, but affected those lower status people who were of marriageable age. They could not marry, the law said, because the city had become too populous. Those people who were without children were all to be punished.

Until the time of Constantine—the originator of positive laws on eunuchs and who, for that reason, was called "The Great"—emperors had banished this practice from the empire. Eunuchs were forced to live outside the empire, because the practice had been totally forbidden.[25]

Do not remind me (a eunuch) again of these carnal laws that speak with a voice coming from the earth and the mouth of hell (Isaiah 8:19), and force eunuchs to carry the burden of guilt because of their stigma and uselessness. Laws more severe than Constantine's condemn eunuchs without mercy. The earlier emperors indiscriminately scorned the people, Christ, as well as the eunuchs, and in so doing greatly enhanced the movement of Christianity.[26] We shall not advance the reasons for official persecution of eunuchs. Otherwise, we would also have to examine their persecution of the Christian martyrs.

The Vices of the Eunuchs

Seeing that you have again referred to the existence of the deplorable passions of eunuchs, as well as accused them of being reduced to the feminine state, I hesitate to respond on this point, because it does not even merit refutation. However, out of my regard for you, I will speak, so that you may not accuse eunuchs of responding with futile and simplistic reproaches. You ascribe to me personally the trifling defects that we eunuchs have, but neglect the huge defects (Matthew 7:3) that many virile men express in their personalities. You believe that in each pusillanimous eunuch the wickedness is insignificant and weak, like the produce of an exhausted earth, which lacks good quality and taste. But in still other eunuchs, especially those who are influential, the malice is strong and unyielding. Eunuchs are reputedly the pirates and brigands; pickpockets and robbers. Or eunuchs who have been installed in the state agencies behave like young lions who roar and terrify other animals by their cries in order to forcibly gain their nourishment (Psalms 22:1, 2).

Who are these avaricious and selfish people? Are they the ones who take care of the widowed and bereft people (1 Corinthians 9:22); who bring up and instruct orphans (Proverbs 23:10, 11); who consecrate their existence to serve others and to love them in words and acts? Or are they the ones who forestalled the heritage of the orphans and who killed the widow and the orphan (Psalms 94:6, 7)? What kind of people are these for whom ambition, anger and jealousy toward their equals is fulfilled by wars against neighboring cities and countries, and by overthrowing all the laws in order to assure that they have the power to impose their will? Such violence is not the conduct of eunuchs.

I will abstain from enumerating in detail the rape of virgins, the adulteries, and other abominations (which must cause the author to blush). If one had time, one could count these evil deeds by non-eunuchs the same as their hollow victories.

The Eunuchs of the Palace

You have discoursed about the scoundrels very well, and enumerated faults we have never committed. Examine the people who are now the most deceitful among the Greeks and the Barbarians and whose great perversity has perpetrated innumerable misfortunes. You will not see one eunuch among these, and so you will learn who is the lowly lizard to compare to an emperor.

You tell me that the eunuchs who live in the palace are the champions of vice, and among them are those who have been chosen to serve the empress because they are discreet and follow the cult of Logos. This permits the royalty to be guided by the eunuchs, and allows them to entrust their charges to them. If those who live in their entourage would only model themselves on these palace eunuchs, they would receive the colors of glory and the divine image, and become representatives of Logos and of honesty. I have heard it said, and I believe it to be true, that many eunuchs are just that. If you do not recognize them, it is not surprising, for many appear quite ordinary. In the same way, Elijah had not known that 5,000 men would be saved by God.[27]

The Eunuchs in the Church

In the same way, if you inquire about men of this type, who as you said, appear to be immoral, your list of charges will immediately confront obstacles. First, they are no worse than non-eunuch men.

Second, who they are is of little interest, for they live in a variety of places—the palace, the Holy Mother Church, the Church of Constantinople, including those who reside in the various monasteries, and live very ascetic and bloodless lives. Other eunuchs belong to other Churches, where they are distinguished by the glory of the episcopacy (ecclesiastical government) and the priesthood.[28] Most of them are only allegedly immoral, although it is to slander Christianity to accuse them.

Third, if you observe the throng of eunuchs and see how many among them are immoral, and subsequently compare these with members of your group, the eunuchs' infamy will be unquestionably lower. To clarify my assertion, examine a number of priests from one or two churches, drawing on both your side and mine. Then observe who are the ones that most closely conform with sacerdotal purity.[29]

You have once again erred in accusing all the stage singers of being corrupted by the theater. You thus fail to distinguish between the singers who charmed God more by their morals, than those who charmed the audience by their singing.

Nevertheless, I concede that you fall under the weight of your accusation. If I examine the ones whom the theater has elected for directors, I can show that this amazing brotherhood is comprised more of men of your sort (normal). See to it, then, that you do not run down our national treasure. Opponents say: many eunuchs are weak. I would add: some are libertines and debauched. But what is the fault of Demas with regard to Luke, the one who abandoned Paul, compared to the one who remained faithful (2 Timothy 4:10)? And what about Phygelus and Hermogenes, compared to Silvan and Timothy (2 Timothy 1:15)? And how does Judas compare to John and all the other Apostles who cried and lamented their master? I will add other significant examples. The betrayal of trust by Esau, so dishonoring Jacob,[30] and the incest of Reuben that dishonored Joseph,[31] although they were brothers, offspring of the same seed.

I again offer this reflection and I do not believe that it is inappropriate. You criticize all of the eunuchs because of having seen some minor debauchery among a few. How many more of them who are justly praised shall I count, crediting castration for having made them vessels of purity (1 Thessalonians 4:3–7)? Above all, I triumph when these good men, the eunuchs, are in the majority. Most certainly, you oppose God's judgment, if you condemn eunuchism because of ten debauched ones, and if you do not allow us to reject your opinion for the sake of those thousands of eunuchs who are both pure and promote purity in others.[32] You should direct your criticism against the sinners and the sarcasm of Momus.[33] It was his habit to harass and not to defend the irreproachable eunuchs.

Every person who sins shall die, as the Scripture says (Ezekiel 18:20). What really concerns me is the greater number of people who have committed serious sins, yet you have accused only eunuchs. This leads me to scorn your insults. I do not tolerate dimwitted fools, but seek those who show who they are—as servants of God. Remember, the adorers of the dimwitted ones were chastised, and God left their bones in the desert, while Caleb and Joshua, hale and whole, reached the promised land and rescued an oppressed and submissive people.

Eunuchs and the Sacred Music

Inasmuch as the eunuchs also sing in the churches, their tunes should contain such licentiousness that they undo saintly thoughts. But why this particular grievance? Answer me, since the Spirit of song has rendered David, the musician, an expert in this art—which we have learned to appreciate—and which heals our animosities toward one another, and restores the divine perspective. Ephraim of Osroene (c. 306–373 A.D.)—another musician who reminds me of Ignatius Theophoros (Saint, martyred in 110 A.D.)—ordered the odes in contra-chant at Antioch because he had heard the angels singing in this manner.[34] This same Ephriam, who also observed that Harmonios, the son of Bardesanes (Bardaisan; Bar Daisan, 154–222 A.D.), had composed some gracious songs that contained a hint of friendly impiety, songs that attracted large crowds.[35] These numerous songs were presented as a succulent dish to the churches of Syria.[36] St. John Chrysostom (347–407A.D.), the prophet that the Aryans were uprooting from Constantinople with their songs, also composed melodious songs.[37] Who was more austere than John, who intuitively knew what the words expressed: praise to David, who is glorified by the Spirit. Besides, it is much more pleasurable when all the ancient songs now used in the churches are sung with harmony and skill. We can also introduce into the books of the saints an ornate scene with an Egyptian richness, which facilitates our passage into the divinity of God.[38] However, if we concede that we banish such images from the churches, they are not the inventions of the eunuchs that we must banish. Instead, I dare say this about the people of your "tribe"—it is the non-eunuchs who are the real transmitters for embellishing harmony.

Attitude of the Early Church

Many early church groups are overly critical, perceiving only bad omens, and are attracted to other nay-sayers. This is how the imbeciles and the foolish ones treat the eunuch monks, because they delight in attacking people different than themselves. Similarly, some Church Fathers criticized the tyrannical eunuchs of their time, and severely stigmatized the archons (community magistrates) of their period. And to what group do the heretical leaders against the early Church Fathers belong—those who have advocated propositions even more damaging than their statements against the eunuchs? Should we criticize the men of today for the sake of the impious archons and of the heretics from earlier times? Let us take account of individual responsibility, and not castigate today's eunuchs because of heretical tendencies among earlier ones.[39] Besides, what good purpose is there in making a detour, when I can go straight ahead? Why not tell you the facts? The most tempting ornaments of the eunuchs are their reserve and their decency, which they have aspired to introduce into their lives. Contemporary eunuchs condemn those who lack these qualities, becoming irritated if one of their own violates the code of proper conduct. Just as the stains on an ornate, rather than plain, vestment are the most visible, a Christian who follows the Gospel most rigorously will become—if they act contrary to their beliefs— easy prey for their accusers. In effect, highly placed men will be purified with little difficulty, but persons whom one depends on for spiritual counsel will demand much more of us (Wisdom of Solomon 6:6; Luke 12:46–52). In sum, it is the same as your criticism of the single bad eunuch, which, when turned around, becomes a eulogy of praise for all eunuchs.

Enumeration of the Eunuch Saints

If you count all the cohorts of the Lord Jesus, you will not find any without some eunuchs. Among the Apostles, that is to say the harbingers of the Word, you will find the eunuch of Candace, who brought all of Ethiopia to Christ.[40] This was attributed not so much to his power and function as imperial treasurer, but because he was named as the Hand of the Spirit.[41] Among the martyrs, you will find Indes who insinuated himself in order to present Christ to the emperor.[42] Before him, Yacinthe, Proteus and his ascetic companion of combat, the valiant Eugene, were saintly eunuchs.[43] Ousthazides and Azades, the companions of Sapor, who were at first his friends for the sake of earthly ties, but afterward became his enemies for the sake of heaven, were eunuch servants of man and God.[44] At the time of Licinius,[45] the valiant Theodore, a saintly eunuch, was vigorous in his courageous resolution for Christ and became even more celebrated than his companions.

There exist many other saintly eunuchs who could be listed if we had the time. And if you say they are not very numerous, it is not surprising. Compared to the multitudes of non-eunuch males, the assembly of the eunuchs would be like a drop of water in the ocean. Eunuchs have been appointed to the patriarchal throne, because of their teaching and profession of faith.[46] They also occupy other high episcopal seats, as well as distinguishing themselves in the churches as bishops and priests. Are you unaware of the many eunuchs who are deacons, or who have acquired other celestial and evangelical ranks?[47] I think that you can see at this point how numerous they are, which is an indication of their growing piety. Among those like Simon from Athens, who as a famous, charming, and most agreeable and prudent monk, commanded the monks according to strict observances on Mount Athos, and who founded a community of eunuch monks there.[48] Consider, too, the number of eunuchs active in politics who are wise, and possess enviable character.

Epilogue

Personally, I suggest that the strongest point in favor of eunuchism is the complete absence of gonorrhea. A man in love with purity, as eunuchs invariably are, will not tolerate being soiled by the involuntary natural discharges. We who enjoy this advantage, avoid the pricking of our conscience, while you (the accusers) for some reason, cannot take the step for yourself that will stop these defilements. You make a case for being able to have an erect penis, and for some reason, take some sort of glory from this. At the same time, do not deny that occasionally your conscience is tormented. Above all, there are those of you who have been persuaded by the words of the great Basil, who so strenuously opposed eunuchism.[49] Surely, it is not that we are chaste reluctantly. In that case, our virtue would not be rewarded. On the contrary, our purity arises from our will, which is reflected by the pure state of our body. This inherent purity is our reward. And I, in my own soul, am proof of that. You have said that many eunuchs are unchaste. This shows that the continent ones are chaste by will. Do you want me to go on with this discussion?

The accuser responds:

That is enough for now. Do not persuade me to become one too, a eunuch to the end of my life.

The eunuch then continued:

Let me at least add this. I do not conclude my statement on eunuchism with the idea that one cannot preserve continence without it. It is possible with great struggle and rigorous abstinence to preserve the sacerdotal celibacy. When we do find such a sublime state, such unapproachable purity, it reduces to silence those who condemn eunuchs. In the eyes of an impartial judge, those who attack eunuchs make reckless and inconsiderate statements because of their envy and sensuality.

Separation of the Interlocutors

The discussion had been most uplifting. The two opponents embraced and kissed each other. The eunuch took a child, his nephew, who had been standing to one side listening to them with rapt attention, into his arms and gave him several kisses, as if he were congratulating the nephew on the debate. The child's face glowed under his uncle's embrace.

I, Theophylactus, then became occupied in thinking about a way to remember the content of their conversation. I asked them what they would be doing in the future, and where they would be going, since they did not seem to be natives of Thessalonica. Yet, I did not keep them, for fear of being bored in the event that they should invite me to participate in their intellectual debate. I let go first, because I sensed they would have seized me like a prize, and continued their contentious debate.

Here is the merchandise that I brought back from Thessalonica, but not without some difficulty, as I must confess I am not Simonides[50] or Hippias,[51] sages of great memory. My own memory, which once was very sharp, is not the same in my old age.

Endnotes—Chapter 7

1. See Deuteronomy 23:1.

2. Castrated males are classified by Balsamone in three categories: Those born without all their genital organs, those rendered impotent by sickness or injury, and those, who by means of a surgical operation, have been deprived of the means to procreate.

3. Canon laws 21–24, especially law 22: "The priest who has had himself castrated should be removed from the clergy because he is an enemy of God's creation." Also Canon 24: "A secular man who castrated himself should be banished from the church for three years because he plots against his own procreation."

4. The most famous is the first canon of Nicea (325 A.D.), similar to the Canon Laws 21–24.

5. Astarte and Chemosh are the ancient goddess and god of a pre-Hebraic religion. Astarte was one of the names for the great mother goddess of the Semitic pantheon, a goddess of fertility, who arose from a castrated god's remains, as cited in one of the myths of that geographic area.

6. Pydna is the ancient name of Kitros, a city situated on the southwest of the Gulf of Thessalonica. One of the bishops of Kitros corresponded with Theophylactus.

7. The eunuch asks his interlocutor if he had heard of these eunuch bishops, and if so, should he appropriately accuse the right persons, and not these saintly persons.

8. See Isaiah 56:3–5.

9. Daniel and his three companions, Shadrach, Meshach and Abednego, were believed to have been eunuchs, although this is not clearly indicated in the Scriptures, because they were the confidantes of King Nebuchadnezzar, king of Babylon. It was foretold in 2 Kings 20:18 and Isaiah 39:7: "Some of your own sons who are born to you shall be taken away; they shall be eunuchs in the palace of the king of Babylon."

[10.] In certain manuscripts, it reads: "I was a servant of the king," in others: "I was a eunuch of the king." 2 Esdras 11:11.

[11.] Jeremiah 38:7: "Ebedmelech the Ethiopian, a eunuch in the king's house, heard that they had put Jeremiah into the cistern."

[12.] See Isaiah 56:3–5.

[13.] The speaker refers to canons 22 and 24 of the Apostles. Castration as a result of sickness or violence was not condemned.

[14.] The author stigmatizes the castrates who allude to canon 22 of the Apostles.

[15.] Another allusion to canon 21 of the Apostles.

[16.] Simon Magus the magician (1st century), the originator of ascetic gnosticism, was considered the first leader of the heretics, and was accused of committing the worst of debaucheries (Eusebius, c. 311 A.D., *History of the Church,* Book II, chapters 13 and 14). See also Acts 8:9–24.)

[17.] These heretics preached the absence of marriage, which they considered to be like corruption and debauchery. Mani (215–277?) was the founder of the religion called Manicheanism, and Marcion (2nd century— excommunicated in 15 A.D.) the founder of the Marcionite church, was related to the Gnostics (Eusebius, *History of the Church,* Book IV, chapter 29). Mani was a former priest of Cybele before his baptism in the Christian religion, and is believed to have been castrated in that religion.

[18.] During the course of the fourth session of the Council of Chalcedon (451 A.D.), 13 Egyptian bishops refused to adhere to Pope Leo I's letter. They were reacting from fear of the Orthodox Greek religious leader of Alexandria, who did not recognize Papal authority. On the matter of their decree, taking an oath to stay at Constatinople—until the new bishop of Alexandria was appointed—they were finally allowed their way. Balsamone also defined it in a similar manner (Rhalli-Potli, *Syntagma,* 2, p. 290).

[19.] Letter 188: "The declaration of the Lord is not to permit the dissolution of marriage, except in the case of fornication, a law equally applicable to men and to women."

[20.] This argument from an historical perspective is not without value. In Byzantium the eunuchs were, nearly always, very numerous in the Church, the army and the administration. (See Rodolphe Guilland, "Les Eunuques dans l'Empire Byzantin: Etude de Titulature et de Prosopographie" in *Etudes Byzantines*, Tome I. Bucharest: Institute Francais D'Etudes Byzantines, Reprinted in St. Cloud, France by Europeriodiques, 1943 pp. 197–235.)

[21.] Etymological explanations, which are popular and traditional, and which we encounter, for example, in a text that is almost contemporary: the *nomocanon* of Nikon on the Black Mountain. (A *nomocanon* is a standard rule of the ancient Eastern Orthodox Church ecclesiastical laws pertaining to the administration of the Church.) Leo VI (886–912) in his Novel 98, proposed another tradition: the guardian of the couch as a position for the eunuchs.

[22.] Tribonian was one of the principal ministers of Justinian I, celebrated for his competence in matters of jurisprudence and his cupidity. He headed the commission responsible for the great codification of the laws, the *Codex Justinianus*, first published in 529 A.D. This is taken by many scholars as the most notable and enduring achievement of the age of Justinian (G. Ostrogorsky, *History of the Byzantine State*. New Brunswick, New Jersey: Rutgers Press, 1969, p. 75).

[23.] Militades (d. 488 B.C.) and Koroibos used to pass in antiquity as the paragons of stupidity.

[24.] Procopius of Caesarea (1st half of the 6th century) and John Zonaras, Byzantine historians, have written that the princes of Abasgi and Lazi in Asia Minor practiced castration on a grand scale as a lucrative business. Most of the eunuchs in the service of the palace originated in Abasgi (or "Absagia"—a region between the Black Sea and Caspian Sea).

[25.] Constantine the Great (323–337) actually renewed the old laws against the eunuchs.

26. Emperor Julian (361–363) put to death the *prepositus* eunuch Eusebius and chased all the eunuchs out of the palace. The author ignores or passes over Novel 60 of Leo VI (886–912), which forbade the practice of castration.

27. The figure is in disagreement with the current biblical text, which says 7,000 men (1 Kings 19:18).

28. See a list of the Patriarchs and other high church officials in Guilland, *Ibid.*, pp. 202–205.

29. I wonder what the results of this test would be in the 1990s? There have been many media reports of priests who are child molesters, homosexuals, perverts and adulterers, along with the hundreds in the priesthood dying of AIDS or contracting other sexually transmitted diseases.

30. Probably an allusion to the marriage of Esau with the daughter of Canaan (Genesis 28:8, 9).

31. Reuben had sex with Bilhah, the concubine of his father (Genesis 35:22).

32. This alludes to the intercession of Abraham with the Lord. For the sake of ten good men, God would not destroy Sodom (Genesis 18:32).

33. Momus in Greek mythology, was the son of Night and the personification of censoriousness, a kind of licensed fault-finder. He found something wrong with all the other gods' words and deeds.

34. This is reported by the historian Socrates (c. 380–c. 445, *Ecclesiastical History*, Book VI:8): "Ignatius of Antioch in Syria saw the angels which sang hymns alternately to the saintly Trinity and introduced this practice into the Church at Antioch. From there it was transmitted to all the other Churches."

35. The author must have found this in Sozomen (contemporary of Socrates, above, Book III:16): "I do not ignore that in Osroene in olden times there were some very wise men, like Bardesanes, author of a heresy which carries his name, and the son of Bardesanes, Harmonios, of whom one relates that he released the Greek culture, in which he was the first to

include the mother language in verse and song in some choirs. Those who sing the Syrian pieces today do not follow Harmonios' text, but rather his rhythm. And it was not entirely foreign to his father's heresy that he muddled the doctrines on the origin of the soul, the corruption of the body, and its resurrection in his own compositions."

36. See again Sozomen (*Ibid.*): "Ephraim having verified that the Syrians were seduced by the beauty of the poetry and the melodic rhythm, and because of this, were amenable to sharing Harmonios' views. He composed other writings, as well, in accordance with the doctrines of the Church. Since that time, the Syrians sang the verses of Ephraim according to the melodies of Harmonios." This is the shortened version of the text of Theodoret (*Ecclesiastical History*, VIII:8), which does not appear to be the author's original source.

37. This fact is related by Sozomen, VIII:8, and Socrates VI:8, which appears to have inspired Theophylactus of Ochrida.

38. This is a first appearance or a part of an unknown hymn.

39. The early Church Fathers have often vehemently attacked the condition of the eunuchs, because they showed that the eunuchs were inclined to follow the heresies rather than orthodox beliefs (Gregory of Naziance, *Orations*, XXI:21).

40. See Acts 8:27–39.

41. Alluding to the prophecy: "The Ethiopian will be the first to tender his hand toward God" (Psalms 68:31; Eusebius, *History of the Church*, Book II: 1).

42. The barbarian eunuch, Indes, was censured and martyred under Maximillian (268–305).

43. The eunuchs, Hyacinthes and Protas, companions of Eugene, were martyred by Commodus (161–192).

44. Ousthades, a eunuch priest, and Azades, a eunuch deacon, were servants of the Persian king, Sapor (Shapur, Sozomenus, *History of the Church*, Book II:9, 11).

45. This probably refers to Theodore the Stratelate, martyred under Licinius (312–324).

46. In brief, several Patriarchs of Constatinople were eunuchs, including: Germanus I (715–730), Nicetas (766–780), Methodius I (843–847), Ignatius (847–858 and 867–877), Stephanos II (925–928), Theophylactus (933–956), Polyeuktos (956–970), Constantine III Leichudes (1059–1063) and Eustratios Garidas (1081–1084).

47. As Chapter 5 discusses, there existed other, lower ranking eunuch clergymen, such as: John, Metropolitan of Side under emperor Michael Ducas (1071–1078), Nicephorus, priest and army commander under Constantine IX Monomachus (1042–1055), the monk Antiochus, tutor of Theodosius II (408–450), the monk Samonas, favorite of Leo VI (886–912), John, priest and monk in service to Romanus II (959–963), and the former *protovestarius* Nicephorus, who became a monk in the reign of Michael IV(1034–1041). There are many other great churchmen whom Theophylactus/Simon the Sanctified could have mentioned who were eunuchs. Perhaps the greatest was Origen of Alexandria (c. 185–c. 254). According to Jerome he was the "greatest teacher of the early church after the Apostles." Also, the treasurers in all of the monasteries and convents were almost always eunuchs because they were more likely to be trusted with funds than the others.

48. There were several other monasteries that were established for eunuch monks, for example, the one founded by Eutropius in Palestine, near Jericho, and the one established at Constantinople by Michael Attelates in March 1077.

49. Saint Basil, the Great (330–379), tenaciously upheld the Nicean doctrine against castration and opposed "ascetical excesses." He was against Eunomius, and wrote a vitriolic diatribe against eunuchs in his Book 16: chapter 17 (per Charles Ancillon, *Traite des Eunuques*. Paris: Editions Ramsay, 1707, Reprinted in 1978, pp. 57 and 58).

50. Simonides of Keos (Kea, Ceos, c. 555–c. 466 B.C.) one of the masters of lyric poetry, spent most of his time in Greece. In spite of his age, he did not hesitate to travel to Sicily, where he met with Pindar. He died at Syracuse at age 89 and left us innumerable works.

51. Hippias of Elis (c. 445–397 B.C.), who plays a significant role in the *Dialogues of Plato* (First and Second Hippias), claimed to know how to do everything. Reportedly, he had been endowed with a prodigious memory.

Chapter 8—The Harem Eunuch

The harem eunuch presents a particularly ancient use of castrated males, which were used partly for profit, as well as for prestige and pleasure. To gain an adequate understanding of these multi-dimensional uses of castration, a highly exotic, closely guarded, clandestine institution must first be examined—that of the harem.

The word *harem* itself is derived from the Arabic *haram*, meaning "protected," or "forbidden." It refers to the physical and spiritual isolation of women confined in a specific place. The same form—pronounced *hareem*—means the group of women themselves. Harems have been in existence throughout recorded history in many Eastern and African cultures. Many other names have been used to describe the harem; the "Forbidden City" in Peking, China refers to the location where the emperor's women were cloistered. In Persia, the harem was called the *enderun* or *zenane* (women's house). The term *purdah* or "curtained" area is used in India. The practice of maintaining harems can be traced back to the first dynasty of Ur, which is the same Biblical Ur of the Chaldees (circa 2,700 B.C.). Harems exist today in some Arab states and parts of Africa. The terms *harem* and *seraglio* (a place of licentious pleasure or palace of a sultan) are most popularly applied to the Ottoman Turkish women's quarters from about 1299 to 1919 A.D., the historical period we consider now.

The arrangements of the Turkish harem were usually the same. A number of smaller rooms surrounded a large hall, where divans, a few small tables provided seating and service for coffee and delicacies. The women slept fully clothed on the divans with a woolen or silk cover in the winter. Enclosed balconies with latticed windows allowed the women to observe what was going on outside without being seen. Roses, jasmine, verbena and fruit trees filled the gardens that surrounded the harem. The lush surroundings included pools with ornamental fish, pathways and coveys of doves, canaries and nightingales; gaudy peacocks, parrots and macaws cackled from the underbrush. Monkeys and gazelles were sometimes kept as pets.

For the most part, harems housed an extended family of women: Mothers, unmarried sisters, daughters, wives, concubines, odalisques, slaves and, on occasion, distant female relatives in need of shelter. The sultan's mother was the most powerful woman in the Ottoman empire, especially when an incompetent sultan was on the throne, which was the case during the so-called "Reign of Women" (1541–1687 A.D.). The Koran allows a man to have four wives, but Muhammad himself had fifteen, suggesting the extent of legalized abuse of the rules.

The first wife was considered most important and often had greater privileges than the other wives. The children of wives were legitimate heirs, but those of the concubines and odalisques could either be recognized as legitimate or not. The Koran permits a man as many concubines ("man's delight," according to Solomon in Ecclesiastes 2:8) and odalisques as he pleased. Wives were the mothers of the recognized children and keepers of the house, while the concubines and odalisques were exclusively for sexual pleasure. The odalisques were all non-Moslem slaves purchased at slave markets or presented as gifts. A Circassian or Georgian girl aged 8 to 16 was worth about 1,000 to 2,000 kurush in the late 18th century—several thousand kurush less than the price of a reliable horse.

The most beautiful and talented of the odalisques were trained to dance, play musical instruments, recite poetry, serve food and coffee to their master, dress him, bathe him, do his laundry and perform the erotic arts that he preferred. Those with strong physiques became servants or administrators. Those who lacked the talent for pleasing their masters in some capacity were likely to be resold in the slave market.

In the sultan's harem, the women wore rich gold and silver brocades, fine satins, velvets, silks, tri-colored cloth and extraordinary jewels. Ideally, the sultan never saw a woman wearing the same dress more than once. All harem women had very fine trousers of linen or muslin, which were dyed red, yellow or blue, and were usually festooned with strings of pearls and gold rings, as well.

Harem women were extremely observant about not having pubic hair, which was considered to be a sin. They removed the hair from their pubic area, underarms, ears and nose with a depilatory paste made of lime. The whiteness of their skin was maintained by avoiding the sun, powdering their necks, applying a paste made of almond and jasmine and scrubbing their skin with pumice stones. They colored their eyelids and lengthened their eyebrows with India ink and reddened their cheeks and lips to appear more exotic.

Eating in the harem was an elaborate ritual. The odalisques were instructed to partake of their meals in a most graceful and elegant manner. Sweets and sherbets, which were made from snow brought in from the mountain tops and flavored with fruit juices or coffee and scented with the essence of flowers, were delicacies reserved solely for those women favored by the sultan.

After the meal, servants delivered a pitcher and basin for washing the hands, and towels for drying them. The women would then take to their divans, partaking of cigarettes and pipes, and drinking either water sweetened with sugar or a kind of beer.

The gustatory excess of harem life fattened the women to a pleasing plumpness—they became the *houris* of Muslim paradise. They were allowed to indulge in sensuous baths, which could last for hours. Sometimes the Sultan would visit the baths and watch his women disporting themselves. After they had been thoroughly pampered, they would luxuriate in the pleasures of hashish and opium. When the later was eaten, instead of smoked, it would induce an intoxicating, dream-like state.

In this exotic and erotic environment, only a eunuch—one who was prepared and trained for the purpose of resisting temptation—was trusted to work among the harem women. Any other male was sure to betray his master, yielding to the pleasures so freely available.

Only eunuchs whose testicles *and* penis were removed were allowed to serve in the harem. The possibility existed that the stump of the penis might rejuvenate and grow into a functioning member, so the eunuchs were checked periodically. Furthermore, only eunuchs who had been castrated before puberty could be attendants, because they needed to have the requisite distinguishing characteristics: a high-pitched voice, soft musculature and the eunuchoid bodily proportions (e.g. enlarged hips and breasts).

Black eunuchs with unattractive faces were preferred for the harem; the handsome "blue" eunuchs of the *One Thousand and One Nights* were romantic inventions. White eunuchs were employed as servants in the men's quarters, where some of them rose to important positions. At first, Turks acquired white eunuchs from conquered Christian areas, but their mortality rate was higher than that of black eunuchs. Black eunuchs were reported to be better able to endure the hazards of the crude surgery and the slave life of a harem guard. The Black African chiefs of Abyssinia and the upper Nile willingly sold young men and boys to the Moslem slave traders, who would have them castrated and brought to the markets in Mecca, Beirut, Smyrna (present-day Izmir) and Istanbul.

Most of the young slaves were castrated on their way to the market by Egyptian Christians or Jews, since every mutilation of man or beast is prohibited in Islam. Muhammad, himself, expressly enjoined his followers not to make themselves or others into eunuchs. Oddly enough, several hundred eunuchs were employed by the mosques in Mecca and Medina, because religious attendants had to come in contact with women while they were visiting the holy places.

Historical accounts indicate that a specific regimen was followed in the course of the castration process. Fluids would be withheld from the boy from shortly before the procedure to three days afterward, so his urge to urinate would be minimal. Tight bandages were wrapped around the upper legs and lower abdomen to reduce the pressure to hemorrhage. A ligature would be tied tightly around the penis and scrotum as close to the body as possible. The genital area would be bathed with hot pepper water or other anti-infection nostrum. The penis and testicles would be cut off as close to the body as the instruments would allow with either a special curved knife, razor, dagger, sword, or whatever other kind of sharp instrument was available.

After the cut was made, the wound would sometimes be cauterized with boiling oil, a hot iron, salt, urine, dung or desert sand. Sometimes, no particular precautions were taken. A metal or wooden plug would be inserted into the urethra of the stump of the penis to prevent it from healing shut. After three days, the plug and any bandages would be removed and the boy allowed to urinate and drink a little water.

The operation was understandably very hazardous under these primitive conditions, and many died from shock, pain, loss of blood, subsequent infection or closure of the urinary canal. The mortality rate of prepubescent boys (age 8 to 12) was generally better than those of older males, and was related to the condition of the genitalia, lack of pubic hair and general state of health. The much higher price that a eunuch brought—versus an uncastrated boy—made the risk of the procedure worth taking for the slave traders.

When the young eunuch was first brought from the slave market to the harem, he was assigned a place for sleeping in the crowded dormitory. Each novice eunuch was subjected to the bastinado sticks, whether he deserved the punishment or not. Youths often disciplined each other until they received their assignments. Once they began working under the tutelage of the Chief Eunuch, they would be given a generous allowance, as well as robes made of silk. They often took feminine names—usually those of fragrant flowers—to reflect their roles as servants to the harem women.

The discipline for the corps of eunuch guards was comparable to that of a military school. At the end of their training, each eunuch, similar to the placement of the odalisques, was assigned to the service of a particular harem luminary—a prince, a wife, a daughter or a sister of the sultan. The young eunuch's dream was to attain the status of the master of the girls, the chief black eunuch.

The main function of the black eunuchs was to guard the women from within the harem. Royal halberdiers guarded the outer walls. The harem was usually the sultan's most valuable possession numbering from a few hundred to nearly 2,000 women at different periods. These women were isolated not only because of their alleged lustful natures, but due to the belief that it was necessary for them to be protected from other men for many reasons—religious, political, moral and medical. A sultan who copulated with hundreds, sometimes thousands, of different women could not take the slightest chance of contracting a deadly venereal disease. (Ironically, Kemal Ataturk, the man who later deposed the sultans and liberated the women of the harems, himself died of syphilis and alcoholism).

The sultan also did not want to allow himself to be cuckolded or be exposed to the moral taint of associating with loose women. The corps of eunuchs reached as high as 800 strong in the Seraglio (harem), and were dedicated to protecting the women from the temptation of outside influences. Contrary to myth, the eunuchs were not neutral bystanders, often succumbing to these very influences. Because eunuchs had a unique position in the palace, they shared an unusual closeness with the harem women, and often had ample opportunity to go well beyond the harem's domain. This freedom allowed them to frequently become embroiled in corrupt and dishonest acts.

The palace dwarf, also a eunuch, was a kind of court jester, a source of amusement for the sultan and harem women. The chief black eunuch was effectively the head of the palace and controlled all communication between the sultan and his women. He exercised great political power in court, serving as a link between the sultan and many other important personages. His position was often equal to that of the grand vizier, which is much like a prime minister.

The characteristic physical effects of castration on the harem guards included a soft, pudgy body and flaccid figure, a high pitched voice, hairless face and body, but usually a full head of hair. They were only seldom bald. The eunuchs usually appeared younger than their actual age, and demonstrated great loyalty to their masters—being both trustworthy and faithful. Some of the black harem eunuchs enjoyed, and became quite skilled in, storytelling, music and dancing; others gained wealth and rose to high positions in the governments. In the Moslem world, eunuchs occupied a privileged position.

> Gang slavery for work in the fields or mines which we knew of in the European and American history, was almost unknown in the Islamic world. Most of the slaves were employed in wealthy households for domestic service and were well treated, in accordance with the prescriptions of the Koran. The one really cruel institution was that of the eunuch, which involved emasculation[1]

The Turkish harem eunuch was reported to be resentful and vengeful for his condition and is said that many of them acquired wives and some strove to continue some sort of sexual relations with women through substitute devices such as dildoes or by performing various sexual acts, including fellatio, cunnilingus and sodomy variations. Some even grew new penises. Such eunuchs were reported to have resorted to fantastic nostrums, such as eating the brains of seven men to re-attain their sexual potency.

While castration usually weakens a man's sexual drive, the eunuchs of the harem were subjected to an environment that was laden with sexuality. They were surrounded by beautiful women who were especially adept at arousing passion in men—women who had all the trappings of wealth and luxury: fine clothing, expensive perfumes, jewels, opium, hashish, scented baths, delightful foods and sweet music. Not only were the senses of the eunuchs assailed with sensuality, but the women had much to gain by subverting the eunuchs, for they controlled their advancement and diversions.

Clearly, the milieu of the harem is something of an unusual circumstance. The temptations of harem life could overwhelm even an emasculated man. After all, removal of the testicles does not remove the sole source of androgenic hormones. Another source exists in the cortex of the adrenal glands, which can be stimulated by such powerful sensory cues as those presented in the atmosphere of the harem. Castration is not necessarily a perfect bar to sexuality, as the procedure has only a 98 percent success rate. Where sexual stresses greatly exceed the norm, the body and brain can be made to respond and sexual interest can develop, despite the overt physical limitations imposed by castration.

Endnotes—Chapter 8

[1.] *Encyclopedia Britannica*, Volume 20, 1968, p. 634a. See also Alev Lytle Croutier, *Harem: The World Behind the Veil, New York: Abbeville Press, 1989. Croutier provides a unique perspective on a way of life for which little information exists.*

Chapter 9—The Hijras of India

In India, eunuchs are usually referred to by the Urdu word *hijra* (also spelled Hijara, Hinjara, Hirjara, Hijada and Khusra), whether the males were congenitally deformed or castrated in youth or later life. In Burma, eunuchs are called *Acault* (pronounced a-chow). Just as in China, eunuchs were a common feature in India from the earliest recorded history until the present day. In Vedic India (c. 1,500 B.C. to 500 B.C.), records indicate that young boys were castrated and presented to the kings and high officials for service in their entourage. The *Mahabharata*, a piece of epic poetry (eight times longer than the *Iliad* and *Odyssey* combined), includes depictions of eunuchs. Bhisma and Arjuna are two characters in the work who acted briefly as hijras.

Throughout both the Hindu and Muslim periods of Indian rulers, eunuchs were employed in the harems and palaces of the queens. In the Vijayanager period (1336–1614 A.D.), the queen's houses were guarded by eunuchs—all other men were excluded. According to Vatsyayana,[1] many of the harem guards were not only castrated, but they had their tongues cut off so they could not speak. If a queen were to go outside the palace, she would be guarded by as many as 400 eunuchs, who were to keep people at a distance from the queen. The cooks and waiters who served the king were also eunuchs. Many eunuchs also rose to important posts.

Malik Kafur, a eunuch, had such influence during the reign of Alau-Din-Khiliji (1296–1316) that he was able to engineer the dismissal of Khizr Khan, the rightful heir to the throne. During the reign of Akbar the Great (1556–1605) and his successors, eunuchs occupied several key positions: Iktiyar Kahn was the chief advocate; Itihar was the chief prosecutor of criminal offenses; Khawaja Saras Hilal built the town of Hilallabad; Feroze Kahn founded Ferozabad; and Yatim Sha had a mosque built in Lohamandi Agra. When Sultan Muzaffar ad din of Gujarat (1896–1907) was sovereign, the eunuch Muhit-ul-Mulk served as commander of the police. Eunuchs were also in charge of caravansaries across India from circa 660 to 1955. The Hindu Marriage Act of 1955 outlawed polygamy and harems were discontinued, and the epoch for eunuch guards and administrators came to an end.

Today, India is very densely populated, with three times the number of people as the United States and less than half of the land area. Its people speak more than 50 different languages and tend to polarize themselves with others who speak the same language and have the same customs and beliefs. The Hijras also tend to join with others of their ilk in bands called "akhadas" in some cities and towns. The hijras' principal shrine is in Bahuchara in northern Gujarat, but even in this location they do not form a majority of the populace. Their total numbers are unknown and estimates vary from 50,000 (*India Today*, 1982) to 500,000 (New Delhi*Tribune*, 1983). Khairati Lal Bhola, who headed the All-India Hijra Welfare Society from 1983 to 1989, estimated the total number of Hijras in India at 300,000.[2] Groups of Hijras live as families with an elderly Hijra acting as mother, lovingly looking after the other members as though they were children, teaching them dancing, singing and the art of begging. A council of Hijras, called a *panchayat,* meets annually to make decisions on the problems facing the community, such as jurisdiction and territory. J It was an international news event when the All India Eunuch Conference met 22 to 29 December 2002 with nearly 5,000 members in the temple city of Varanasi about 450 miles southeast of New Delhi. Several eunuchs have been voted into city and state legislatures as an expression of frustration with corrupt politicians. Most of the thousands of eunuchs in India are born without male genitalia, while a few are castrated as babies. They typically dress like women and live on tips for dancing at weddings and Hindu festivals and blessing newborn babies.

The main profession (of sorts) of Hijras is to attend marriage and birth ceremonies, singing and dancing for the guests. Not only do they congratulate the bride and groom, but ascertain whether a child is born sexually intact, as well. Upon encountering a hermaphroditic or cryptorchid baby (a boy with undescended testicles), they take the child away. In India, a strong stigma is attached to families when such a child is born, so by removing the child, they also remove the stigma. In this manner, the Hijras recruit new members into their own families and provide a service to society at large.

Just as in China and Byzantium, the process of castration is outlawed in India, yet still performed frequently. Emasculation is the source of the uniqueness of the Hijras, and provides the very origin of their ritual powers. Only after castration do Hijras become vehicles for the power of the Mother Goddess. Nanda writes:

> The hijras call the emasculation operation nirvan. Nirvan is the condition of calm and absence of desire; it is liberation from the finite human consciousness and the dawn of a higher consciousness. The Hindu scriptures call the beginning of this experience the second birth, or the opening of the eye of wisdom. ...Ideally, the emasculation operation is performed by a hijra called a *dai ma* (midwife), a clear and strong symbolic statement of emasculation as rebirth. ...Prior to the operation there is a preparatory stage, in which the dai ma and client seek the Mata's blessing in a *puja* (ritual of worship). ...The dai ma asks the prospective nirvan to look at the Mata's picture. If the Mata appears to be smiling and laughing, that is a sign that the operation will succeed. ...Clients who do not receive these positive omens translate this into their own lack of courage, and some have gone two and three times for this puja before the signs were propitious. Given the irreversible and life-threatening nature of the operation, it seems reasonable to interpret the puja as a way of attempting to resolve the ambivalence that anticipation of the operation generates.

Nanda then describes the operation.

> If it is decided that the operation will take place, the client is isolated for a period of several days to a month. ...The operation takes place at about 3:00 or 4:00 in the morning, a usual time in India for auspicious ceremonies, such as

marriages. Only the dai ma and her assistant are present, along with the client. ...The client's clothes and jewelry are removed; 'they must be as naked as the day they were born.' After being given a bath the client is ready for the operation. She is seated on a small stool and held from the back by the dai ma's assistant, who crosses the client's hair over her face for her to bite on. The client's penis and scrotum are tightly tied with a string, so that a clean cut can be made. The client looks at the picture of Bahuchara and constantly repeats her name, Mata, Mata, Mata. This apparently produces a trancelike state during which the dai ma takes the knife from her sari and makes two quick opposite diagonal cuts. The organs—both penis and testicles—are completely separated from the body. A small stick is put into the urethra to keep it open. None of the hijras who had the operation told me that they felt any pain when the cut was made; it was variously described as 'a small pinch' or 'like an ant bite.' When the cut is made, the blood gushes out, and nothing is done to stem the flow. ...the blood is considered the 'male part' and should be drained off.

The hour just after the operation is considered to be the critical time during which the client's life or death is in the balance. This uncertainty is conceptualized by hijras as a 'tug of war' between Bahuchara Mata, who gives life, and her elder sister, Chamundeswari, 'the goddess who sits on a lion in Mysore,' who takes life. During this hour the dai ma's assistant secretly disposes of the severed organs, which are placed in a pot and buried under a living tree. ...No stitches are made in the wound after the surgery, and the wound is healed through repeated applications of hot sesame oil and heat to prevent infection. ...On the 40th day the reincorporation stage of the ritual takes place. The facial hair, which by now may have grown very long, is pulled out with tweezers. Turmeric is applied to the face and body and then washed off.

The spiritual transformation processs is at the heart of the ritual, Nanda explains.

> It is the emasculation ritual that transforms an impotent male into a potentially powerful person. The renunciation of sex and the repression of sexual desire are, in the Hindu belief system, associated with the powers of the ascetic, and it is this association that is at the heart of the powers of the hijra. Hijras explicitly recognize this connection: They frequently refer to themselves as 'other worldly' and as sannyasis, people who renounce society to live as holy wanderers and beggars. This vocation requires renunciation of material possessions, the social relations of caste, the life of the householder and family man, and the worldly attachments of normal men and women, most particularly, sexual desire (kama). The importance of chastity to the religious ascetic is that sexual desire is seen as a distraction from spiritual purposes. Also, sexual activity, which involves a loss of semen, results in a loss of spiritual energy. The hijra's emasculation is their culturally defined 'proof' that they do not experience sexual desire or sexual release as men. This proof of renunciation is the basis of the hijra's claims on society. ...not all hijras, or even most, live up to this ascetic model; it is nevertheless the most powerful idea that legitimates their ritual functions in Indian society.

> *In Hindu mythology, impotence can be transformed into the power of generativity through the ideal of tapasya*, the practice of asceticism. Tapas, the power that results from ascetic practices and sexual abstinence, becomes the essential feature in the process of creation. Ascetics appear throughout Hindu mythology in procreative roles, and of these, Shiva is the greatest creative ascetic. In one version of the Hindu creation myth, Shiva carries out an extreme, but legitimate, form of tapasya, that of self-castration.[3]

The castration ritual is linked to the fertility cult of the linga (phallus) worship. It may be startling to recognize that strong similarities exist between the Hindu myths of Shiva and the worship of Cybele, the Great Mother and her son Attis, in Asia Minor. Attis is also believed to have castrated himself. "The widespread association of the powers of asceticism with self-castration in Hindu mythology, particularly as associated with Shiva, provides the background through which we can understand the legitimacy of the hijra emasculation."[4]

Nanda mentions the debate in the psychological, anthropological and sociological literature over the Hijras' homosexuality, which has gone on for at least 100 years.[5] Certainly, the question of homosexuality is the most visible and notorious issue surrounding the Indian Hijras. The question remains unanswered as to what percentage of the hundreds of thousands of Hijras regularly indulge in homosexual prostitution. Similarly, few know the precise numbers of Hijras that are bisexuals, hermaphrodites, transsexuals or transvestites. The assumption exists that a percentage of Hijras have chosen to adopt one of these gender identity roles. However, respect for the Hijras continues most likely because of the "true Hijras," those who are eunuchs and had their male genitalia surgically removed for ascetic purposes.

The incidence of homosexuality in the Hijra population is probably small. There may exist an estimated hundred times the number of homosexuals in the country who are *not Hijras, and do not profess to be such. Likewise, there must be at least 20 times as many transvestites and transsexuals, and probably about 10 times more hermaphrodites in the general population as compared with Hijras. It could be concluded that only a tiny portion of these groups elect to join the Hijras. It must be inferred that reasons other than gender identity and birth morphology exist that induce these men to face the perils of castration in order to join this unique sect.*

Burton wrote:

> There are two kinds of eunuchs, those that are disguised as males and those that are disguised as females. Eunuchs disguised as females imitate their dress, speech, gestures, tenderness, timidity, simplicity, softness and bashfulness.

The acts that are done on the jaghana, or middle parts, of women...are done in the mouths of these eunuchs, and this is called Aurparishtika. These eunuchs derive their imaginative pleasure, and their livelihood, from this kind of congress, and they lead the life of courtesans.[6]

Thus, without naming the homosexuals as eunuchs, Burton indicates that some references were made to the Hijras by Vatsyayana, writing some time before the third century, A.D.

Several other authors have tried to pierce the shroud of secrecy that surrounds the Hijra society in India; Shingala[7] researched the literature and questioned 40 Hijras in Baroda, India, concerning their life styles. Jeffrey[8], an American of Indian descent, used the records of police in the region of Hyderbad to investigate the Hijras; Sharma[9], professor of Sociology at the Panjab University, investigated the roles and institutionalization of the Hijras. On the 23rd of February 2001, my newspaper published an article that showed that five Hijras had recently won executive positions in India from town mayor to state legislator. By electing eunuchs to public office, the people of India have found a way of dispensing with some of the leadership flaws that our President William Clinton and Reverend Jesse Jackson have brought to us in the United States.[10]

Endnotes—Chapter 9

1. N. K. Sagar, editor, *The Kama-Sutra of Vatsyayna.* New Delhi, India: Capital Book Co., p. 174.

2. Arthur R. Kroeber, "Half Man, Half Woman." *Far Eastern Economic Review,* March 2, 1989, p. 76.

3. Serena Nanda, *Neither Man Nor Woman.* Belmont, California: Wadsworth Publishing Co., 1990, pp. 26–29.

4. *Ibid.,* p. 31.

5. *Ibid.,* pp. 9–12.

6. Sir Richard F. Burton made a translation of *The Kama-Sutra of Vatsyayna* from the original Sanskrit of Vatsyayna in 1838 for the Kama Sutra Society of London and Benares. The work been repeatedly re-published in slightly different forms. This excerpt is from the 1962 edition reprinted by Dorset Press in 1986, p. 124.

7. Shingala, MD Vyas Togesh. (1987). The Life Style of the Eunuchs. New Delhi, India: Anmol Publications.

8. Jaffrey, Zia. (1996). The Invisibles: A Tale of the Eunuchs of India. New York: Vintage Books.

9. Sharma, S. K. (2000). Hijras: The Labeled Deviants. New Delhi, India: Gyan Publishing House.

10. The Eunuch Tactic. Northwest Florida Daily News. February 23, 2001. Page A-4, and Letter to the Editors, Victor Cheney Trust vs. Virility. Northwest Florida Daily News. March 1, 2001, p. A-7.

Chapter 10— "The Most Splendid Sound Ever Raised from Earth Toward Heaven"

Surely the most splendid sound ever raised from earth toward heaven was the singing of the *Castrati*—singers castrated in boyhood to preserve the soprano or contralto range of their voices. "A eunuch can, therefore, sing in a treble or soprano range with greater power than a woman owing to their greater body bulk and lung capacity."[1] Even with the aid of electronic amplification, contemporary sopranos most likely could not produce the range and utter beauty of the sound of the castrati. The great twentieth century Peruvian soprano, Yuma Sumac, with her surprising vocal capabilities might be a comparable example of what the castrati could achieve vocally. Mozart is said to have perceived the special quality of the castrati and written some of his most exalted music especially for their voices. "Their timbre is as clear and piercing as that of choirboys and much more powerful: they appear to sing an octave above the natural voice of women…they are brilliant, light, full of sparkle, very loud, and with a very wide range."[2] Goethe exhibited great enthusiasm about the castrati for still another reason: "…the concept of imitation and of art was invariably more strongly felt, and through their able performance a sort of conscious illusion was produced. Thus a double pleasure is given…."[3]

Choir leaders of the Christian churches knew of the tremendous impact of the castrati and kept them in the world's great choirs, including the Sistine Chapel in Rome itself, more than 1,500 years after the Church had officially condemned the practice of castration at the Council of Nicea in 325. Pope Leo XIII finally brought an end to the tradition with his edict in 1878. In seventeenth century Italy, some 4,000 boys were sexually altered each year by destitute parents hoping to capitalize on their son's talent.[4] In the eighteenth century, more than 2,000 boys had been castrated in a year in the Papal States of Europe—more than 1,000 a year in Naples alone[5]—in order to sing the soprano parts in opera and the great hallelujah choruses. These demanded a high, powerful voice to rise above the hundreds of other voices in order to achieve their full effect. Neither the tenors, nor the falsettos, nor the female sopranos could compare to them. As many as 70 percent of the singers in opera in the eighteenth century were castrati. The Pauline proscription against women in church forestalled their performance in church choirs for a considerable period of time: "As in all the churches of the saints, the women should keep silence in the churches" (I Corinthians 14:33, 34). In addition to the qualities of their voices, the castrati were noted for their loyalty, perseverance and dedication to the task at hand, for they were relatively immune to many of the temptations of virile men.

As with many of the earlier rules of the Christian church against castration, Pope Leo's edict did not immediately eradicate the practice of using castrati. For example, Dominico Mustafa (1829–1912), a celebrated male soprano, was director of Papal music until his retirement in 1895.

> The last castrato of all seems to have been Alessandro Moreschi (1858–1922), noted for singing of the Seraph in Beethoven's oratorio 'Christus am …lberg,' who performed at the funerals of two kings of Italy—Victor Emmanuel II in 1878 and Umberto I in 1900. Moreschi retired in 1913.[6]

Various attempts were made, however, to conceal the fact that the late nineteenth century castrati had been purposely castrated. Some were alleged to be merely falsettists, others were encouraged to marry, while a few were provided with medical certificates that they had been born with cryptorchidism, or had suffered some childhood injury or illness. To assure that the voice would remain high, the operation had to be performed before any symptoms of puberty (visible or invisible) appeared. This meant that most of the castrati were operated on before the age of eight.[7]

The period for the initial use of castration to provide the high voices needed for the most exquisite singing remains a matter of hypothesis. It probably began in the most ancient antiquity. Only brief notations and references to the practice exist, but it most likely began in early biblical times. Tompkins quotes the late drama critic, C. J. Bullet, as saying that Plautinianus, an African by birth, had castrated and trained several young boys as choir singers. These sopranos performed at the wedding of the Emperor Caracalla (211–217 A.D.) with Plautinianus' daughter. The author also quotes Sozomenus (Book VIII, Chapter 18, 325–415) as telling the story of how Eudoxia, wife of the Emperor Arcadius (395–408), ordered her eunuch, Brison, to organize a choir of Christian castrati to replace pagans. Saint John Chrysostom, then bishop in Constantinople, objected, but the empress persisted and only the Christian castrates were allowed to continue in her church. Theodore, the eunuch tutor and patricius under Constantine VII (913–959), wrote a book, "For Eunuchism and Eunuchs," which also mentioned the practice of castrating young boys for later use as singers.[8]

Castrated singers first appeared in the Catholic world in the service of the popes at the end of the twelfth century, according to Matteo Fornari, whose work, "Narrazione Historica...della Pontificia Cappella...col Catalogo dei Cantori," was published in the eighteenth century. This treatise contained a complete catalog of the castrati in pontifical service dating back to the twelfth century, and was guarded in the famous Liceo Musicale at the Bologna academy of music. Mysteriously, it has become "lost."[9] Other terms for the castrati were *evirati* (the emasculated ones), *ch trŽs* (geldings) or *incommodŽs* (the invalids), and Kapaune (capons)—in Italian, French and German, respectively. The term *falsetti* was sometimes used later, as was *musici* (connoisseurs of music), which denoted a certain respect for the singers, as they became recognized as stellar composers, vocal artists and teachers. Some were vocal virtuosi, with a range of four octaves to A-three (A above the female high C).

The inconsistency between the laws against castration and its continuing practice is thoroughly difficult to understand and nearly impossible to reconcile. Not only were the church laws against castration clearly archaic and severe, but the Italian civil law also imposed heavy penalties on anyone guilty of causing the castration of a boy or of even having specific knowledge of the act without telling the authorities. Concurrently, the Italians were very ashamed of the unnatural act of making a castrato as well as particularly proud of their singing talents. Civil law provided penalties up to death, and Church law called for the excommunication of all those concerned with a castration, unless it was required specifically for some disorder and with the consent of the boy.[10] The profound adulation Italians expressed for the singing of the castrati is captured in the words of musical historian Enrico Panzacchi (1840–1904):

> What singing! Imagine a voice which leaps and leaps like a lark that flies through the air and is intoxicated with its own flight; without the slightest sign of forcing or the faintest indication of artifice or effort; in a word, a voice that gives the immediate idea of sentiment transmuted into sound, and of the ascension of a soul into the infinite on the wings of that sentiment. ...a calm, sweet, solemn and sonorous musical language that left me dumbstruck, and captivated me with the power of a most gracious sensation never before experienced.[11]

The symbolism of the purity of the castrati singing their praises to God should not be ignored. Many of the popes and other religious personages down through the ages must have been conscious of this aspect and found in it a sense of rightness and delight. The castrati tended to be innocent of sexual sin and desire—untainted with lust—unsoiled much like a virgin, and even angelic. A contemporary approximation of the castrati might be the dedicated youths of the Vienna Boy's Choir. It should be noted that a golden age of the castrati existed—where the practice of castration was actually recognized in Italian churches and operas—lasting about 200 years. The age, which began about 1599 when the names of Pietro Paoli and Giralamo Rossini appear in books as the first *admitted* castrati, reached its apogee in about 1790, and died away after 1844, when the castrato, Pergetti, was last heard in London.

In no way should it be implied that castration magically creates a wonderful singer in itself. A great deal of training, study and practice is required to produce a majestic voice. Castration merely eliminates the hormones that cause the voice to deepen during puberty, allowing it to stay in the high juvenile register. The rigorous training required to produce a professional singing voice was provided by the numerous Italian conservatories. The poorest families would sell their male children outright into a kind of musical slavery if they demonstrated a vocal gift. Those who could afford it started their son off with a reputable singing master, or sometimes attached their son to the court of one of the members of the aristocracy for his support and training. The Dukes of Parma and Modena were lavish supporters of opera, as were many of the dukes, electors and Margraves of Germany. The Duke of Wurtemberg had 15 castrati and two surgeons in his service in 1772.[12] These surgeons were from Bologna, where the doctors of the time were the most esteemed for the performance of the castration operation.

Due to its illegal and infamous status, the actual castration operation was performed surreptitiously, usually at a remote location. Historians have only limited descriptions of the exact medical procedures. One discussion offered by Heriot refers to Ancillon for some details: "This operation is ordinarily performed by putting the patient in a bath of warm water to soften the parts and make them more manageable.... After the patient has been there for a while, his jugular veins are compressed and that way made unconscious...then it is easy to cut him without his feeling anything."[13]

Heriot continues:

> The ducts (veins) leading to the testicles were then severed, so that the latter in course of time shrivelled and disappeared. Eunuchs of this type were...in contradistinction to eunuchs proper who had been subject to full castration. The later operation does not seem ever to have been practiced in the case of the castrato singers. It was often supposed that, the later the child was castrated, the lower its voice would be: others, however, and more convincingly, have supposed that those who would naturally have been tenors became sopranos,

and those who would have been baritones or basses became contraltos.[14]

The fact that the castrati retained their penis is especially trenchant, as this prevented a host of problems that eunuchs frequently had with urination.

The singer touted as the world's finest is thought to be Carlo Broschi, a soprano, who was recognized throughout Europe by his nickname, "Farinelli" (1705–1782).[15] So grand was the power and brilliance of his voice that he won impromptu contests several times with one of the most famous trumpet players of his day. The poet, Rolli, wrote of the singer:

> I cannot, because of his merit, forbear to say that Farinelli has surprised me so much that I feel as though I had hitherto heard only a small part of the human voice and now have heard it all. He has, besides, the most amiable and polite manners, and I take the greatest pleasure in his acquaintance.[16]

Farinelli was tall, handsome and had tremendous success with the female members of his audience, yet he was not interested in amorous intrigues. His extreme placidity and gentleness of character was well-known. He earned the unprecedented sum of 5,000 pounds a year while he was in England between 1743 and 1747.

The queen of Spain secured Farinelli to sing for Philip V, who suffered from such acute melancholia that he could scarcely attend to the business of governing and was in danger of dying. Upon hearing the miraculous voice, the king quite forgot his troubles and was spared another nine years of life—a life whose only solace was the frequently heard singing of Farinelli.[17] Ferdinand acceded to the throne in 1746 and Farinelli's influence over the affairs of state became, if possible, even more significant. In 1750, he was made Commander of the Order of Calatrava—a signal honor, normally reserved for those of noble blood.

Caffarelli (nŽe Gaetano Majorano), who lived between 1703 and 1783, was another of the most lauded castrati singers. A soprano with as beautiful a voice as Farinelli, Caffarelli lacked Farinelli's courteous, gentle manner; but instead acted capricious, proud and quarrelsome. Caffarelli's influence helped shape the public's image of the Castrati as temperamental prima donnas, which was usually undeserved. It has been said that he adored music from an early age and may have been one of those strong-willed children who insisted on the operation for the sake of his voice and career.

Giovanni Battista Velluti (1780–1861) also was classed among the leading castrati sopranos of Italian opera. Handsome in face and figure, Velluti presented himself as a lady's man. He was also unusually intelligent, if sometimes conceited and demanding. Velluti was believed to have been castrated as a result of the doctor's misunderstanding of his parent's instructions concerning an illness.

The majority of the famous castrati of Italian opera lived between 1610 and 1922. About half were tall, good looking men with a pleasant disposition, although a few—perhaps 10 percent—were badly formed with heavy hips and breasts. Most lived to an advanced age and continued singing until very late in life. According to the records available of the 38 most widely recognized castrati, the mean age at the time of death was 72. This was considerably higher than the average life expectancy for men of that region and era, which was 35 to 40. It has been theorized that high testosterone levels are linked to high incidence of atherosclerosis, one of the primary causes of death in men. A few of the castrati (five of the sample of 38) were priests or monks.[18]

So great was the singing of the castrati, that many people in the world of opera still yearn for its beauty. Several articles about the castrati have appeared in the trade journal, *Opera News*, in recent years, and a book about the subject by Robert Baher, titled *Castrato*, was published in 1987. Ultimately, nostalgia for their singing has endured since they last graced the stages of Europe. A particularly sensitive poem, "Castrati in Caesar's Court," by James Reiss appeared in the

July 13, 1987 issue of *The New Republic, in which four castrati tell of their experiences:*

I. Remus

Of all court singers Caesar loves me best.
He makes me sing to him in his atrium
after festivals and Senate meetings.
Away from his bodyguards,
he reclines on cushions.
I set a stool beside him and begin:
'Hail Caesar, godlike, indestructible.'
The higher my voice soars
the more his features soften.
'Give me your paw, Remus,' he murmurs,
guiding my hand to his head
where I finger his thinning curls
and stroke his forehead smooth.

II. Gracchus

He treats me like a jester.
Fat Bacchus, he calls me.
I once was a sullen boy soprano, thin
as an olive pit, well-known in Etruria.
The day his envoy entered the temple
and summoned me to him,
I knew years of learning to treat
my voice like a vestal virgin
would cost me my manhood.
Now I hide behind smiles
and fast no longer as I did back home.
At dawn I enter Caesar's wine cellar
with a key he gave me
and drink my fill, with honeyed bread.

III. Caius

Whenever he boasts about the wars
or makes me chant hymns
to Caesarion his son,
I feel his sword between my legs.
I am young, I will never again see home.
Yet I have sung with the best musicians
in the Republic, while my mother and sister
live on sesterces I send them.
In Umbria, where spring comes late
to the mountain passes, I picture them
hard by a fire whose wood I provide for,
my mother carding wool,
my sister spinning.

IV. Septimus

I am old, yet my skin is still soft,
clear as it was when his legions
stripped my countrymen of their rags
and bundled me off in a cart
as a prize capon from the provinces.
In Gaul I sang for shepherds
and begged better fare as a minstrel
than I do at his banquets in Rome.
How many cities sacked and villagers taxed
to pay for his evening repast.
Caesar never patted my knee
or called me his Gallic cantor.
The gods will set him straight
when I sing at his funeral.

Undoubtedly, the history of these castrated singers dates back to the time of the Roman Caesars, yet tracing the actual records of their existence has proved difficult.

The singing of the last Italian castrato, Alessandro Moreschi, was recorded on 10 gramophone recordings in 1902 and 1904. Some recordings were reissued by Opal in 1988. As might be expected, these extant works are of relatively poor quality and by a castrato who was far from the best of his kind, but they are the only source for contemporary audiences to glimpse the stunning splendor of the castrato voice.

It seems apparent that a significant lesson can be learned from this examination of the castrati as applied to the present age: a wide disparity exists in our sense of values. If the Italians could castrate hundreds of thousands of young boys over the course of several hundred years for the relatively frivolous purpose of enhancing their singing voices, is it possible we moderns may consider using castration for the purpose of preventing serious crimes, diseases, and the loss of vital spiritual and moral values?

Endnotes—Chapter 10

1. *Encyclopedia Britannica*, 1968, 23–100a.

2. Charles de Brosses, *Lettres Familiares sur l'Italie*. 1931. Quoted in Angus Heriot, *The Castrati in Opera*. New York: Da Capo Music Press, Inc., 1974, p. 14.

3. Heriot, *Ibid.*, p. 26.

4. Matthew Warshaw, "My Son, the Diva." *Esquire*, November 1991, p. 58.

5. Ida Franca, *Manual of Bel Canto*, New York: Coward-McCann, Inc., 1959, pp. 96, 100–123.

6. Heriot, *Ibid.*, pp. 21, 22.

7. Franca, *Ibid.*, p. 100.

8. Peter Tompkins, *The Eunuch and the Virgin*. New York: Clarkson N. Potter, Inc., 1962, p. 127.

9. Franca, *Ibid.*, p. 92.

10. Heriot, *Ibid.*, pp. 42, 43.

11. *Ibid.*, pp. 36, 37.

12. *Ibid.*, pp. 44, 60.

13. Charles Ancillon, *TraitŽ Des Eunuques*. Paris: Editions Ramsay, 1707, Reprinted in 1978, p. 63.

14. Heriot, *Ibid.*, p. 44 (footnote).

15. *Ibid.*, pp. 96, 99.

16. *Ibid*, p. 98.

17. *Ibid.*, p. 100.

18. *Ibid.*

Chapter 11—Asceticism Through the Ages

A Brief Overview

One of the alleged benefits of castration lies in the realm of asceticism: the doctrine that expresses the belief that through renunciation of the desires of the flesh and pleasure in worldly things, and through self-mortification, one can subdue one's base appetites and discipline oneself, so as to reach high spiritual, intellectual or educational states. Mysticism, Puritanism, cynicism, gnosticism and yoga might be aided by removing the sexual appetite. Peter Abelard (1079–1142), the renowned French theologian, wrote of his own castration: "So when divine grace cleansed, rather than deprived, me of those vile members; which from their practice of utmost indecency are called the 'parts of shame'...what did it do but remove a foul imperfection in order to preserve perfect purity. Join me in thanksgiving...."[1]

Our earliest human ancestors may well have associated sex with evil—long before recorded history and the formulation of religious doctrines. The anatomical fact that humans' sexual organs are also sources for the elimination of waste could well have instilled considerable revulsion in early humans. The shameful, low status of women in the majority of ancient ethnic groups was due to the many superstitions concerning her monthly flow. Even today, a woman is considered unclean and should not be touched for two weeks of each month by Orthodox Hasidic Jews. These types of beliefs were reinforced by primitive religions down through the ages, such that sex and evil have become entwined in the minds of men. Many of our notable authors and artists have vividly portrayed this close association—Dante's *Inferno*, Milton's *Paradise Lost*, Hogarth's *Satan, Sin and Death* and Blake's *Satan Comes to the Gates of Hell*.

The world's great religions recognize the dualism of the human condition: Man is both mind and body, good and evil, spirit and matter, sacred and profane and body and soul. We have been taught that evil and sin are inherent in the human body. The Judeo-Christian religions, especially, have the idea that sex is sinful, basing their beliefs on the story of Adam and Eve eating the forbidden fruit of the tree of life in the Garden of Eden (Genesis 3). The stern commandments handed down in fire and thunder include: "Thou shalt not commit adultery" and "You shall not covet...your neighbor's wife..." (Exodus 20:14, 17). All sex is deemed sinful, for we are all born into sin (Psalm 51:5). Only Christ was born of a virgin and untainted. Sex and sin are often synonymous.

Catholic religious law, which was established by Saint Thomas Aquinas and the Apostolic Cannons, acknowledges that "...every sexual act for mere voluptuous pleasure is a mortal sin." Co-habitating men and women are often referred to as "living in sin." Some forms of sex were once spoken of as "a fate worse than death." We are all passengers on a "streetcar named desire" (Tennessee Williams, 1947). Removing a man's sexuality through castration could eliminate the sinful part of him. Asexualization theoretically solves the problems of evil by rendering us as *sinless..*

Although ascetics may benefit from castration, certain difficulties persist in assessing the merits of the procedure. Men are so different in their spiritual, mental and physical characteristics that the effects of the operation can vary with individuals. Of course, relatively little has been written about the beneficial qualities of castration because of its prohibition by the Catholic Church since the first Council of Nicea in 325 A.D. In addition, records of the positive effects have been destroyed and those who have undergone the surgery have tended to maintain secrecy about their condition.

The Teachings of Jesus Christ and the Apostles

In his profound Sermon on the Mount, Jesus Christ clearly identified sexual sinning, and urged the removing of a part of the body as a means of preventing it:

> You have heard that it was said, 'You shall not commit
> adultery.' But I say to you that everyone who looks at a
> woman with lust has already committed adultery with her in
> his heart. If your right eye causes you to sin, tear it out and
> throw it away; it is better for you to lose one of your members
> than for your whole body to be thrown into hell. And if your
> right hand causes you to sin, cut it off and throw it away; it
> is better for you to lose one of your members than for your
> whole body to go into hell (Matthew 5:27-30).

It should be kept in mind, though, that in the Middle East, removing
offending body parts is customary; i.e. if one has been convicted of
stealing something, one's hand is literally chopped off.

Other parts of Jesus' sermon support the interpretation that he was
referring to the removal of the testicles because the effect of castration
is to reduce a man's aggression and make him more humble.

"Blessed are the meek for they will inherit the earth" (Matthew
5:5).

"Blessed are the poor in spirit, for theirs is the kingdom of heaven"
(Matthew 5:3).
"Blessed are the peacemakers, for they shall be called the children
of God" (Matthew 5:9).

Earlier religious figures were noted for their meekness: "Now the
man Moses was very humble, more so than anyone on the face of
the earth" (Numbers 12:3). Also consider: "The meek shall inherit
the land, and delight themselves in abundant prosperity" (Psalms
37:11). The wisdom of Solomon comes to mind, as well: "Toward the
scorners he is scornful, but to the humble he shows favor" (Proverbs
3:34).

Jesus, as well as other Biblical writers, encouraged castration as a
means to achieving a higher spiritual state and to worship God more
fully. Josephson refers to the beliefs of the Skoptsi and gives several

other references to the often repeated words in Matthew (18:8, 9; 19:12) and Mark (9:43–47). Josephson goes even further than other Biblical scholars in stating that Jesus repeated this more insistently and frequently and more at length than any of his other teachings.[2] Ancillon wrote that Christ was referring to the Essenes and the Pharisees when he spoke of eunuchs for the sake of the kingdom of heaven, quoting Josephus book 18, chapter 2 on the ancient Jews as his authority.[3] Most of the biblical reference to the Pharisees is uncomplimentary, with the exception of Acts 5:34–40; little or no reference is made to the Essenes.

The Apostles also contributed to the lessons of Jesus by teaching that evil lies in our body parts. Paul wrote in Romans (7 and 8) of the evil nature of the body in "…making me captive to the law of sin that dwells in my members….with my flesh I am a slave to the law of sin." This early belief in the sinful nature of the body led to the elimination of the testes, asserted to be the most sinful part of the male.

Jesus himself uses castration as a metaphor for the power of faith in that a man who is completely dedicated to his religion can accomplish any deed. When asked by the disciples why they could not cast out the demon from the epileptic boy, he offered them the parable of the mustard seed: "Because of your little faith. For truly, I say to you, if you have faith as a grain of mustard seed, you will say to this mountain, 'move hence to yonder place,' and it will move; and nothing will be impossible to you" (Matthew 17:17–21; Mark 11:20–24).

Aspects of Human Nature

The three recognized parts of every personality are body, mind and spirit. Freud called them id, ego and superego. It could be contended that the body is basic to the other two. That is, ego and superego do not exist—they do not have a life of their own—without the body, as far as we are able to observe. In the angels, no doubt, spirit is paramount, but in man, body is the first consideration. From this perspective, the body largely controls mind and spirit. Sometimes the mechanisms are particularly apparent, and the body's control over the mind can be easily observed. For instance, pain and pleasure are felt by the body. The body influences the mind to move the body in such a way as to avoid pain and seek pleasure. Some of the mechanisms are not so clear. Of course, many claim that, conversely, the mind controls the body, or the spirit controls the mind, or at least the spirit ought to control the mind and body (see Paul's exhortations to the Romans and Galatians 5:16–24). D. H. Lawrence wrote: "My great religion is a belief in the blood, the flesh, as being wiser than the intellect." In highly conscious persons, the body, mind and spirit are integrated and unified. However, most humans behave through the body, usually in unconscious ways.

The philosophical debates have occupied learned men for centuries. Adrenal, gonadal and pituitary hormones circulate in the blood stream and exert their influence on the brain, which controls our behavior in many more ways than are immediately apparent to us. Furthermore, the body is very selfish—much like a baby—it cries "Me!" all the time. In the unconscious state, the body is demanding: it is perverse, capricious and exerts painful retribution if its demands are ignored. "Take care of Me first; feed, clothe and rest Me!" In the hierarchy of all our needs, body's needs come first: air, nourishment, sleep, shelter, sex. Most psychologists assert that the mind resides in the brain. Among religious seekers, the belief is that the spirit resides in the mind and, without question, all reside in the body. Subduing some of the body's hungers through castration thus serves to elevate the mind and the spirit over the physical imperatives of the body.

If even a fraction of the tremendous life forces of energy that are frittered away each day in sexual activities were to be concentrated in another higher goal, then it should be reasonable to assume that much more power could be exerted to reach such goals. In this culture, young people expend many hours thinking, fantasizing and dreaming about sexual subjects. A similar amount of mental and psychic energy devoted to a more productive goal could contribute much that is positive to society. James Allen taught: "As a man thinketh in his heart, so he is." Reduction or removal of the hormonal impetus of sexual brain activity could greatly facilitate thinking on almost any other field or endeavor. Voluntary castration, with foreknowledge of the full effects of the operation, offers the most promise for men who are troubled with a deviant sexual orientation, and wish to change.

We have seen how castration has been used in many ancient cultures to sublimate the sexual urges, so that ascetic and religious individuals could devote themselves more completely to a higher power. The Hijras of India and the priests of Byzantium exemplify this, as well as a sect of early Jews, as we will see later.[4]

Early Mythology

Debasing the body in order to purify it of its unholy and profane attributes and striving for higher states of piety and purity have led men in many ancient religions and cults to utilize castration as a means of better serving their beliefs. The first to clearly set down this notion was likely Plutarch (c. 46–c. 120 A.D.). He was one of the most popular of the Greek writers, particularly in the Eastern Church, and had been initiated into the mysteries of Osiris (the Greek Dionysus).[5] Familiar with the relationship of the divine state and castration, Plutarch wrote in his *Essays* that "…Normal eyes cannot see the truly holy Osiris, for men still in possession of bodies and passions cannot rise to divine heights. When men are released from their carnal impediments, they will rise to purer and unimagined heights."

Along with the virgin priestess and other virgins who tended to the needs of the temples, the origins of the eunuch priests are buried in the history of the ancient cultures that flourished in Babylon, Lebanon, Cyprus and Syria. Beliefs and practices varied widely even in the same cult over time and are difficult to trace. In the mythology of Egypt, for example, the worship of Set (Setekh) was popular in parts of the country during the Second Dynasty (c. 2,890–2,686 B.C.), but fell from favor with the end of the reign of the Hyksos kings. Worship of Set was reinstated by the Ramessides (c. 1,320–c. 1,200 B.C.) and again vilified in Tanite times (c. 1,085–c. 945 B.C.).

Myth had it that Set castrated and murdered his brother Osiris and then suffered the same fate at the hands of the son of Osiris, Horus. The name for the Egyptian priests who worshipped these deities meant "pure" and bodily purity was assured by ablutions—shaving all face, head and body hair, circumcision of some, and castration of others. The tomb of Per-N-Ankh, dated at 2,328 B.C. and identified by its hieroglyphics as a "Purification Priest," was found in January 1990 near the pyramid of Giza (Ft. Walton Daily News, January 18, 1990).

Beginning about 1,576 B.C., the priesthood formed a separate caste and in each major temple there was a hierarchy of perhaps 20 to 50, from the humblest servants of the threshold up through the keepers of the interior chambers to the high priest himself. Each level of priest would have his special rituals and authority, observing dietary taboos and wearing pure white linen garments. Shaving all body hair is also prescribed in the Christian Bible (Leviticus 14:8, 9).

Not unlike the story of Set is a primitive Greek myth reported in Hesiod's *Theogony*. Uranos was castrated by his son, Chronos, with a scimitar and the parts thrown into the sea. Aphrodite sprang from the severed member as it floated in the spume. Chronos reigned as king until he was later similarly deposed in a bloody manner by Zeus.

Worship of the Goddess

Pre-dating even the Egyptian eunuch priesthood of Osiris is the worship of the ancient Asian Great Mother of the Gods by eunuch temple servers throughout Mesopotamia. Her cult appears to have been nearly universal in the earliest days of this ancient land. She was the preeminent goddess, worshipped by great and small alike; even the famous Hammurabbi and his antecedents were recorded to be among her followers. She was called Inanna in Sumeria and Ishtar as the great goddess of the Sumero-Babylonian-Akkadian pantheon. Traces of her worship extend back to the Neolithic period—circa 6,000 B.C.[6] Characteristic clay statues of her with lions from this very early period have been found at Hacilar (near present Konya) in southwest Turkey. Alabaster figurines of her priests, which plainly showed their eunuchoid features, from the temple of Eanna (house of heaven or "house of date clusters") near Uruk were found, and are thought to date back to 2,600 B.C. She was worshipped in Phrygia, but most of the records of these people have been lost or purposely destroyed. The royal Assyrian annals indicate that the Phrygians settled the area of present Turkey about 1,160 B.C. and worshipped her by the name of Kabula or Agdistis ("She of the rock").

The Great Mother was worshipped by different names throughout ancient history around the entire region. She was called Arinna, Wurusemu or Ma among the "thousand gods of the Hittites." The Phoenicians and Hebrews referred to her as Ashtaroth, Ashtoreth or Ashtar. She was recognized as Athar by the Sabaeans, Astarte and Atargatis in Syria, Cyprus and Ascalon, Cybeba by the Lydians, Kubaba by the Luwains, Tanith by the Carthaginians and Artemis by the Ephesians. The ancient writer, Apuleius of Madauros, listed several other names of the Great Mother in his work, *Metamorphoses, Book II, stanza 5:*

Thus, the Phrygians that are the oldest human stock call me Pessinuntia, Mother of the Gods. The aboriginal races of Attica call me Cecropian Minerva. The Cyprians in their island-home call me Paphian Venus. The archer Cretans call me Diana Dictynna. The three-tongued Sicilians call be Stygian Proserpine. The Eleusinians call me the ancient goddess Ceres. Some call me Juno. Some call me Bellona. Some call me Hecate. Some call me Rhamnusia. But those who are enlightened by the earliest rays of that divinity the sun, the Ethiopians, the Arii, the Egyptians who excel in antique lore, all worship me with their ancestral ceremonies and call me by my true name, Queen Isis.[7]

The Bible mentions the temple of Ashtoreth, dating to about 1,020 B.C. (I Samuel 31:10). It also makes reference to the temple for his foreign wife that Solomon built in 920 B.C. to honor the Goddess, located east of Jerusalem, and Josiah destroying it about 622 B.C. (I Kings 11:3–8 and II Kings 23:13). Euripides noted in his play *Iphigenia in Tauris* (411 B.C.), the immolation of strangers as a sacrifice to Artemis at her Crimean temple. The eunuch priests who served the Great Mother Goddess at Ephesis were called "Bugabuxsa"—"having salvation through the deity." These priests had not been mutilated by men, but were eunuchs by congenital malformation, as were the effeminate priests of Cotys (Cotytto), the goddess of Thrace.[8]

In most of the Greek and Latin literature, the favorite name for the Great Mother of the Gods (Mater Deum Magna or Mater Deum Magna Idaea) was Cybele, and the name of her consort, or son, was Attis. The worship of Cybele was known in Boeotia by Pindar in 474 B.C. (Pythian IX). Hippolytus (c. 165–235 A.D.) reported on Naassenian authority in his *Refutation of All Heresies*, V 17 that Attis, by his castration, was raised to "celestial essence, where, they say, there is neither male nor female, but a new creation, a new man, who is androgynous." Gruppe, a sixteenth century writer, supposes that "the castration of the priests of Cybele and Attis was to secure chastity, in conformity with an ascetic desire to renounce the joys of the world."[9]

As is invariably the case, many other names for Cybele and Attis exist, reflecting the various languages and peoples who adhered to the goddess religions. Several versions of their origins exists, as well. Other names were sometimes derived from the place where her sanctuaries were located; i.e., the name "Dindymene" came from Mt. Dindymus in Galatia. Mt. Ida and Mt. Sipylus, as well as the cities of Cyzicus, Sardis, Hierapolis, Baalbeck (Heliopolis) and Pessinus, were other early seats of her worship. One version of the Goddess legend was recorded by the elegiac poet, Hermesianax of Colophon (c. 320 B.C.). In this version, Zeus had a nocturnal emission and his semen fell to earth, generating a hermaphroditic creature called Agdistis. The other gods feared Agdistis, so they cut off his male member. An almond tree sprang forth from the severed parts and, when the tree's fruit ripened, the daughter of the river Sangarious gathered the almonds and put them in her bosom. The almonds disappeared, and she found herself pregnant. In due time, she brought forth a divinely beautiful but impotent son, Attis, who became a priest of the Mother of the gods. Attis spread the cult of his patron with such zeal that Jupiter became angry and sent a boar to kill Attis. Diodorus of Sicily (c. 100–c. 21 B.C.) relates in his *Biblioteca Historica* III, 58–59, the same legend, minus the Phrygian elements, as a love story between Cybele and Attis, and without the androgynous attachments of Agdistis.

Ovid also recounted the story of Cybele and Attis about 2 B.C. in his *Fasti* (*Calendar*) IV, 221–233:

> In the middle of the forests, a Phrygian child of such beauty as Attis, chained up because of a pure love for the goddess of Towers (another one of Cybele's names), she wanted to attach him to her and she said to him: 'always stay a child!' He promised to be faithful to this order—"If I lie, may the first love which makes me fail, be my last.' He committed failure in the arms of the nymph, Sagaris, and he ceased being what he had been. The Goddess, irritated, exacted punishment and the Naiad died of her wounds near her tree which also died. Attis became insane and fled to the summit of Dindymus crying 'Take these torches—carry away these whips.' He cut his body with a sharp stone, he dragged his long hair in the dust crying 'I have deserved it, I pay with my blood the deserved punishment. Ah! Let the parts which caused my downfall perish!' He suddenly cut off the part attached to his groin and left no sign of his virility. From that madness came an example, and the effeminate priests, their hair disheveled, also cut off the members which they despised.[10]

The version of the myth written by Pausanias about 170 A.D. in his *Book VII* is similar to that of Hermesianax, but it has Agdistis and Attis as lovers. Attis is sent to Pessinus to marry the daughter of the king. The wedding has already started when Agdistis arrives. Attis mutilates himself, as do some of the others present, amongst the commotion. Arnobius Afer, a Christian Apologist, who had been a pagan himself before 300 A.D., adds to the intrigue of the tale in Book V of his *Adversus Nationes* (*Against the Pagans*): "Attis, having seized a fragment of a vase, withdrew under a pine tree and did away with the marks of his sex, saying: 'Receive cruel Agdistis, receive the fatal object of your terrors.' His life ebbed away as his blood flowed."

Numerous other religions existed that held certain rituals or beliefs in common with those who castrated themselves for Cybele. The Artemis cult is one of these (Artemis resembles Diana of the Romans). The Greek goddess of wild animals, vegetation, chastity and the hunt, worship of Cybele flourished from the second millennium B.C. and included cults that had practices similar to those of the Great Mother, with wild phallic dances, scourging of youths at her altar, immolation of strangers, figures flanked by lions, and a many-breasted Ephesian version.

Many scholars believe that the Goddess was originally a mother goddess of the mountains, analogous to the Asian Magna Mater. Rhea is another Greek and Roman goddess who has been associated with Cybele through her attributes of providing fruitful crops, herds and families. She married Cronus in a relationship comparable to that of Cybele and Attis. Demeter is a Greek mother goddess of grain who is sometimes identified with Rhea and Cybele. Ops was Roman goddess of fertility who was equated in the early period with Rhea and Cybele in the later period. The goddess, Hecate, was worshipped by eunuch hieroduli (temple slaves) at Lagina, an archeological site in southwest Turkey, as far back in time as 540 B.C.[11]

The Hymn of Hecate—attributed to Hesiod (411–352 B.C.)— represents the goddess as having power over heaven, earth and sea, hence she bestows wealth and all the blessings of daily life. Vestiges of her worship existed well into the eleventh century A.D.[12] Gaia was a particularly early Greek personification of the earth and a mother goddess who was the wife of Uranus before the cult of Zeus. Gaia was worshipped by some Greeks as the mother of Hermes by Zeus. Mithra was an Indo-Iranian god of light. His worship advocated a vigorous morality code, which was similar in some respects to the one that caused the priests of Cybele to castrate themselves. Mithraism ranked about equal with the cult of Cybele and the cult of Issis as the most widespread of the religions of the ancient world before Christianity. In fact, Mithraism is still practiced in India by a tiny sect, the Parsis.

The Greeks and Romans clearly reveled in sensual pleasures, as their erotic paintings, statuary, pottery and writings attest. Since manly vigor was more admirable than ascetic attributes, they generally reviled those who were eunuchs. They considered the priests of Cybele to be foolish for castrating themselves, calling them Galli after the river Galles—he "who drinks of the water becomes insane" (Ovid, *Fasti IV*, 361). The water of the river "must be drunk wisely, for fear of madness" (Pliny, *Natural History V*, 147).

The Galli had the characteristic appearance of eunuchs and wore distinctive clothing. Juvenal alludes to the "gigantic priests of Cybele" who walk at the head of a cohort of the lower priests—"they had become effeminate and lost their manly characteristics" (Sat. V). He added that they were dressed like women in long, pale yellow robes, the color of a "dead leaf." Augustine had met them in the streets of Carthage with their long "hair perfumed, face powdered, their members weakened, their walk lewd" (*The City of God*, VII, 26).[13] However, their life was one of devotion with daily morning and evening prayers, chanting interminable litanies in their sharp, thin voices, accompanied by the beat of a drum. They also fasted regularly and observed the dietary taboo of bread and pork.

During the Second Punic War, the enemy had invaded Italian soil and the people were beginning to lose hope that the old gods could save the country. The Sibyllene oracle was consulted and it was prophesied that whenever the country had been penetrated by an enemy, he could be expelled if the Idaean Mother were brought to Rome from Pessinus. Accordingly, in 204 B.C., the silver statue of the Great Mother with her sacred stone—reputed to have fallen from heaven—was installed in the temple of Victory on the Palatine hills along with her Galli and other attendants from Phyrgia. The Great

Mother's identification with Maia, Ops, Rhea, Tellus and Ceres by the Romans contributed to the firm establishment of her worship in that region of the world.[14]

The main public event in the worship of the Great Mother was the annual spring festival from March 15 to March 27. March 24 was known as the "Day of Blood" and is described by Lucien (*Dea Syria*, 49–51) (125–c. 190), who claimed to be an eyewitness to the event:

> Of all the feasts I know, the greatest is the one that is celebrated at the beginning of spring. This feast attracts a large number from Syria and surrounding countries. A great number of Galles and men attached to the service of the priests slash their arms and beat each other on the back. Several musicians play the flute, others beat the drum, others sing inspired religious chants. The fury spreads and many men join the acts. The young man who has decided to become a Galle, throws down his clothes, advances to the middle of the assembly, shouting loudly and seizes a knife reserved long ago for this use. With this cutlass he castrates himself briskly and runs through the village holding in his hands that which he has cut off. The house, whatever it is, where he is going to throw himself, will furnish him a woman's dress and everything used to ornament women. That is how castration is practiced.

Contemporary accounts by others who also observed the ceremony first-hand vary. Catullus (Roman) (34–54 B.C.)., Ovid (43 B.C – 18 A.D.), and Juvenal (c. 60–128) state that a broken stone was the instrument used (*Attis* 5; *Fasti* IV; 237; *Sat.* VI). Pliny (c. 23-79) (XXV 455) maintains a broken bottle served as the implement. Arnobius (*Prudent*, V 7, 1083) writes that the parts were removed, washed, embalmed and put away in a special temple chamber. The now transformed Galle was then presented with his new yellow robe, which had long sleeves and gathered at the waist by a sash. The activities of the Galles were not confined to their sanctuaries alone, as they could be seen circulating across the country from town to town dressed in their robes, carrying the divine statue on a donkey

(Apuleius, *Metamorphoses* VIII, 35) (Greek) (B.C. 125 A.D.). They would stop at public places, play the flute, dance, take up a collection and prophesy.

Discrediting Castration

The annual spring festival of Cybele was such a major public spectacle that it endured for literally hundreds of years and was written about widely. The festival was so well-known that it could not be completely effaced from the historical record, as so many other religious practices had been, by the anti-heretical movement of the early Christians. However, every effort was made to discredit the practice of castration for the purpose of purifying the priesthood.

Castration was a prime target of the "Apologists," which consisted of 15 or 20 Latin and Greek authors who wrote treatises in letter form addressed to the governmental ruling bodies. The Apologists attacked the procedure with special vehemence because it changes a creature of God. Saint Jerome wrote that the Galles do not castrate themselves through vice—"they are fools." Saint Augustine refers to emasculated men as "perverts" who must be hated. Lactus Firmianus was even more vitriolic in his description of these men, writing in his *Divine Institutions* that, "They are not all human and they insult divine will." In Arnobius' *Adversus Nationes*, which the *Encyclopedia Britannica* styles a "mordant critique of pagan religion by a half-educated Christian," the author calls the Galles: "Vile beings, impure people who bring bad luck. They are drunkards and frequent the slums in company of sailors, thieves, assassins, fugitive slaves and they are coffin makers for the poor. …They are infamous debauched people."

How curious that the alleged dreadful men portrayed by the Apologists have perpetuated a religious practice for 6,000 years in many cultures and countries. This practice would one day gain popularity in eighteenth century Russia (discussed later in this chapter). The ascetic life, the burning faith, the austere disciplines of the Galles and other similar holy men must have appeared as a beacon of light to many of the spiritual seekers, who were inspired to go and do likewise. And what can be said about the vitriolic language directed against the eunuch priests? Such scurrilous abuse is clearly against the scriptures—e.g., second commandment of Harmas, 1 Corinthians 5:11; 6:10; Leviticus 19:15–18; and Titus 2:3.

Representations in Various Faiths

Hinduism is the world's oldest religion, and still flourishes today. It has an estimated 500 million devotees; most of whom are located in India. Hinduism encompasses an enormously complex variety of beliefs and practices ranging from simple silent meditation to extremes of asceticism involving rich displays of suffering to actual orgies of all sorts. Walker mentions some of the ascetic practices of the Hindus:

> Several types of Tapasains are named after their dietary habits. ...There are some who haunt graveyards and cremation grounds and eat human flesh, and others who supplement their diet with cow dung and urine or human excreta. ... Because of its many perversions, Tapas was condemned by most progressive reformers, including Buddha, Kafir, Guru Nanak and many modern leaders.[15]

Weston La Barre offers additional insights into the sexual beliefs of Hindu mysticism:

> Hindu asceticism derives immediately from its believers' cosmophysiological fantasies about sexuality. The direct equation of semen with life emerges from the medical texts, where semen is expressly said to promote longevity; therefore, to live long, one must retain semen (Caraka 1.25.39). This is merely a reformulation of the Vedic hypothesis: Soma promotes immortality: to become immortal, one must drink Soma. The Upanishads teach that a man's power, sakti, enters him in food and is stored in semen: to increase and retain

this sakti, males must retain their semen and hence lead an asceticlife![16]

These are not arcane myths, but rather, popular beliefs that still exist in India today. Although acted upon by a relatively small esoteric section of Indian society, such ideas are subscribed to and known among most Indians, even illiterate villagers.

A thread of fanatical Hindu asceticism, which involves castration, can be traced back to Vedic times. A tortuous form of splitting the penis is discussed in the *Arthavaveda III*, ix and VI, cxxxiii. Eunuchs are mentioned in the *Great Tale of the Prince Bharata* (*Mahabharata III ci, 46*), a work which deals with events before the tenth century B.C. Eunuchs were dedicated to the goddess Huligamma in Madras, Mysore and Dharwar districts.[17] The Yoniga sect is said to see castration as a step to unification with the higher state of being, as delineated in their religion.

In the early Hindu Vedas, ascetics were said to be able to achieve states of ecstasy and perform extraordinary feats, such as flying through the air. The Upanishads (c. 600 B.C.) mention ascetic practices that are necessary to achieve other goals, including happiness, spiritual liberation, magical powers, prolongation of life, foreseeing the future, healing infirmities and dispelling evil. Even today, some ascetics are said to be able to achieve a transcendental state of awareness and thought, which allows them to pierce the barriers and limitations of this world. For example, they are able to travel out of their bodies at high speeds, move backward or forward in time so they can relate historical incidents with great accuracy, reveal future events, and are said to be capable of other karmic wonders. The Hijras, an ascetic sect whose members castrated themselves out of devotion to the Mother Goddess Bahuchara Mata, are mentioned in the Hindu epic, the *Ramayana*, which was written about 300 A.D. (see chapter 8).

Buddhism, presently numbering some 245 million adherents, began as a reform movement within Hinduism in the fifth century before Christ. Guatama, the Buddha, was an Indian prince who renounced the pleasures of the world and gained enlightenment. He later attained Nirvana—the obliteration of desire—and was delivered from all suffering henceforth. The doctrine of Buddhism is unique among the world's faiths, in that it does not center on a god or gods; rather the religion teaches a deliverance of suffering through the annihilation of desire. Although castration eliminates the basest of bodily desires and thus, serves the Buddist's objective of sexual detachment, the practice is not advocated by any but the most ascetic Buddhist sects.

In China, ancestor worship and the worship of various spirits of nature were dominant until about the fifth century B.C., when two other systems of religious beliefs emerged among the upper classes. One was the ethical system of Confucius (Kung Futzu, 551–479 B.C.); the other was the mystical faith of the Tao. Tao means "the way" and calls for humans to be in harmony with Tao through the practice of quietude. These two religions are estimated to have about 305 million adherents. In China, eunuchs were regularly employed by the rich classes to attend to the men's wives and concubines (see chapter 2). Eunuch priests were also employed to minister to these women's religious needs. The Emperor Yang of the Sui dynasty (c. 600 B.C.) regularly utilized 18 of these eunuch priests for his harem because intact men were not allowed contact with these women.[18]

The beginnings of Judaism can be traced to Abraham's migration into Canaan some 20 centuries before the birth of Christ. Judaism has forbidden castration in all its forms in men and animals since the time of Ezra—about 428 B.C. Marriage is an unconditional duty, especially for Rabbis. "Be fruitful and multiply, and fill the earth and subdue it…" is taken as a command of God. According to Gerhard Kittel, the author of *Theological Dictionary*, Judaism has had only one celibate rabbi.[19] Explicit disqualification of the Rabbis and temple servants, who castrated themselves in order to promote their spirituality, illustrates how repulsive the practice is in this religion.[20] Nevertheless, a thread of ascetic celibacy can be found in Judaism.

The Essenes were a Jewish religious sect that had its foundations in the region that is northwest of the Dead Sea from around 200 B.C.

to 100 A.D. Ancillon quotes Josephus, the historian of the Jewish people and the Bible (I Maccabees 2:27–30), who discussed the ascetic, celibate lives of the Essenes.[21] Josephus himself underwent three years of preparation in the desert to become a member of the sect, but resigned before completing all of the requirements. The Purity Laws of the Essenes, recorded on one of the Dead Sea Scrolls,[22] describe an especially "pure" man who may well have been a eunuch.[23] The Essenes also practiced a communal living arrangement where everything was shared equally among all. The Skopzy followed this custom of the Essenes 1,700 years later. It has been established that the Essenes practiced purification ceremonies, although it has not been proven whether castration was involved, as it was with so many of the ancient religions.

Although most of the information concerning the Essenes has been lost to us, the famous psychic, Edgar Cayce, has shed considerable light on their contribution. He called the Essenes, the hated ones, the lowest of the Jews, but at the same time reveals that John the Baptist was an Essene; Zacharias joined that group and Elizabeth, the mother of John the Baptist was the first to be told of the coming of Christ by her cousin, Mary.[24]

Religious castration was practiced by the early Christians, despite its practice being seen as an anathema. In Phrygia, the ancestral home of the worship of the Great Mother, a Christian sect called "Montanism," the "Cataphrygian heresy," or the "new prophecy" arose about the year 156 A.D. Montanus, the founder, is referred to in Jerome's letter (41) to Marcella as "abscisum et semiverum" (castrated and half a man). Montanus is also mentioned in Eusabius' *Church History* (5, 16, 17) and Didymus' *De Trintate* (3.41) as a pagan priest, so he was probably a former priest of Cybele who had converted to Christianity. A majority of the Phrygian Christians belonged to the Montanist sect, and by 207 it had spread to Carthage where Tertullian (c. 155–220 A.D.) adopted some of its precepts. Montanism encouraged martyrdom, fasting and moral rigor. Its dogma forbade second marriages and likely allowed castration as a means of assuring piety. Tertullian declared that the kingdom of heaven was open to eunuchs. Vestiges of Montanism remained in the rural areas of central Asia Minor into the sixth century.

The best known of the early Christian priests who were castrated was Origen of Alexandria (Origenes Adamantius, c. 185–c. 253 A.D.). Origen was a brilliant scholar; he read widely—including the ancient manuscripts in his father's library as a boy, as well as those in the Library of Alexandria later in life. Origen castrated himself when be was about 18 years old, as an outcome of his studies. He was influenced by the words of Christ in Matthew 19:12, as well as by two essays on the high ideals of purity. One essay was written by Philo of Alexandria (c. 30 B.C.–c. 40 A.D.) titled, *Evil Often Attacks Good*; the other was by a Pythagorean named Sextus titled, *The Sentences. According to Rufinus, Origen authored 6,000 books. Saint Jerome considered him to be the greatest theologian and teacher after the Apostles. In his seventh Treatise on Saint Matthew 18, Origen wrote:*

> As for us, we are filled with spirituality…those who, appealing to a moral system, abstain from the pleasures of love for reasons of morality, must be called eunuchs. Those who are chaste by virtue and piety, to be better disposed to the service of God are being more pleasing to Him.

His life was devoted to strict asceticism, which included poverty, a frugal diet, walking barefoot and sleeping on the floor. He was arrested, tortured and stretched "four spaces" on the rack on orders from the pagan emperors for his religious activities. In spite of his faultless life and significant contributions to the Church, he was denied admittance to the priesthood in 231 A.D. and forbidden to preach by a synod of bishops. This action was instigated by his own bishop, Demetrius, because of his self-mutilation. Three centuries later (in 542 A.D.), Origen was again regarded as an anathema by the pope and emperor for this same act.

The question remains whether another early church official, Militon, was castrated, inasmuch as he was referred to as "the eunuch saint" in a letter of Polyrate, the bishop of Ephesus in the third century. It may be that the ecclesiastical language of that particular period simply meant "celibate," instead.

The Christian scholar, Valesius, castrated himself and formed a sect, the Valesii, in the Arabian desert circa 240 A.D., which advocated castration for the laity as well as the priesthood. Saint Epiphanius (313–403) wrote in his study of heresy, *Advertus Octaginta Haeres,*[25] that the Valesian heresy was spread among the inhabitants of Dachatis, a large town in the territory of Philadelphia (modern Amman), beyond the Jordan River, and that they were wrongly confused with the Gnostics.[26] He also wrote that not only were the followers of the sect all castrated, but that castration was considered a necessary part of the priesthood. At the beginning, most of the adherents attended church up to the time that "their madness went too far," and the authorities of the church were obliged to rout them out. In the words of Saint Epiphanius:

> They pretended to follow what the Evangelist said: 'If one of your members disgraces you, cut it off, etc.' (Matthew 18É8, 9). They believed it their duty to practice the operation not only on their adherents, but on all those who fell into their hands. In this way, whether by persuading the former, or forcing the latter, they guarded their followers, attracted pilgrims and travelers and this is how their doctrine spread. Those whom they recruited were thrown into fetters and their organs violently mutilated. Thus they speak of these heretics and thus they recognize them. …[T]ravelers would do anything to escape their country, where they risked falling victim to their fanaticism.[26]

Although Epiphanius was highly critical of the Valesians and all other heresies, his study is the only original source available on this sect. All of the later writers who have written about the sect only paraphrased what he had written.

In 313 A.D., Christianity emerged as the dominant religion of the Roman Empire, after Constantine the Great decided to stop persecuting the Christians. Uncertainty existed from the earliest period of the faith about castration for the priesthood, so it was ruled on at the very first major convocation of the Church at Nicea (May 26 to June 25, 325 A.D.). "If anyone has become a eunuch, either by surgery during illness or by the barbarians, let him remain in the clergy, but the one who castrated himself, though in good health, must be forbidden to remain in the priesthood, and from then on must not be moved ahead."[27] Constantine later went even further with the civil law: "If anyone shall anywhere in the Roman Empire after this decree make eunuchs, he shall be punished by death. If the owner of the place where it is perpetrated was aware of it, his goods shall be confiscated."

In 391 and 393, Theodosius I issued edicts forbidding the practice of all pagan cults. In 395, Pope Leon I issued a papal decree forbidding voluntary emasculation, even if it were done with the intention of "avoiding sin." After many millennia of almost guaranteeing the celibate purity of the priesthood, religious castration was legislated nearly to the point of extinction. Nonetheless, traces of the practice can still be found throughout Christian history.

A regular practice in Christianity consisted of expunging all records of "heretical practices" that were in conflict with current dogma, leaving few remains of the religious history of castration. The great library in the temple of the Serapis (the Serapion) in Alexandria, Egypt was willfully destroyed by the zealous Eastern Orthodox Catholic patriarch, Theophilus (391), under the edict of Byzantine Emperor Theodosius I. This loss probably had the single greatest impact on the knowledge of early religious practices. The Sarapeum had been a branch of the great library of Alexandria since 235 B.C., when it was established on the palace grounds in the southern part of the city by Ptolemy III (246–221 B.C.). The long succession of the Ptolemies of Egypt maintained it for more than 600 years. This particular library may have been damaged when Caesar besieged the city in 47 B.C., but it was not destroyed as some accounts would have it.[28] At the time, Theophilus' burning of this grand library was taken as the final triumph of Christianity over the old pagan religions.

Byzantine Orthodox Christianity suffered a similar fate a thousand years later when Constantinople fell to the Ottoman Turks on May 29, 1453. The Muslim conquerors destroyed the records in the ancient religious libraries, and sold the treasured books for whatever coins they would bring. These lost books could surely have told us much more about Byzantine religious eunuchs than we now know.

In spite of the deliberate destruction of the records concerning the use of castration to assure purity in religious leaders, a certain amount of information on religious eunuchs is still available to contemporary scholars. In addition to the discussion in Chapter 5, research indicates that two other prominent religious figures were eunuchs—an abbot of Medicium in Bythnia in 824 and Photius, a Patriarch of Constantinople (858–867; 878–886). The possibility exists that castration, as part of religious practices, also occurred in other ascetical sects such as the Manichaens, Massalians, Paulicians and Bogomils, but the record is not clear on this.

The eunuch priesthood of Byzantium continued, but only sporadically in the Russian Orthodox lineage. Two bishops of Kiev, Ivan and Jephren, encouraged the faithful to castrate themselves for the kingdom of Heaven. Ivan had been brought from Greece by Princess Wsewolodowna in 1089. He was referred to in the Chronics as *nawje*, meaning "corpse."[29] Boccaccio wrote a story about one of these eunuch priests—one who carried his dehydrated testicles with him in a little box so that no one could accuse him of "not being in possession of his manhood."

Byzantine religious customs were passed on to the Russians beginning with the missionary work of the Orthodox church during the reign of Basil I (867–886). Olga, regent of the Russian realm, was baptized in Constantinople in the autumn of 957.[30] Russian Norman warriors (Varangarians) sent by Russian Prince Vladimir greatly helped the Byzantine emperor in quelling a rebellion in 989. Vladimir received the hand of Anna, the emperor's sister, in marriage as a reward. The Varangarians remained a vital part of the Byzantine army for well over a hundred years. After the fall of Byzantium, Moscow became the center of the Orthodox world. Ivan III, the great consolidator of Russian lands, married the niece of the last emperor of Byzantium and introduced Byzantine ceremonials into Moscow. The traditions of Byzantine faith and politics endured through the centuries in the Russian Empire.[31]

Browe[33] mentions several others of lesser stature who castrated themselves. St. Epiphanius of Salamis (d. 403) spoke of "those who are of not inconsiderable number who castrate themselves in youthful folly, against the laws." There was the bishop of Antioch, Leontius (344-357) and two monks mentioned in the Vitae Patrum who castrated themselves "for the sake of the kingdom of heaven." About 550 A.D., a monk named Jacob at a monastery near Jerusalem cut of his testicles with a sword and he was thrown out of the monastery for the act, but later forgiven and returned. The synod of Limoges recorded in 1031 that there were "certain clerics" who had also done that thing. It is also recorded in a biography of Thomas a Becket that another German monk had done the same thing at the end of the 12th century. Pope Clements III reported it of a priest in the diocese of Ravenna, and later Thomas of Eccleston reported one of the first English friars to castrate himself. Popes John XXII and Benedict XII granted dispensations to monastic and secular priests for their mutilations. The Spanish historian Ambrose Morales (d. 1590) castrated himself after the example of Origen Richard Wagner (1869-1930) in his opera *Parsifal*, Klingsor lays his hand against himself to slay sin and his most horrible urges to make himself worthy of the Holy Grail.

Purification & Penance in Religious Sects

In the early Christian Church, those who did not believe in actual surgical castration as a means of assuring the purity of the priesthood, advocated "spiritual castration." Early church fathers, such as Saint John Chrystostom (Bishop of Constantinople from 398 to 404), Saint

Anthony and Saint Jerome, believed that those who were in the priesthood should be able to overcome temptation by strength of mind, rather than by physical means. If a priest were to succumb to his sexual desires and commit a sin, he could rely on the sacrament of penitence to cleanse his troubled conscience. The concept of penance through voluntary suffering and flagellation is as old as history itself and almost as widespread as religion. Men who burned with passion for holiness have resorted to various means to punish the "soul's evil yoke-fellow" (the body) from ancient times until the present day. The followers of the Ayatollah Khomeni could be seen on television in 1985 parading through the streets of Tehran whipping themselves with leather scourges. Eight young men of a fundamentalist Islamic sect were pictured in the *U.S. News and World Report* (July 6, 1987), smashing their heads with stones and bleeding in memory of Imam Hussein. News media also depicted six Philippine citizens in Cutud nailing themselves to crosses on Good Friday (March 29, 1991), as thousands watched; hundreds of others beat their backs bloody with whips.

Flagellation within the Christian faith had been practiced to a limited extent since the beginning of the religion, but not until 1259 did it become a primary tenet of a Christian sect. Public self-flagellation of the naked body for the absolution of guilt became epidemic that year in the Italian city of Perugia. The Church first accepted the notion that men might purify themselves of sin with the practice, but later condemned it. The sect of flagellants came to be viewed by both Church and state governments as a threat to their authority because the punishment was self-prescribed and self-administered without the mediation of their auspices and control. Pope Clement I condemned the practice in 1349, as did the Council of Constance in 1414, and the sect was persecuted to extinction.

Another flagellant sect flourished in seventeenth century Russia, which was called the *Khlisti* (sometimes spelled Khylisti, Klysty, clisti or chlisti), meaning "flagellants" in Russian. Beginning about 1645 with the Khlisti, a whole series of rigid sects split off from the official Russian Orthodox church in protests against the liturgical reforms of the Patriarch Nikon (1605–1681), including the discrediting of orthodox priests, the "Europeanization" of the Russian church, and other perceived evils. The collective name given to these was *Raskolniki*, which is the Russian term for "dissenters." They were divided into the Skoptsi, Doukhobors, Molokani, Stundists and Judaizers. The Kylisti referred to themselves by the equivalent of "Men of God" and practiced severe, protracted fasts, complete sexual abstention even with their wives, and mortification of the flesh in many ways, including whipping while they were dancing and singing.

The Skoptzy

The Khylisti were the precursors of the Skoptsi, a religious sect of "the castrated ones" (also known as the Skoptzy, which is the plural form of the Russian word *scopets*, meaning "eunuchs"). *Skopiti* is akin to the term "to castrate." The Skoptzy originated in Russia shortly after 1700, and lasted until at least 1959.[37] Members of the sect became the most extensive users of castration for the purpose of purification known in the history of Christianity. The Skoptzy, who do not refer to themselves by this term, but rather call themselves "white doves" (*belyie goloubi*), managed to endure well into the twentieth century in Russia and Rumania, despite severe persecution. Members of the Skoptzy were forced to go underground, concealing their practices, rituals and beliefs because the church and state were intent on suppressing the sect. While the Skoptzy usually had the reputation of being industrious, amiable, honest, model citizens, a controversy would arise that would bring them to the attention of the authorities. On occasion, a new convert might die as a result of castration, or they might be indicted for proselytizing converts from other religions. Inasmuch as they were celibate, they were required to recruit new members from other faiths—much like those in the Shaker and Oneida communities. This was likely to bring them into conflict with the leaders of these other religions. The Skoptzy were ardent missionaries, and they would sometimes employ coercive measures, such as contracting poor peasant children as servants and requiring their conversion (and usually castration) for non-payment of loans. Most of these converts were originally Russian Orthodox Catholics, but about 6.5 percent had been Lutherans. Token members also came from other faiths. Records show that at least two converts had been Muslims and two had been Jews.

The number of Skoptzy have varied widely at various times and places, likely due to the internments and forced expulsions with which they have contended. Pelikan reports a population in the 1805 to 1839 time period around Koursk of .014 percent, and in the 1860 to 1870 period around St. Petersberg of .031 percent of the total population.[36] Stein maintains that their total number was 10,488 in 1875.[34] A census taken in Rumania in 1865 indicated 8,375 Skoptzy were in the country; a 1871 census showed their numbers at 16,098. Vrouzevitch estimated their total numbers in 1905 at more than 100,000.[35] Pelikan also reports the dispersion of 100,000 Skoptzy in the periods 1840 to 1858, 1805 to 1839 and 1860 to 1871.[37]

The sect first came to the attention of the authorities when Prokop Lupkin and 20 others were arrested because of performing genital mutilations in Moscow in 1717. The central figure in the development of the Skoptzy sect was originally known as Andrei Ivanov (c. 1732–1832), a fugitive serf from Brasovo in the district of Sevsk. He later took the name Kondrati Selivanov (sometimes spelled Selivanoff or Sseliwanow). He was arrested the first time in 1771 and exiled to Siberia. He returned to Moscow in 1795 and was again arrested and interred at an insane asylum from 1797 to 1801, but he continued to preach and make converts even while his movements were restricted.

Czar Peter III was a Skoptzy who was ousted by his wife, Catherine the Great, in 1762 for being "less than a man" and thus unable to perform the duty of royalty—that of providing progeny. Many have claimed that he was murdered, but the Skoptzy believe another man was killed in his place and Peter escaped, continuing to preach the necessity of the "baptism of fire" in Siberia, where he officiated with a hot iron at a number of emasculations.

The "golden age" of the Skoptzy, or at least when they received the most favorable treatment, was from about 1801 to 1820, during the reign of Alexander I. According to Joseph Wieczynski, author of the *Modern Encyclopedia of Russian and Soviet History:*

> The Tsar was strangely indulgent of Selivanov, even conversing with him privately at least once, and permitting him to direct the activities of his sect in the capital, free from interference by police, subject only to the promise that he would not indulge in sexual mutilation. These activities consisted of regular meetings, called 'radeniia', often held in aristocratic mansions, which featured frenzied dancing and singing, accompanied by ecstatic verbal utterances. Despite Selivanov's promise, they also included cases of castration at the times of intense hysteria...Alexander who had encouraged various mystical religious expressions, accepted from a former Polish courtier who supported Selivanov, one Elenskii, the draft of a proposal to grant state patronage to the sect of the Skoptzy with a view to transforming the Empire into a theocracy governed according to the principles of the sect. Elenskii's patron in Alexander's entourage was none other than Nicholas Novosil'tsev. That such an ambitious proposal could gain even brief consideration at the highest levels of government reflected the considerable sympathetic attention which Selivanov's teachings had aroused among certain wealthy and influential members of St. Petersburg society. But Elenskii's project was short lived; he was exiled to the Monastery of Souzdal in 1813. Selivanov's freedom of action was ended in 1820 and he too was sent to Souzdal when the Governor-General of St. Petersberg learned that two of his nephews and several Guards officers had been castrated in radeniia. During the reign of Nicholas I (1825–1855) the Skoptzy were declared to constitute an 'especially harmful sect', and this designation remained in effect until the fall of the aristocracy (c. 1917). Decrees of religious toleration of 1883, 1905 and 1906 specifically excluded the Skoptzy from their purview.[37]

Selivanov's principal writings, "Poslanie" and "Strady," were published by I Nadezhdin in 1845 in St. Petersberg in Issledovanie o skipcheskoi eresi.

Throughout their history, the Skoptzy were repeatedly consigned to the work forces, mines, Siberia and the Caucasus. Even in Siberia they were sometimes oppressed by the local administration.[38] They were shut up in jails and fortresses, but throughout all of their persecutions, they were somehow able to recruit new converts and continue. Many emigrated to Rumania during one period of severe Russian persecution in 1840. In Bucharest, they became quite prominent as carriage drivers. Here they were celebrated for their fine horses and harnesses, their grand air and their fine long velvet garments. Some of them were able to accumulate great wealth. The police found a hoard of 48 million rubles in the house of a Skoptzy named Plotzine in 1869.

In the early days of the Bolshevik revolution, many Skoptzy joined with the Bolsheviks because of a common belief in the communal way of life. Whenever conditions would permit, the Skoptzy lived in this manner, in accordance with the New Testament teaching, as discussed in Acts 4:31; 5:11. Some Skoptzy were elevated in the new order and were said to occupy as many as four seats in the Supreme Soviet council in 1921. However, their other religious tenets were incompatible with Soviet ideology and several dozen members of the sect, including their leader, D. Lomonsov, were imprisoned in 1929 and 1930 for opposing socialism and "spreading religious superstition." Some resurgence of Skoptzy activity was thought to have occurred after World War II, and the existence of scattered groups was documented as late as 1970.

Georgi M. Malenkov, the premier of Russia from March 1953 to February 1955, may well have been a Skoptzy castrated before puberty. He showed almost all of the appropriate physical features: Beardlessness, high pitched voice, eunuchoid fat distribution, and the like.[39] Malenkov was replaced by Kruschev, who was later expelled from the presidium and dropped from the party ranks in 1964. Another story of castration of a communist leader was published in the *New York World Telegram* (June 4, 1957. This article told of the castration of Janos Kadar, the Hungarian premier from 1956 to 1958, on Russian orders to make him subservient to the Kremlin. Alexei Obukhov, the leading Soviet bargainer on both the INF and Strategic-arms talks in 1987, is another prominent Russian who was almost certainly a Skoptzy. His photographs reveal that he has the characteristic height and bodily features. Men like Obukhov are reputed to be well suited as vicars or heads of state, as they are supposedly less inclined to yield to temptation, and are both reliable and trustworthy.

In the United States, people have difficulty understanding the suffering and turmoil of the Russian people that may have helped foster the emergence of the Skoptzy sect. At least 20 million Russians died in wars against invaders. Until roughly 1876, most of the citizens were serfs who lived in bondage to the land, in a condition that was like slavery. The Russians have not only suffered at the hands of their own rulers, but in warfare with other nations. Ivan the Terrible (1530–1584) tortured and murdered entire village populations. Rapaport (1948) quotes an earlier work, Tienturier's *Les Skoptzy* (1876), as saying that, "Material and moral suffering, poverty and slavery prepared ignorant minds, marvelously, to believe those inspired apocalyptics who promised them an end to their miseries."[40]

Most Westerners do not share the religious background of the Skoptzy, which is directly linked to Byzantine practices through the Eastern Orthodox Catholic rites. Nor do we understand the power of the Biblical statements that inspired hundreds of thousands of Skoptzy to seek castration. The single most important influence on the Skoptzy are the words of Jesus (translated literally from the Russian):

> Not everybody holds these words, but those to whom it is given. For there are eunuchs, who were born such from the mother's womb; and there are eunuchs who have been castrated by people; and there are eunuchs who have castrated

themselves for the Heavenly Kingdom. Who contains (holds), he then contains (Matthew 19:11, 12).

Note that Jesus' message shows no equivocation. He says and *means* castration to these Russians. Somehow the same verses in Western culture have been altered to imply that the word "eunuch" means one who does not enter into the marriage relationship.[41] Consider the same quotation in the majority of American Bibles:

Not everyone can understand this word, but (only) those whom it has been given. For there are those who were born eunuchs from their mother's womb, and there are those who were made eunuchs by men, and there are those who have made themselves eunuchs because of the kingdom of heaven. The one who is able to accept (or understand), let him accept.

Another interpretation is that Jesus meant that whoever is able to remain celibate should do so, but only if the person is especially gifted for the choice.[42] The precise meaning of the passage remains ambiguous. Perhaps Russians have been misled as to the exact meaning of Christ's words, or Westerners have been misguided by the Roman Catholic interpretations of the Bible, which intended to encourage castration for purity's sake. Conceivably, the final translations of the Dead Sea Scrolls will offer the last word.

It seems apparent that Westerners have been deceived on the intent of Christ's words. How could a man be made celibate by other men? Or how could a man be made not to enter the marriage relationship by other men unless it was by castration? This matter has been seemingly glossed over in the Roman Catholic teachings, but squarely faced by the Russian Orthodox Church. Several other quotations of Christs' words (Matthew 5:27–30 and 18:8, 9), indicate that it would be better for us to sacrifice a bit of our flesh than have our whole body thrown into hell, "…where the worm does not die and the fire is not quenched." Many other biblical references emphasize the need for bodily purity and celibacy (such as Romans 12:1, 2, I John 2:16, 17, Revised version, 1952, and Revelations 14:4, 5). The Apocryphal

Scriptures also stress the need to be undefiled by lust for salvation. (See Clement III:18; IV:2; Barnabas 14:7, 8; 2 Hermas 4:27; 3 Hermas 5:58, 59; and Wisdom of Solomon 3:14.)

Castration was not the only mutilation that the Skoptzy inflicted on themselves. Some of them had cuts and burns in the form of a cross on their thighs, stomach or shoulder blades. They also mortified themselves by wearing chains or 24-pound coats of mail. Many of the Skoptzy women also subjected themselves to the removal of their nipples, labia or clitoris. The biblical quotations of the words spoken to the women of Jerusalem by Jesus were taken to heart by the Skoptzy: "For behold, the days are coming when they will say, 'Blessed are the barren, and the wombs that never bore, and the breasts that never gave suck!" (Luke 23:29); "Blessed are the womb that has not conceived and the breasts that have not produced milk" (Gospel of Thomas, Saying 77); and "Blessed is the barren woman who is undefiled..." (Wisdom of Solomon 3:13).

In addition to the Scriptures, the Skoptzy had their own books of dogma. Their *Guide to the Kingdom of Heaven* stated: "In anyone evil is so deep and dangerous that it is better to be healed by the iron and the fire..." to assure oneself and others eternal happiness. It also clearly prescribed the essential need to remove those organs by which one loses the chance of genuine, lifelong happiness. Such was the strength of these exhortations that 14-year-old boys were known to go out into the woods after a religious meeting and operate on themselves with a hatchet against a tree trunk.

The Skoptzy were, for the most part, rigidly disciplined observers of all of the rules of their religion. Austere in their eating habits, they were mostly vegetarian, but ate fish, at times. They would practice their fasting with extreme rigor and never indulged in alcohol, the use of tobacco or drugs. They did not play cards or attend shows, as well. The women were even more sober and fanatical than the men, seldom going outside their own fences, or speaking with others outside their own family. Adultery, fornication and corruption were unheard of in the community. The Skoptzy religious customs, rituals and ceremonies varied to some extent from place to place. In the cities, their places of meeting might be a large building capable of holding 300 people. In the rural areas, it could be a special room at the residence of one of the members, where there would invariably be singing of hymns and chants, dancing and preaching about purity.

The castrations usually took place in a ceremony at the place where the Skoptzy habitually met. The dancing and singing seemed to have the effect of reinforcing the candidate's resolve and to prepare him in some psychological and physical manner to tolerate the pain and shock of the operation. The knife or razor used was sometimes heated to cauterize the wound. Often, the instrument was whatever was at hand and the conditions of the surgery were primitive and far from antiseptic. In spite of this, though, the number of deaths due to the procedure were minimal.[43]

On the vital question of the mortality due to castration, estimates are extremely variable: Millant was probably the most extreme, citing an estimated 98 percent of those operated on in Turkey and its environs, dying from the procedure.[44] Pittard quotes a rumored 90 out of 100 succumbing, but adds that this is "too pessimistic." He quotes Thevenot as declaring that one of four survives the surgery and Cardin one of seven only. He also mentions Clot Bey, the chief doctor to the ruler of Egypt, estimating that one in three resist the operation. This was also the opinion of Paul Itschke. Pittard's observations indicated that these estimates very much exaggerate the death rate, and argues that few deaths follow the operation. Pittard quotes Matignon, who had examined many Chinese eunuchs: "Unfortunately the procedure of the operation is very primitive, accidents are rare and death occurs in only 3 percent or 4 percent of the cases." Pittard also quotes Demarquay as saying that the number of recoveries is incomparably superior to those that died. He cites Dupuytren in a similar comment: "However abominable the conditions in which the operations were made, almost always recovery followed."[45] Rapaport quotes Matignon: "It should be said in spite of the brutality of the operation and the ignorance of those in charge, mortal accidents are rare." He also quotes Pelikan as knowing of only nine cases (out of

588) where death resulted. Rapaport rationalized that, "Perhaps these cases are kept quiet by the Skoptsi and the bodies are buried secretly to escape judiciary investigations."[46]

Sometimes the penis, scrotum and testicles were removed at the same time, but more often it would be only the scrotum and testicles first, with the penis cut off in a second operation at a later date. A ligature would be tied tightly around the member to be removed to minimize bleeding. After the cut was made, the necessity existed for inserting a zinc nail into the urethra of the stump of the penis to assure that it would not close during the healing process. The patient would be kept very quiet and allowed little or nothing to eat or drink for several days after the procedure. Normal activity and healing were usually assured within two months.

Pittard studied 50 Skoptzy who were castrated before puberty and 50 castrated after, and found that the observable physical effects of the operation on the Skoptzy were highly age-related and variable to a lesser degree with the size of the individual, his family, ethnic group characteristics and lifestyle. The effects were far more numerous and dramatic when the operation was performed before puberty (about age 11) than after (age 21 or older). The morphological changes that were definitely attributable to the prepubescent removal of the testicles were comparable to those observed in the clinical conditions of acromegalic gigantism or anorchism:

- Parts of the skeleton continued to grow well beyond their ordinary term, causing a considerable elongation of the legs, arms, hands, feet and face. The stature and arm span of the Skoptzy were observed to exceed that of their uncastrated cohorts by an average of four inches. However, their craniums were generally smaller;

- Total absence of the male hair patterns. No beard, chest, arm, shoulder or leg hair, but heavy and abundant head hair and never any baldness;

- Retention of the high-pitched, infantile voice throughout their lives;

- Eunuchoid fat distribution with larger than normal breasts, broad hips and buttocks. Also a characteristic soft and undefined musculature; and

- Soft, clear skin with no acne and a tendency for facial wrinkles at a somewhat earlier age than normal.

Those Skoptzy who were castrated after puberty generally did not show the skeletal modifications, high-pitched voice or loss of beard, but some of them did gain some of the eunuchoid fat distribution (especially the development of their breasts), fineness of skin texture and a tendency to premature wrinkling.

Most of the Skoptzy were of peasant stock. The members of the sect were industrious, yet largely unlettered—probably as many as 95 percent of them could neither read nor write. They were not unlike the peasants who recruited them. Their enterprises prospered because of their rare sobriety and sense of solidarity. In Jassy, many of them were grocers. In Bucharest, they were coachmen and later, taxi drivers, when horses were supplanted with automobiles. They characteristically performed all their public and familial duties with zeal and punctuality. Many of them worked on their own farms. Jacobs, author of *Eunuchs, the Keeper of the Bed, quotes a nineteenth century Russian saying:*

> If I were a banker, I would choose Skoptzys as cashiers, for the cash register, as for the harem, a eunuch is a perfect guardian. In all embezzlements and in all irregularities of the accounts, a woman will have influenced the man; with the Skoptzy looking after the money, this will not occur, and one can sleep in peace.[47]

Such was their reputation.

Certainly the throttling of the sex drive and aggressive instinct, which castration accomplishes, had something to do with the finer character traits attributed to the Skoptzy. However, most of the observers who have written on the subject have not been able to detect appreciable changes in their character that were unequivocally due to the procedure itself. With regard to psychopathologies, it had often been hypothesized that there existed a high frequency of coincidence between morbid types of religious hysteria and voluntary castration. Although, the classical symptoms and progression of these psychoses have only rarely been verified among the Skoptzy. In the cases of individuals, who may have performed the operation on themselves in a fit of melancholy, psychosis may have been present. This is probably not the case with most, who were castrated in the ritual manner. It should be noted that the ancient priests of Cybele were called Galli because they were considered foolish or crazy for castrating themselves.[48]

The study of mental morbidity among those who castrate themselves for religious reasons has been highly convoluted. Some psychologists, for example, Halberstadt, has said, "Religious or political fanaticism is not in the domain of clinical psychology," and have simply avoided the issue.[49] Others have tried to explain the Skoptzy and Galli motivation as collective behavior; related to mental excitation among a mass of people, thereby provoking delirious or convulsive social phenomena, such as the Salem witch hunts of 1692 or the London and Cologne demonstrations. Rapaport maintains that these sorts of collective psychoses are not a major factor with the Skoptzy. Collective mental disorders do not operate in a social vacuum. Although, social pressure is not enough to impose the mutilation by itself, it paves the way for it and adds its force to the unconscious impulse. "Collective madness is only a straw fire. Society is thrust into the current of containing that which was in confusion. The morbid is normalized. It is a spontaneous cure, the calm follows the storm." Rapaport also points to the low number of suicides, nervous disorders, drunkenness and mental defects among the Skoptzy as evidence that the morbid pathological factors are very minor.[50]

The words of the Skoptzy themselves bear testimony to their motivations. Kartamychev said at his trial in Melitopol in 1876: "When I received purity, I felt relief. Before, I tormented myself and worried all the time, and now everything has become pleasant for me, my wife, my children, my freedom, and the prophets sing! I castrated 10 people and I never did it by force—they always begged me to do it."[51] Another Skoptzy, from Paveletz, who had learned to read, commented at his trial in 1903:

> We mutilate ourselves; no one taught us anything...I followed the word of the Evangelist and the teaching of our savior, Matthew 19:12...I understood that I had castrated myself for the kingdom of heaven...If castration had not been necessary, Christ would not have spoken. But he said clearly: 'There are some Skoptzy who have made themselves Skoptzy themselves for the kingdom of heaven.' Christ poured out his precious blood twice; the first time eight days after his birth, when they mutilated him. Holy God teaches us all that is necessary for the salvation of the soul.

Rapaport notes that what the psychoanalysts refer to as the "castration complex" is accentuated in the case of the Skoptzy by their religious upbringing. The natural sexual curiosity of the child and his first investigations are severely repressed by his parents. The gravity of the threats with which they pursue the boy makes the disorder in the child more intense. The need for mutilation, already implanted in his unconscious, is increasingly irritated each time he is reprimanded. The condition is also exacerbated by the holy books, the chants and the churchly exhortations, such that mutilation eventually presents itself as an inescapable necessity.[52]

If hundreds of thousands of simple peasants and ancient priests were able to purify themselves of sexual deviancy by castration for the glory of their God, why not utilize the same treatment for persons in the modern era who are unable to restrain their sexual impulses.

Endnotes—Chapter 11

[1]. C. K. Scott Moncrieff, *Abelard's Letters to Heloise*, 1925.

[2]. Emanuel M. Josephson, *The Unheeded Teachings of Jesus or Christ Rejected*. New York: Chedney Press, 1959, pp. 9–11, 61.

[3]. Charles Ancillon, *Traite des Eunuques*, Paris: Editions Ramsay, 1707, Reprinted in 1978, p. 98.

[4]. N. A. Gur'ev, *Skoptsi Siberskte* (Siberian Skoptsi), 1900. From the library of Michael Vinokouroff; donated to the Library of Congress, filed at BX 9798.S47G8. Gur'ev sketches the history of the sect and details their Siberian exiles, particularly in the region of Yakutsk and Oleminsk.

[5]. The worship of the god, Osiris, has existed in Egypt since circa 1,580 B.C.

[6]. Maarten J. Vermaseren. *Cybele and Attis*. London: Thames and Hudson, Ltd., 1977, p. 15.

[7]. Translation by Jack Lindsay, *Apuleius: The Golden Ass*. Bloomington, Indiana: Indiana University Press, 1962.

[8]. The eunuch priests of Atargatis are mentioned by several writers: Ctesia (c. 400 B.C.), Judas Maccabaeus (c. 164 B.C.), Lucian (*Da Dea Syria*, c. 185 A.D.) and Apuleius (*Metamorphoses*, Books VIII & IX).

[9]. Gruppe, *Greek Mythology and Religions*. Munich, 1906.

[10]. Ovid. Quoted in Ionel Rapaport, *Introduction a la Psychopathologie Collective: La Secte Mystique des Skoptzy*. Paris: L. Rodstein (Edition Erka), 1948.

[11]. Gruppe, *Ibid*.

[12]. *Encyclopedia Britannica*, Volume 2, pp. 110, 111; Volume 19, p. 558, 1968.

[13]. Juvenal and Augustine. Quoted in Rapaport, *Ibid.*, p. 26.

[14]. *Encyclopedia Britannica, Ibid.*

[15]. Benjamin Walker, *An Encyclopedic Survey of Hinduism*. London: George Allen and Unianim Ltd., Ruskin House, 1968, p. 80.

[16]. Weston La Barre, *Muelos, A Stone Age Superstition About Sexuality*. New York: Columbia University Press, 1984, pp. 96, 97.

[17]. Fawcett, *JASN* ii, 1890, pp. 331–334.

[18]. Peter Tompkins, *The Eunuch and the Virgin*. New York: Clarkson Potter Inc., 1962, p. 40; Mary M. Anderson, *Hidden Power: The Palace Eunuchs of Imperial China*. Buffalo, New York: Prometheus Books, p. 309.

[19]. Gerhard Kittel, *Theological Dictionary*, Volume II. 1964, p. 765.

[20]. *Encyclopedia Judica*, 1972.

[21]. Flavius Josephus (c. 37–c. 98 A.D.), *Antiquities of the Jews*, Book 18, chapter 2; *History of the Jewish/Roman War*, Book 2, chapter 7. Quoted in Charles Ancillon, *Ibid.*, pp. 97, 98.

[22]. Dead Sea Scroll number 4Q276–277, Manuscript B, Fragment 1, lines 6–7.

[23]. See also Numbers 19:9

[24]. Cayce, Edgar. (1998). The Second Coming. Future Inward. January/February, pp. 21-22.

[25]. The Dead Sea Scrolls of the ancient Essenes were found near here.

[26]. Epiphanius. Quoted in Rapaport, *Ibid.*, p. 35.

[27]. Canon I, Council of Nicea; Canon 7, Second Arles Council; Apostolic Canons XXI–XXIV.

28. Earnest A. Savage, *The Story of Libraries and Book Collecting*. New York: Burt Franklin, 1909, pp. 9, 10. Reprinted in 1969.

29. *Chronics* is probably an abbreviated name for the book of chronicles titled, *Povest Vremennykh Let* (*The Tale of Bygone Years*), first published in English as *The Primary Russian Chronicle* in 1930. The original version of this book is believed to have been compiled by Nestor, a monk of the Kiev-Crypt Monastery about 1112.

30. George Ostrogorsky, *History of the Byzantine State*. New Brunswick, New Jersey: Rutgers Press, p. 283.

31. *Ibid.*, p. 572.

32. Josephson, *Ibid.*

33. Browe, Peter. (1936). Zur Geschichte der Entmannung, Breslau, Poland: Verlag Muller and Seiffert, pp. 23-26.

34. Von Stein, *Die Skopzensekte in Russland, in Ihrer Entstehung, Organisation und Lehre*. Berlin: Zeitsch. f. Ethaol, 1875.

35. Vrouzevitch. Quoted in Ionel Florian Rapaport, *La Castration Rituelle, L'etat Mental des Skoptzy*. Paris: Librarie Lipschutz, 1937.

36. E.V. Pelikan, *Gerichtliche Medizinishe Untersuchungen Uber das Skoptzenthum in Russland*. St. Petersburg: J. Ricker Schug Buchhandlung, 1876. (German translation by Dr. Nicolas Iwanoff.)

37. Joseph Wieczynski, *Modern Encyclopedia of Russian and Soviet History*. Academic International Press, 1983.

38. Gur'ev, *Ibid.*

39. Tompkins, *Ibid.*, pp. 156–164.

40. Teinturier, *Les Skoptzy. Progres med.*, 1876, pp. 878, 896, 916; 1877, pp. 301, 323. Quoted in Rapaport (1948), *Ibid.*, pp. 23–24. Rapaport studied the psychological effects of the procedure.

41. John P. Lange, D. D., *Commentary on the Holy Scriptures*, Volume 8. 1960, p. 399.

42. Michael R. Cosby, *Sex in the Bible: An Introduction to What the Scriptures Teach Us About Sexuality.* Englewood Cliffs, New Jersey: Prentice-Hall, 1984, p. 98.

43. Three or four percent, according to Matignon, *Les Eunuques du Palais Imperial de Pekin.* Clinical Archives of Bordeaux, No. 5, Fifth Year, May, 1896.

44. Richard Millant, *Les Eunuques a Traverse Les Ages.* Paris: Vigot Freres, Editeurs, 1908, p. 224.

45. Eugene Pittard, *La Castration Chez L'homme et les Modifications Morphologiques Qu'elle Entrain. Recherches sur les Adeptes d'une Secte D'Eunuques Mystiques. Les Skoptzy.* Paris: Masson et Cie, Editeurs, Librairies de L'academie de Medecine, 1934, p. 29, 100. Pittard has documented many measurements of the physical results of castration.

46. Rapaport (1948), *Ibid.,* pp. 10, 109.

47. Joseph Jacobs, *Eunuchs, the Keeper of the Bed.* London: Arlington Books, 1973.

48. See also: Millant, *Castration Criminelle et Maniaque.* Paris: These, 1901, 1902, p. 293; Davidson, "Amputation of the Penis." *The Lancet,* 1884; Charles Blondel, *Les Automutilateurs.* Paris, 1906; Laignel-Lavostine, "Les Troubles Psychiques dans les Syndromes Genitaux Males." *Rev. de Med.,* 1909; N. Lewis, "The Psychobiology of the Castration Reaction." *Psychoanalytical Review,* xiv-XV, XVIII, 1927, 1928, 1931; Albert Sweitzer, *The Psychiatric Study of Jesus.* Boston: Beacon Press, 1978; E. Goldenberg and G. S. Sata, "Religious Delusions and Self-Mutilation." *Current Concepts in Psychiatry* 4: 2–5, 1978; Robert A. Clark, "Self Mutilation Accompanying Religious Delusions: A Case Report and Review." *Journal of Clinical Psychiatry*, Volume 41, Number 6, June 1981.

49. Hendrika C. Halberstadt-Freud, *Het Sadomasochisme: Proust En Freud.* Amsterdam: De Arbeiderspers, 1977.

[50]. Rapaport (1937), *Ibid.*, p. 237.

[51]. Soukhomline, *Les Procs De La Secte Mystique Des Skoptzy, Les Procs Celebres de la Russie.* Paris, 1937, pp. 65–102.

[52]. K. K. Grass, *Die Weissen Tauben Oder Skopzen.* Leipzig, 1914, pp. 557–558.

[53]. Rapaport (1937), *Ibid.*

Chapter 12—The Current Era

Bringing the situation of castration into the current era, or roughly the past one hundred years, opens up a contradictory, confusing and ambiguous discourse, just as it did in ancient and medieval times. Although the former purposes of the procedure—that is, profit, punishment, prevention of crime and disease, pleasure, piety and purification—remain, the old religious objections, canons and customs still hold sway. As a result, the entire concept of castration remains an anathema, and banished into obscurity. The recent history of castration contains irregularities; it has swung in and out of favor at various times and places with the changing winds of politics and academic fashions.

Today, castration is still employed surreptitiously for profit in the harem guards of the Muslim world in Arabia, Morocco and other parts of Africa. The Anti-Slavery Society reports that boys were still being castrated and sold in Afghanistan in 1971[1] Boys continue to be castrated in Bombay, India and other areas in that country, partly for profit and partly for pleasure, where they are used as catamites and prostitutes for a deviant segment of the homosexual population. Castration also remains a necessary part of the surgical procedure that converts males to females in the roughly 1000 transsexual operations a year that take place in the United States. Castration is used as a treatment for prostate cancer, as well.

Castration is probably more familiar to the public as a form of punishment. The Nazis employed it from about 1935 to 1945 as a "security" measure to protect Germany's racial purity from the Jews, Gypsies, homosexuals, lunatics and "others." The harsh manner of its use has seemingly given the entire practice a negative reputation that still prevails. In more recent years in the United States, several attempts have been made by state legislatures to enact castration laws for the punishment of sex offenders.

On March 5, 1979, state representative Joyce Lewis proposed a bill in the Maine House of Representatives seeking to asexualize child molesters. It failed to pass; however $5,000 was approved for the study of the use of "chemical castration" with Depo-Provera. In 1981, state representative Frank Shurden offered a bill that would authorize voluntary castration of rapists; it passed in the Oklahoma house but was voted down in the senate in 1982. A bill was introduced in the Indiana House of Representatives by state representative Richard L. Worden on January 11, 1989 calling for the castration of rapists, criminal deviates and child molesters. Despite its failure, it managed to stir considerable interest across the country. Oregon state senator Ellen Craswell introduced a bill that called for the voluntary surgical castration of sex offenders on January 22, 1990. The bill passed the senate but was effectively tabled by a one-year study proposal in the house. Craswell's bill provided that the court should not impose greater than 25 percent of the presumptive sentence for the sex offender who was voluntarily castrated. In 1990, Oregon and Alabama also considered similar legislation to help stem the worsening crime problem, accompanied by a lack of adequate prison facilities.

In general, castration is mentioned frequently on occasions where the public has been stirred up by reports of especially heinous sex crimes—namely those perpetrated by offenders who have been "treated" and released.

Judge Lawrence Neil Turrentine experimented with voluntary castration as a treatment for sex offenders, offering them probation after having undergone the procedure in 1938. After 20 years, Turrentine proudly claimed that "not a single probationer has 'backfired' with any criminal case of consequence" (San Diego *Evening Tribune*, November 14, 1958). Following the judge's retirement, the castration program was continued by another judge, John Hewicker, in the same jurisdiction. Turrentine told the San Diego *Union* of November 14, 1958 that he has supervised approximately 140 such cases. Hewicker commented that he had granted probation in 100 cases under his tutelage. A report conducted by the state of California in 1952 stated:

"Approximately 60 convicted individuals had been castrated in San Diego county. The record reflects that not one of these individuals has committed a further sex offense."[2] Tannahill (1980) maintained that 397 sex offenders had been castrated in San Diego between the years 1955 and 1975 rather than serve the typically extended prison sentence.[3]

Florida state senator Robert Wexler filed a bill proposing the castration of repeat rapists on February 4, 1994. He immediately came under strong opposition from feminists and the American Civil Liberties Union (ACLU). The president of the Florida chapter of the National Organization for Women (NOW) commented: "Rape is a crime of violence, not a sex crime.... Castrating rapists will not cut down on incidence of rape" (*Pensacola Journal*, February 6, 1994). Nearly 60 percent of respondents of a poll conducted by the National Broadcasting Company (NBC) said they favored legislation to castrate rapists convicted of a second violent sexual assault (Pensacola *Journal*, February 22, 1994). The senate committee passed a watered-down version of Wexler's bill calling for chemical castration with Depo-Provera rather than surgical castration on March 1, 1994 by a 6 to 2 margin. The senate voted 29 to 10 for it but it never came before the house before adjournment. Florida later passed a bill for castration, which became effective 1 October 1997.

The Los Angeles *Daily Journal* reprinted an article (December 1, 1983) from the New York *Times titled, "The Castration Option," which discussed a judge from Anderson, South Carolina, who gave three rapists the option of being placed on probation if they were castrated.*

> The men were reported to be leaning toward the latter. Their choice is scarcely surprising. Why serve 30 years when an operation could give you five years probation? Besides, the deprivation may not be as drastic as it first appears. Surgery would render the men infertile, but given later hormone treatment, not necessarily impotent.

The article maintained the idea of castration was misguided because the procedure would not reduce the men's hostility, and it could, possibly, increase it.

Another piece, "Supervisors Order Study of Castration of Rapists," which appeared in the Los Angeles *Daily Journal* (March 26, 1986), claimed that castration would not deal with the hostility and violence that typically underlie the crime of rape. These and similar articles have repeatedly molded public opinion, leading the public to beliefs about castration that may be erroneous. Dozens of closely controlled studies with hundreds of cases, as well as centuries of experience with man and beast clearly demonstrate the gentling effects of castration.

Much progress has been made in the use of castration for the prevention of sex crimes and disease. Several European countries, including Denmark, Germany, Sweden, Norway, Holland, Switzerland, Finland and Estonia, have had statues in effect since the late 1920s and 1930s.[4] Results over some 3,000 cases indicate that the recidivism rate among those castrated has been consistently low—about 2.3 percent.

In the United States, California and Nebraska had castration laws on the books in 1937, but by 1971, such laws were repealed.[5] Among the 185 cases in California that were followed up, the rate of recidivism was zero. The majority of those castrated in this study, an estimated 57 percent, were very satisfied with the results, some were dissatisfied, and still others experienced unexpected side effects (about 29 percent).[6] Several thousand orchidectomies were performed in the 1960s and 1970s to arrest the progress of prostate cancer. Currently, although most of the aforementioned countries in Europe still have laws permitting castration on the books, surgical castration is rarely employed. Instead, chemical castration is frequently utilized as an adjunct to psychological counseling for sex offenders.

Several other states followed California's January 1, 1997 lead in passing laws for the use of castration for sex offenders. Most of these were for second-time offenders to be treated with chemical or surgical castration. Florida and Montana's laws became effective October 1, 1997; Georgia on July 1, 1997; Texas on May 20, 1997; Oklahoma on March 5, 1998; and Wisconsin's law was signed by the governor in May 1998. At least 12 other states have discussed similar laws in their legislatures: Louisiana, Michigan and Minnesota were among these.

The use of castration for purposes of piety and purity were carried into the modern era by the Skoptzy sect in Russia and Rumania— continuing until at least 1943.[7] It is entirely possible that members of the Skoptzy still practice castration "for the sake of the kingdom of heaven." In India, "holy men" in the Jain sect and Khoja caste of the Cult of Shiva continued to castrate themselves for ascetic purposes until 1927,[8] and may still continue the practice.

Volumes of material shedding light on precisely how castration causes the somatic and behavioral changes in men—noticed since ancient times—have reopened the discourse. C. Ray Jeffery,[9] Lee Ellis[10] and other noted criminologists have provided insight into several ways in which androgenic hormones produced by the testicles are responsible for serious crimes. However, very little of this information has been channeled into the popular media, and has been utilized to an even lesser extent in the formation of public policy. In the years ahead, we can anticipate a vigorous re-examination of castration as a treatment for medical and behavioral problems.

With reference to my first edition of this book, there has been quite a shift in the availability of information on the castration treatment in the past 10 years. More than 1,800 entries were available for printing on the world wide web computer system. . .Google part. Some of the entries were duplicated and there was more on chemical castration than surgical.

Also, the Heaven's Gate Cult in the United States resorted to castration to improve their religiosity, but they had to go to Mexico to find a surgeon to do the procedure.

By the year 2000, seven states had enacted legislation for the use of castration, mostly the chemical type. By the year 2005, at least three more states had similar laws.

Several people took up the arguments for using the castration treatment. Inmate Larry Don McQuay of Texas, had the surgery March 8, 2004 and wrote articles about it.

Several other inmates besides those that volunteered for the surgery took up an advocacy.

Israel Siev published several articles in his Crucial Concepts and the New York Street News periodicals.

Dr. Alan Peterson of New Jersey put several notices of my books on the World Wide Web computer network and his own web pages, including this one.

Frank Shurden of Oklahoma legislature worked to get a law passed there.

Ruth Anne Castle of Minneapolis became an activist. She had been raped as a young woman.

Judge McSpadden gained considerable television and news media when he offered a young black rapist parole instead of prison if he would have himself castrated in 1999.

Dr. Felix Spector of Philadelphia has performed hundreds of castration surgeries.

Endnotes—Chapter 12

[1]. Joseph Jacobs, *Eunuchs, the Keeper of the Bed*. London: Arlington Books, 1973, p. 192.

[2]. California Assembly (1952). *Report of the Subcommittee on Sex Crimes*. Interim Committe on Judicial Systems and Judicial Process. Published by the Assembly of the State of California, Sacramento, California, p. 47.

[3]. Reay Tannahill, *Sex in History*. New York: Stein & Day Publishers, 1980, p. 247.

[4]. Marie E. Kopp, "Surgical Treatment as a Sex Crime Prevention Measure." *Journal of Criminal Law, Criminology and Police Science*, Volume XXVII, Number 5, January–February, 1937, pp. 700, 703.

[5]. Sol Rubin. Quoted in Robert S. Brown and Richard W. Courtis, "The Castration Alternative." *Canadian Journal of Criminology and Corrections*, 1978, p. 160.

[6]. California Assembly (1952), *Ibid.*.

[7]. Ionel Rapaport, *Introduction a la Psychopathologie Collective: La secte Mystique des Skoptzy*. Paris: L. Rodstein, 1948.

[8]. Catherine Mayo, *Mother India*. New York: Harcourt & Brace, 1927, p. 9; C. D. Daly, *Hindu-Mythologie und Kastrationskomplex*, Leipzeig: Internationaler Psychoanalytischer Verlag, 1927.

[9]. C. Ray Jeffery, *Criminology—An Interdisciplinary Approach*. Englewood Cliffs, New Jersey: Prentice-Hall, 1990, pp. 370–383.

[10]. Lee Ellis, "Toward Neurologically-Specific Theories of Criminal Behavior." *Contemporary Sociology,* Volume 8, 1979, pp. 372–376; *Androgens, The Nervous System and Criminal Behavior*. Florida State University Dissertation, 1983; "Neurohormonal Bases of Varying Tendencies to Learn Delinquent and Criminal Behavior." In E. Morris

and C. Brankmann (Editors), *Behavioral Approaches to Crime and Delinquency*, Plenum, 1987, pp. 499–517.

Postscript

Since the purpose of this work is to present an overview of castration across cultures through history, certain issues were not addressed in the main body of the text. However, I would be remiss if I failed to discuss two issues critical to castration: The crisis of sexual deviancy in the Catholic Church and why castration is, indeed, an effective means to dealing with, one, this crisis; and, two, with the problem of sexual deviancy in the culture at large.

Sexual Deviancy in the Church

A frequently heard question is whether or not we should hold our spiritual leaders to a higher moral standard of sexual morality than for the average individual. The answer would have to be a resounding yes—we should and we do. Foucalt has meticulously traced this concept in several ancient Greek writings: The more a man was in the public eye, the more a man wanted to have authority over others—the more necessary it was for him to maintain rigorous standards of sexual conduct. Sexual moderation was always represented as among the essential qualities that belonged to those who had rank, status and responsibility in the city. Controlling one's passion was always a mark of leadership, and this was particularly true for those in the religious and moral leadership. The inferior populace and slaves could be intemperate in wine, food, sleep or lust, but the minority who were best by nature and education must be virtuous and hold themselves above the ugly and bad weaknesses of the flesh.[1]

However, many of the religious persons today, most notably celibate priests in the Catholic Church, are engaging in clearly unacceptable, if not socially abhorrent, behavior. Beginning in the early 1970s, Father David Holley (even as he was completing a stay in a so-called treatment center) was molesting boys. According to court testimony, Holley fondled, masturbated and performed oral sex on the boys on secluded roads or in his own home. In March 1993, at the age of

65, Holley pleaded guilty to sexually assaulting eight boys. In June 1993, a judge in Alamogordo sentenced him to 275 years in prison (*Newsweek*, August 16, 1993).

On November 13, 1993, the headlines thundered across the national news: The leader of the nation's second largest Roman Catholic archdiocese, Cardinal Joseph Bernardin, 68, was accused of sodomizing a 16-year-old boy

17 years earlier (Pensacola *Journal*, November 13, 1993). In the 19-page complaint filed in U.S. District Court in Cincinnati, Ohio, Stephen Cook, an unemployed mental health counselor who has AIDS, also implicated the Reverend Ellis Harsham. Cook claimed that Harsham had abused him for a period of time, then took him to Bernardin, who sexually assaulted him. Cook and his lawyer were seeking $10 million and Bernardin's removal.

Cardinal Bernardin denied all of the charges against him, asserting that in his 42 years as a priest, "I have lived a chaste and celibate life. I know the allegations are totally false." Bernardin, ironically, was one of the nation's most visible prelates in the fight against pedophilia in the priesthood. He had appointed a panel to review 59 similar allegations of abuse. The priests involved in those cases were removed, forced to resign, or to retire or died. Bernardin had also set up a toll-free telephone number for the reporting of priests who had molested minors, as well as convened a nine-member board to investigate allegations of abuse. Cook later removed Bernardin from his accusations.

Several other religious personages, although not so well-known, have been found to be sexual deviants in recent years. Jonathan Franklin, a 61-year-old monk who was accused of sexually molesting an altar boy, shot himself in Cullman, Alabama on August 1, 1986, three days before his scheduled trial. He wrote in a note to his fellow monks: "My friends, the presumed guilty are an embarrassment. The dead are soon forgotten, so I take the liberty of being a dead memory rather than a living symbol and disgrace to the church...." In another letter addressed to the district attorney he revealed that he had had a psychiatric evaluation around 1959, which indicated that he was "overly sympathetic to children." His superiors had known he was a pedophile for at least 30 years.

Reverend Andrew Christian Anderson was convicted of 26 counts of child molestation in Santa Ana, California in 1986 and sentenced to probation by Superior Court Judge Luis A. Cardenas. He was again convicted of sexually molesting an altar boy on July 18, 1990 and sentenced to six years in prison. "I gave you a chance to straighten out your life. You let me down," Cardenas told the priest at his sentencing (Pensacola *Journal*, July 20, 1990). Reverend Lucien Meunier, 74, of Lake Worth, Florida was extradited to Nelson, British Columbia for trial on charges of molesting six boys while he was a parish priest there more than 30 years previously (Pensacola *Journal*, January 14, 1990).

Annie Laurie Gaylor's book, *Betrayal of Trust: Clergy Abuse of Children*, documents 100 cases of sexual abuse of children by clergymen between 1982 and 1988. She reported:

In 1984, Dr. Jay Fierman, a psychiatric consultant at the Servants of the Paraclete Hospital in the Jimez Mountains of New Mexico, the largest church-owned facility for treating pedophilic priests, testified in a miminal case that the facility had treated 300 priests in the past 8 years for 'various sexual problems.'[2]

Jason Berry, an investigative journalist for the National Catholic Reporter, said in an interview with the Houston *Post* that 130 cases of pedophilia by priests and monks had been reported to the Washington Vatican Embassy between 1983 and 1987. In a television appearance in 1990, Berry stated that some $100 million had been paid out in legal suits by the Catholic Church for cases involving priests accused of sexual assault in the past 20 years. In his book, *Lead Us Not Into Temptation*, which was published in 1992, Berry notes that a grand total of $400 million for all court costs had been paid out by the

Church in the past decade.[3] *Time* quoted the sum of $300 million paid out during the same period (August 19, 1991).

Richard A. W. Sipe, a former Roman Catholic priest, and now a psychotherapist and lecturer at Johns Hopkins University, interviewed 1,500 persons over a 25-year period, and published his findings in *A Secret World—Sexuality and the Search for Celibacy. Based on his research, Sipe assessed:*

- The homosexual component among supposedly celibate clergy was twice as high as in the general population, with the estimates increasing in the 1978 to 1985 period from 38 percent to 42 percent;

- Approximately 50 percent of the clergy fit the general category of homosexual according to several sources, with the highest, unconfirmed estimate in two dioceses between 1982 and 1985 of 75 percent;

- Two percent of Catholic priests (about 1,240 men) could be called pedophiles in the strictist sense of the definition, with another four percent of priests sexually preoccupied with adolescent boys or girls;

- "Several" cases exist of priests who indulge in sadomasochism—primarily involving the paddling and whipping of students;

- The number of priests who are involved in heterosexual relationships (and marriage) has remained relatively stable at 20 percent worldwide;

- 80 percent of priests masturbate as least occasionally; and

- One percent of priests indulge in some form of transvestitism.[4]

The truth that emerges from Sipe's research is that those in the priesthood are at least, if not even *more*, sexually deviant than those in the general population.

This situation is clearly desperate and becoming progressively more grave. The time may have come for priests to return to the ancient practice of making themselves eunuchs for the kingdom of heaven.

The disgust and revulsion felt throughout the populace about the crimes of pedophiles are reflected in the severe sanctions meted out by the courts since 1989—25 years to life is not an uncommon sentence. Our religious faith should not be destroyed by having such deviant practices among our clergy. Loss of our religious foundations in the past has typically led to widespread crime, sensuality, self-interest and social chaos. The penalty is far too high to pay for a few individual's sexual pleasure. The priesthood should be strongly encouraged by the courts to cleanse itself by purging its ranks of sex offenders—either by eliminating them from the church hierarchy or by permitting them castration so they will no longer indulge in their deviant behavior. No other alternatives merit the public's confidence.

Catharsis is needed and readily available through the medium of castration, if we would only recognize its many advantages. The words "castration" and "catharsis" may have had a common meaning at one time. The word catharsis comes from the Greek *katharos*, which means "pure;" inasmuch as the Cathars were an ascetic sect in medieval Europe. The records of the sect were obliterated and they were persecuted during the Inquisition. It remains unclear if they ever practiced castration for purity's sake.

It has been historically established that a man who has troublesome sexual urges may use castration to bring a life-giving release. The ablation of the testicles allows a man to ascend to a level of spiritual renewal. Rather than using a simple, tried and true expedient of ameliorating addictive and dangerous sexual practices, we have allowed men in trusted positions in this country to undermine the morals and health of our youth. Moreover, a strong tendency exists for the victims of incest and pederasty to become victimizers in later life.

Through education, the public's perception of castration can be changed, such that it no longer is viewed as a repugnant act, but as a therapeutic measure. Education must confront centuries of negativity—the obvious benefits of orchidectomy have been repeatedly denigrated, scorned, refuted and ignored by psychiatrists, psychologists, sociologists, doctors, educators, theologians, popes, priests and saints for hundreds of years despite widespread use. Those who have attempted to point out the advantages of castration have been persecuted, rudely shunted aside and reviled; their writings destroyed, discredited, expurgated, or misinterpreted. In other words, a wholesale scientific and religious denigration of castration has occurred. Nonetheless, the words of Christ in Matthew 5:27–30 and 19:10–12, as well as the ancient scripture from Isaiah 56:3–5 (about 732 B.C.) and Jeremiah 38:7–13 (about 580 B.C.) remain—and Jesus himself encouraged castration for the sake of purity (see Chapter 10). Perhaps the time has come for us to take his words to heart, so as to reduce the moral, spiritual and social crisis in our culture.

The religious leadership needs to gain an adequate understanding of the benefits of the procedure. The Roman Catholic Church is obviously suffering from the revelations of having so many deviant priests in its midst. McLaughlin performed a study to determine the degree of disaffection this abuse has caused. She found that prior to the abuse, 95 percent of Catholics and Protestants had a very positive spiritual view. After the abuse, 77.1 percent of the victims said their faith was seriously damaged. Their relationship with God and/or the local church was disrupted to the extent that 58 percent of the Catholics no longer attended church services, 14 percent changed their religious affiliation and 32 percent were no longer involved with any church after the abuse.[5]

Theologians and ecclesiastical leaders should recognize that castration is an effective way of purging the priesthood. Emasculation not only protects the public from the legions of deviant clergymen, but it also protects the clergymens' reputations, as well as the Church's standing from the taint of sexual transgressions. The cleric gains respect for his courage, purity and dedication to his God by submitting to the act of castration.

Those clergymen who are practicing their sexual deviance and exposing thousands of children a year to loss of innocence could easily be relieved of their temptations. Their physical, spiritual and mental health would be greatly improved by the expedient of the operation. Admiration for the virtuous, ascetic man could be reclaimed in the culture. I would argue that the purified body and mind of the castrated man could make him morally superior, in view of the sacrifice offerred. He has chosen sanctuary in forgiveness and asceticism, rather than iniquity. The eunuch is, in fact, a superior organism—thousands of years of history have shown this to be so. C. C. Hawke, a medical doctor, summarized the conclusions of several prominent physicians in stating: "Physically, the castrate is an improved organism."[6]

Why Castration is Beneficial

Castration is beneficial for several reasons, but primarily because "general health and longevity are increased."[7] Castration offers a greater life expectancy for the average human male: an additional 14 to 15 years. Cherfas and Gribbin report that the inmates of American sanitariums who were castrated lived an average of 14 years longer than the other male inmates. Harem guards who were eunuchs in the Ottoman Turk seraglios lived considerably longer than the other male servants. Noted eunuchs in history—including Narses, the great Byzantine general, and Selivanov, the Skoptzy religious founder—lived to be 100 years old. Antonio Mannieri (1643–1740) was still singing for Louis XVI at the age of 97. This is remarkable, considering that the average life span for a man of that era was 35 years or less.

The reason castration prolongs life and promotes health is because it serves to reduce the level of males' androgenic hormones by approximately 95 percent. This, in effect, lowers testosterone levels, and testosterone increases blood-clotting in males. Nearly 80 percent of males deaths in the United States are due to cardiovascular diseases brought on by blood clots.

Estelle Ramey, a physician, theorized during a televised presentation to the National Press Club (June 13, 1987) that the evolutionary process led to males having a physiology designed for fighting. Being bigger, stronger and more aggressive than their female counterparts, males required greater clotting capacity to prevent bleeding from frequent wounds.

Testosterone is thought to contribute to such behaviors as aggression, frustration, irritation, impatience, competitive drive and urgency. Chronic emotional upset leads to excessive biochemical changes in the body that are detrimental to the heart, which, in turn, leads to increased risk for heart disease, the nation's leading cause of death. Research shows testosterone pushes up production of stress hormones and LDL, the "bad" cholesterol, which increase blood pressure, as well. In addition, the heart is a target organ for the androgens.[8] By reducing testosterone levels, the male is less likely to engage in risky behavior, as well as promiscuous sexual behavior. High levels of testosterone and adrenaline are linked with the predisposition to engage in dangerous acts and serious sex crimes.

Castration effectively circumvents the more than 25 sexually transmitted diseases (STDs) that are being spread at an increasingly rapid rate today. An estimated one in every six adults is infected with a sexually transmitted disease (STD) at any given time. Several other diseases, which are not classified as STDs, can also be prevented or cured by castration: Testicular cancer, prostate cancer, epididymitis, breast cancer (in males), lymphedema, testicular torsion, hemospermia, balanitis, hydrocele, viral hepatitis and glaucoma. Other conditions, which may not be classified as diseases, may also be averted by castration, including priapism, baldness, acne and some signs of aging.[9]

Testicular cancer was one of the leading causes of cancer death in men between the ages of 15 and 45, and it remains the most common form of cancer in males between the ages of 20 and 40.[10] This form of cancer appears to be rising, particularly in men of higher socio-economic groups. Testicular cancer tends to spread rapidly, and about 88 percent of the cases are not detected until the cancer has spread to other parts of the body. Between 2,000 and 3,000 cases of testicular cancer occur annually in the United States.[11] Men who have cryptorchidism, or undescended testes, in early childhood are especially at risk of contracting testicular cancer—although this condition affects only one to two percent of the male population. Testicular cancer was once considered fatal, but now is largely curable. Usually only one testicle is infected, and after it is removed (a procedure called an orchidectomy), the remaining testicle is capable of supporting all the normal male functions.

While most men will not be affected by testicular cancer, virtually all American men will face prostate cancer, provided they live long enough. In a study of 4,004 cases, 32 percent in the 60–69 age group had prostate cancer, and 43 percent were infected in the 70–79 age group.[12] According to Allan Bruckheim, a physician, 75 percent of all men are affected by age 80 (Pensacola *Journal*, October 10, 1990). And by age 90, all men are purported to have the disease.[13]

In 1988, the estimated number of deaths due to prostate cancer was 28,000, and the number of new cases was 99,000. As of 1990, cancer of the prostate now surpasses lung cancer as the most frequently diagnosed form of cancer in men in the United States. Its death rate is also significantly higher in African-Americans than Caucasians.[14] In fact, the rate for African-American males is six times that of Nigerian men.[15] Prostate cancer occurs approximately 40 percent more frequently in African-American men than in Caucasian men; this may be due to higher levels of testosterone in African-American males.[16]

Some evidence exists that suggests sexual activity is related to the incidence of prostate cancer, but currently, the conclusions are vague. Foucar suggests that engaging in sexual behavior generally stimulates the rapid release of sex hormones in men.[17]

Research indicates that testosterone and dihydrotestosterone (DHT) are the carcinogens that are causing prostate cancer and metastic disease in the seminal vesicles, bladder, bones, brain and other organs. The testicles normally produce about 6,000 micrograms of testosterone and 150 micrograms of DHT daily. The cortex of the adrenal glands produces about 100 micrograms of testosterone and other tissues convert testosterone into about 100 micrograms of DHT daily.

Orchidectomy removes the source of the majority of these hormones, although the output of the adrenals surges temporarily to compensate for the loss of the testicles, producing as much as half of the pre-operative level in some individuals, according to Labrie.[18] Consequently, adrenalectomy, or its chemical equivalent, flutimide or cytadren, is often used to remove the residual effects of the remaining androgens in patients with prostate cancer.

Orchidectomy remains unpopular, although the procedure is generally the most inexpensive and most effective treatment for prostate cancer. Physicians perform an orchidectomy usually after the other treatments have failed, if at all. The removal of the testicles—that is, castration—causes the prostate to atrophy, thus eliminating the source of the problem. Only one case of prostate trouble is known in men who had undergone the procedure before age 35.

In other treatments of cancer of the prostate,

> Reasons can be cited for the simultaneous use of orchidectomy and estrogen, orchidectomy and adrenal blockage, or antiandrogen therapy plus medical or surgical castration. In large collected series of patients with metastic disease,

three-and five-year survival rates of treated patients with stage III and IV disease were always better than those of untreated patients. The difference among regimens of castration, estrogen therapy and combined treatments were not significant. Among recent studies using randomized assignments to therapeutic regimens, no difference was found among the three regimens; however, the daily use of five milligrams of diethylstilbestrol was associated with increased mortality from cardiovascular disease.[19]

Vasectomies have been advocated as providing some of the benefits of castration without the apparent disadvantages, but some studies have shown that, rather than diminish cardiovascular diseases, they tend to increase them. Thus, one of the greatest benefits of castration would be negated (*Time*, March 20, 1989). In addition, two recent studies suggest that vasectomies actually increase the likelihood of developing prostate cancer.[20]

Finally, castration may be beneficial in treating mental disorders. Modern science is beginning to find the underlying physical factors that lead to psychoses. Becker, Breedlove and Crews have shown that testosterone effects the growth of many body parts, as well as the formation of the brain.[21] Rugen C. Gur, a professor of neuropsychology at the University of Pennsylvania, published the results of his studies in the *Proceedings of the National Academy of Sciences* (1991). Gur and his associates measured the brain tissue of 34 men and 35 women, ages 28–80, using the magnetic resonance imaging (MRI) machine, and found that the brains of the men atrophied two to three times faster than the women.

Gur's findings suggest that the hormonal differences were the cause of the increased atrophy associated with aging in men. The greatest amount of atrophy in elderly men occurred in the left hemisphere, while the change in women's brains was symmetrical. "What we have to do is relate that behavior in order to understand what that means," said Susan Resnick, an assistant professor of psychiatry, who worked on the study (Pensacola *Journal*, April 2, 1991). Crow demonstrated that the origins of psychoses, particularly schizophrenia and manic-depression, are related to brain symmetry, and initially occur most often in males at the age of puberty, precisely when the sex hormones begin to surge.[22]

Conclusion

Castration has the potential to help alleviate sexual deviancy in the Catholic Church, as well as in the general population. Both history and modern medicine have proven that castration can effectively remedy the numerous problems associated with high levels of testosterone in males. Ultimately, the time has come for a serious consideration of the applications of such a simple and safe—if controversial—procedure.

Endnotes—Postscript

[1]. Michel Foucalt, *The Use of Pleasure*. New York: Random House, 1985, pp. 60–66.

[2]. Annie Laurie Gaylor, *Betrayal of Trust: Clergy Abuse of Children*. Madison, Wisconsin: Freedom from Religion Foundation, Inc., 1988, p. 76.

[3]. Jason Berry, *Lead Us Not Into Temptation*. New York: Image Books, 1992, p. 368.

[4]. Richard A. W. Sipe, *A Secret World—Sexuality and the Search for Celibacy*. New York: Bruner/Mazel, 1990, pp. 71, 74, 101, 107, 108, 133, 139, 147, 175, 195, 262.

[5]. Barbara R McLaughlin, "Devasted Spirituality: The Impact of Clergy Sexual Abuse on the Survivor's Relationship with God and the Church." *Sexual Addiction & Compulsivity*, Volume 1, Number 2, 1994, pp. 154, 155.

[6]. *California Sexual Deviation Research*, January 1951, p. 109; Horace E. Campbell, "The Violent Sex Offender." *Rocky Mountain Medical Journal*, Volume 64, Number 6, June 1967, pp. 40, 41. Campbell was a medical doctor.

[7]. *Ibid.*

[8]. H. C. McGill, V. C. Anselmo, J. M. Buchanan and P. J. Sheridan, "The Heart is a Target Organ for Androgen." *Science*, Issue 207, February 15, 1980, pp. 775–777.

[9]. Gilbert Cants, *Male Trouble: A New Focus on the Prostate*. New York: Praeger, 1976. Cants was awarded the Nobel Prize for some of these discoveries.

[10]. Neil H. Baum, "The Testicular Self-Examination." *Medical Aspects of Human Sexuality*, Volume 24, Number 8, 1990, p. 15.

11. David Culp and Stefan Loening, *Genitourinary Oncology*. Philadelphia: Lea & Febiger, 1985, p. 351.

12. Culp and Loening, *Ibid.*, p. 416.

13. *Ibid.*, p. 426.

14. David E. Crawford and William L. Nabors, "Total Androgen Ablation: American Experience." *Urologic Clinics of North America*, Volume 18, Number 1, February, p. 61.

15. Leslie J. DeGroot, *Endocrinology*, 2d Ed., Philadelphia: W. B. Saunders Co., 1989, p. 2717.

16. Lee Ellis, "The Sex Paradox in Crime Victimization: A Neurohormonal Hypothesis." Presented at ASC Meeting, Phoenix, Arizona, October 29, 1993. Also quoting Ross, *et al.* 1986 study of and Ellis and Nyborg 1992 study.

17. Elliott Foucar, "Prostatic Neoplasms," in Culp and Loening (Eds.), *Ibid.*, p. 423.

18. F. Labrie, I. Luthy, R. Veilleux, *et al.*, "New Concepts of the Androgen Sensitivity of the Prostate Cancer." *Progress in Clinical Biological Research*, 243A, 1987, pp. 145–172.

19. DeGroot, *Ibid.*, p. 2718.

20. *Journal of the American Medical Association*, February 17, 1993.

21. J. B. Becker, S. M. Breedlove and D. Crews, *Behavioral Endocrinology*. Massachusetts Institute of Technology, 1993, chapters 2, 4, 5, 6 and 9.

22. T. J. Crow, "Sexual Selection, Machiavellian Intelligence, and the Origin of Psychosis." *Lancet*, Volume 342, September 4, 1993, pp. 594–598.

Glossary

BASILEUS (basileis, plural): The ruler of the Eastern Roman Empire. The emperor of Byzantium.

CATAMITE: A boy kept for purposes of sexual perversion. Ganymede, sometimes spelled catamitus.

CRYPTORCHID, CRYPTORCHIDISM: A birth condition in males in which one or both testicles fails to descend from the body cavity into the scrotum normally.

CYROPAEDIA: An account of the education of Cyrus the Great, founder of the Persian Empire, written by Greek historian Xenophon (c. 430–c. 354 B.C.).

ETYMOLOGY: The history of language and the tracing of the origins of word formation and development.

EVIRATION: Removing the virility and manhood; castration; emasculation.

GANYMEDE: An archaic term used to denote a young man used as a sexual object. Taken from the mythological Ganymede, the handsome son of the King of Troy, who was so beautiful that he was carried off to become the cupbearer for Zeus. His kidnapper was supposed to have had a homosexual passion for him, hence the connotation that Catamitus, the popular Latin form of his name, has had.

HERMAPHRODITIC: Relating to, or characterized by having the genitals of both the male and female sex. The word comes from the mythological son of the Greek gods, Hermes and Aphrodite, who was named Hermaphroditus. Hermaphroditus is supposed to have become joined in body with the nymph, Salmacis. Also meaning ambisexual.

ICONOPHILE: A believer in the power of icons. Icons are sacred images venerated in churches—particularly the Eastern Orthodox Catholic churches. The icons usually depicted Christ, the Virgin Mary or a saint, and were painted on small wooden panels or enameled on metal.

KOITONITE: A high Byzantine religious official near the level of abbot.

LOGOTHETE: An administrative official under the Byzantine emperor. Beginning about the 8th century, the logothete of the drome handled important functions pertaining to foreign affairs. In the 12th century, this minister was virtually the chancellor of the empire. But after that time, the name simply indicated a title of rank.

PARADYNAST: One of the titles of a high government official, who arranged and resolved the questions relating to state marriages of Byzantine royalty.

PARANYMPH: A friend who went with a bridegroom in a chariot to fetch home the bride in ancient Greece and Byzantium. The best man at a wedding. One who speaks for another; an advocate.

SERAGLIO: The harem or place of licentious pleasure. Usually one of the buildings at the palace of the sultan, particularly of the Ottoman Turks.

Index

About the Author

The author was born in Lynn, Massachusetts in 1918. He joined the U.S. Army in 1938 and became a commissioned officer in 1944. He was transferred to the newly created U.S. Air Force in 1947. After a decorated military career that took him around the globe, he retired in 1965 as a lieutenant colonel.

Colonel Cheney received his undergraduate degree in law enforcement in 1975 and a Master's Degree in Criminal Justice form Alabama's Troy State University in 1976. He went on for further studies in criminology at Florida State University.

Colonel Cheney, who makes his home in Fort Walton Beach, Florida, had two wives (deceased), three grown children, seven grandchildren and four great-grandchildren. He has studied the castration treatment for 28 years and had it himself in successful treatment for prostate cancer in 1993. He has written three books, four booklets, 10 articles and has been on television three times, on radio three times, and was an expert witness in a court case once.

www.ingramcontent.com/pod-product-compliance
Lightning Source LLC
Chambersburg PA
CBHW061346280526
45784CB00001B/151